Praise for
Uprisings for the Earth

"*Uprisings for the Earth* creates new, vibrant ground that holds within it keys to finding our way to a meaningful and vital relationship with the natural world in modern civilization. Osprey Orielle Lake's unique, personal, and inspiring perspective on current and historical events makes us proud to be human as we search for self-responsibility and renewal while defying apathy and cynicism. Her book presents a philosophy that is both rich in nature poetics and filled with good sense. Within compelling and dynamic verse, Lake makes a call to discover and uphold what she has named an 'Earth etiquette.' This is a call we need to answer, and Lake makes us thrilled to do it."

—Riane Eisler, author *The Chalice and The Blade* and *The Real Wealth of Nations*

"If you are searching for your 'ground of being' in these turbulent times, this is the book to read. Osprey Orielle Lake shares with us how to listen to the natural world in our midst and offers some penetrating philosophical nuggets, while tantalizing us occasionally with her poetic flare. The result is a healthy dose of wisdom and a dynamic process for renewing our cultural narrative in a time of societal and environmental change. *Uprisings for the Earth* is the kind of ecological literacy we need today."

—Tony Clarke, co-author *Blue Gold* and author *Tar Sands Showdown*

"Seeing both the peril and the promise of this moment in time, Osprey Orielle Lake brings us stories infused with her passion for life. Like winds off the mountains, they renew our energy and summon our will to rise up together for the sake of Earth."

—Joanna Macy, author *World as Lover, World as Self*

"*Uprisings for the Earth* is a book for leaders and for those who feel the call to lead in this historic moment. The unity of Earth's biological functioning has been broken, and thus all intelligent humans are united in a search for planetary healing. What you will experience in *Uprisings for the Earth* you will experience nowhere else."

—Brian Swimme, California Institute of Integral Studies, co-author *The Universe Story* with Thomas Berry

Uprisings for the Earth

Reconnecting Culture with Nature

OSPREY ORIELLE LAKE

WHITE CLOUD PRESS
ASHLAND, OREGON

White Cloud Press
PO Box 3400
Ashland, OR 97520
800-380-8286

Cover and interior design by Christy Collins,
Confluence Book Services.

Library of Congress Cataloging-in-Publication Data

Lake, Osprey Orielle.
Uprisings for the earth : reconnecting culture with nature / by Osprey Orielle Lake.
p. cm.
Includes bibliographical references.
ISBN 978-0-9745245-9-7 (pbk.)
ISBN 978-0-9793840-9-7 (cloth)
1. Human ecology--Philosophy. 2. Philosophy of nature. 3. Human beings--Effect of environment on. I. Title.
GF21.L345 2010
304.2--dc22
2010027033

Contents

For my beloved mother, N'ima,
and the Pacific Ocean and Coastal Redwoods
of Northern California

Acknowledgments

I magine a tree in a wild forest. The tree is nourished, grows and propagates because of the gifts of sunlight, nutrients in the soil, underground rivers, rainfall, bees and wind that carry its pollen, birds that carry its seeds, the change of seasons, and hundreds of other interwoven ecological happenings that are fundamental to the existence of the tree. Similarly, the fruition of this book is the result of inspiring and essential gifts given to me by many remarkable people.

I wish to offer my deep gratitude to Riane Eisler, who has been a treasured friend and mentor. Her seminal work concerning dominator and partnership models of society continues to be at the core of some of the most transformative ideas of our day. I give a mountain of thanks to Martín Prechtel, who is one of the most eloquent thinkers of our time. The history and indigenous knowledge he shares is vital to building a healthy culture and sustainable future. David Orr's elegant writings and forthright conversation concerning the need for environmental education for our young people and an urgent call for all of us to awaken to the climate crisis are messages we ought to heed, and they have helped hone my own thinking. I so appreciate Brian Swimme for his encouragement while I was working on this manuscript and for *The Universe Story* that he and Thomas Berry have presented to the world.

Vandana Shiva, Wangari Maathai, Joanna Macy, Tony Clarke, Janine Benyus, Al Gore, Tom Hayden, Paul Hawken, Terry Tempest Williams, Leonard Cohen, David Korten, Georgia Kelly, Belvie Rooks, Bill McKibben, Lester Brown, Nina Simons, Kenny Ausubel, Lynne and Bill Twist, David Suzuki, and Gary Snyder have also been important to my thinking things through—either directly in conversations or indirectly through their writings. I thank them all, not only for their invaluable wisdom, but for their brave and meaningful work in the world.

Although Rachel Carson and Thomas Berry are no longer with us, these two profound individuals have shaped not just my views but an entire generation and generations to come. I salute them both with my cup lifted in praise.

Thank you to Joan Wages, president of the National Women's History Museum, who took time from her fierce schedule to answer my many questions. I offer deep thanks to Sherrie Smith-Ferri, director of the Grace Hudson Museum, who shared her Pomo basket stories with me and kindly took me into the back room of the museum to reveal some of the most exquisite baskets I have ever seen.

It is with the utmost gratitude that I thank Robin Bishop for her tremendous editorial skills and commitment to this project. Robin was an early enthusiast of the original manuscript and kept me laughing in the long writing hours with her impeccable wit. She is an extraordinary wordsmith and I am honored to call her a friend.

Big thanks to Susan Griffin, Andy Courtier, Matthew Gilbert, Linda Powers, John Gray, Michael Bell, Kaye McKinzie, and Patty Montmorency for valuable feedback and encouragement while the book was in process.

Lydia Papageorgiou and Kosta Bagakis have my appreciation for their kind support and help in untangling several historical knots in the chapter about Greece.

Heartfelt appreciation goes to everyone at White Cloud Press for believing in this book. I offer great thanks to Gary Kliewer, Stephen Sendar, and Steve Scholl for their support and good wisdom in framing the project. Christy Collins handled the production with true grace and artistry. I thank Raina Hassan for her excellent ideas, editorial work, and ensuring that every point was clarified and polished. It was a pleasure to work with such a thoughtful editor. These are all wonderful, caring folks.

It is difficult to find enough words of appreciation for my dear, long-time friend and business associate, Wyolah Garden. Her dedication not only to this book, but also to the larger cause of protecting the Earth is something that touches me everyday. I thank Bonnie Gray for her extraordinary friendship and support throughout the entire project. Her wise words were always welcome.

I am forever grateful to Blaise Johnson, whose love came across the oceans. Her support was critical in the development of this book. I thank my dear friend, Gabriele Schwibach, particularly for her magical soups that kept me well-fed while writing throughout the winter. I thank my lovely friends and family Aviva and Rick Longenotti, Elley Coren, Mira Rose, Linda Adams, Kim Weichel, Matia Brizman, Runa Basu, Larry Thomas, Anne Hedges, Alana Conner, Jan Coleman, Lenny and Vairagya Eiger, Valentin Burgmann, Ginny Stearns, and Carole and Russ Burns for their encouragement.

My heartfelt thanks go to each and everyone from the art years in the madrone and fir forests of California.

I thank my dear father, Alan, for his kind love and support.

Several names have been changed where I was unable to request permission for their appearance in this book, specifically some of my acquaintances from China and Russia. I give thanks to these individuals and appreciate the stories they shared with me.

A special note of gratitude to Tom Adams for his loving support, which has meant so much to me, as well as his careful editorial read that helped shape the final manuscript. I give an ocean of thanks to my dear sister Annie, who is the best sister ever—I am grateful for her irreplaceable love. This book is dedicated to my late mother, N'ima—a truly remarkable woman who I loved with all my heart and who continues to mean the world to me.

Finally, I want to acknowledge and honor all the courageous advocates in a plethora of disciplines and organizations who work countless hours every day to protect people and planet at this extraordinary juncture in history.

1 The Big Quiet

Our history and presence on Earth, both individually and collectively as a species, is greatly shaped and forged from the realm of a remarkable force we call choice. At this critical moment in our human journey, these choices have a profound effect on the destiny of the Earth and all who live here. As I deliberate over the meaning and consequences of these choices, I recall the following words, written by one of the most important founders of the modern environmental movement, Rachel Carson:

> We stand now where two roads diverge. But unlike the roads in Robert Frost's familiar poem, they are not equally fair. The road we have long been traveling is deceptively easy, a smooth superhighway on which we progress with great speed, but at its end lies disaster. The other fork of the road—the one "less traveled by"—offers our last, our only chance to reach a destination that assures the preservation of our earth.[1]

As I see it, Carson gave these words to our generation and those to come as a clear directive. Her entreaty to us—to choose the road less traveled—seems even more prescient now than it was when she gave warning a half-century ago. At times, we have been dawdlers and plodders, reckless stumblers and careless ramblers, insistent on dangerously marching down the opposite track.

Yet, more of us each day become aware that we must somehow traverse the less familiar but life-sustaining road. With a mixture of appropriate apprehension, curious enthusiasm, and growing determination, we are realizing that the route out of the thicket is one we ourselves must design. We are learning that the way forward requires a new depth of courage, imagination, hope, and maturity—and that we must move decidedly, now.

As our climate rapidly heats up and all signs point to a world that no longer supports life as we know it, we see that it is vital to our new direction that we respond immediately to what scientists are telling us about the gravity and speed of global warming. To this end, we must address the actions required to mitigate environmental crisis as well as the long-term societal and personal transformation needed for creative, systemic, and enduring change. We will need inner clarity combined with sound action to move through the uncertain passage ahead.

I received wise words concerning this new road, quite unexpectedly, from not only Rachel Carson but also several other remarkable women. In 2004, thirteen indigenous elders—all distinguished leaders from around the world—met in the countryside of upstate New York. These women, from the Arctic Circle, the Americas, Africa, and Asia, agreed to form an alliance to work together locally in their communities and globally to care for the Earth and for future generations. They came to be called the Thirteen Indigenous Grandmothers.

Several years after their initial convening, the elders spoke at the Bioneers Conference in California. A conference participant asked Maria Alice Campos Freire, one of the Grandmothers from the alliance, about illness. Freire is a traditional healer from Brazil and an activist in the Alliance of Peoples of the Rainforest. She was asked, "What can be done about so much physical and emotional illness of people in our time?"

The elder's voice was soothing, filled with the resonance of birdsong and forest flute of her homeland. To paraphrase, she answered by saying, "In the way of traditional people in Brazil, we do not work with illness. We instead focus on what is actually well and healthy. No matter who the person is, there is a part inside, maybe only a very small part, but it is there, that is well. I focus on this, nurturing and caring for this person's wellness. I focus on what is healthy in them, allowing this part to grow."

As I heard her speak, I felt the armored wall of cynicism, all too common in Western society, suffer a healthy crack in my psyche. I then pictured in my mind's eye images of our modern civilization. I imagined many caring people and all their concerted efforts in communities around the world bringing their collective intelligence together. In the center of our cities, I imagined islands of green-wellness and I imagined these islands growing into healthy, environmentally sustainable bioregions.

I closed my eyes and welcomed this new perspective washing over me as if from a clear mountain spring. This kind of renewal, however it comes, is essential because no matter which country we call home, we are bombarded daily by disheartening news about societal and environmental demise. The devastating effects of climate change, poverty, water scarcity, severe economic downturns, oil spills poisoning the ocean, species extinction, the destruction of rainforests, the disappearance of Indigenous cultures, and the declining health of our children confronts and often overwhelms us. On this "road we have long been traveling," it is startling to comprehend the assault we as a species have inflicted upon our home planet and ourselves. In this cascading turmoil, how should we respond to the news and to what the scientists are telling us about the state of our world?

When environmentalist and entrepreneur Paul Hawken is asked if he is pessimistic about the future, he answers this way: "If you look at the science about what is happening on earth and aren't pessimistic, you don't understand the data. But if you meet the people who are working to restore this earth and the lives of the poor, and you aren't optimistic, you don't have a pulse."[2]

We live in a time that requires tremendous courage to recognize the peril of our existence while simultaneously generating the hope and innovation needed in order to fundamentally change our course. Hawken encouragingly reminds us in his book *Blessed Unrest* that millions of people the world over are doing extraordinary work on behalf of environmental and social change. It is empowering to think of these efforts as the "Great Work" of our time, so named by cultural historian Thomas Berry.[3]

While teaching seminars and university classes and giving public presentations over the past decade, I have found that people who are involved in restorative work primarily engage in two different pathways as a response to our global crises.[4] I like to think these two pathways are both heading down the new road, the one that is, as Carson describes, "our chance to reach a destination that assures the preservation of our earth." Both pathways are indispensable and together provide a comprehensive way toward a healthier future. Traveling on one does not preclude simultaneously traveling down the other, and indeed, some traverse both.

The first pathway focuses on the immediate and urgent need to stop the destruction of the planet and the imperative to help those most in need. These efforts range from campaigns to mitigate climate destabilization and preserve rainforests to fighting for the rights of Indigenous people, from battles to improve environmental laws and preserve wildlife to protecting seeds and food sovereignty. This includes the development and implementation of a wide spectrum of innovative and inspiring solutions: green energy technologies, social media platforms for connectivity, new sciences, eco-buildings, clean energy economies, ecological restoration projects, and micro-lending organizations, to name a few.

Equally important, the second pathway involves nothing short of a profound individual and societal transformation of consciousness—a "new dream" for the modern world, as Ecuadorian elders in the Pachamama Alliance have called for. This is the delicate and extended work of reconstituting Earth-honoring cultures and worldviews in modern societies. This enterprise requires a revolution in our educational institutions to ensure that ecological literacy is central to our young people's curriculum. It begins by examining and transforming the deleterious attitudes and beliefs that led us to this perilous moment in the first place. It simultaneously requires creating a new understanding and narrative of how humanity might better live in a mutually enhancing manner with the Earth and all species. This book primarily addresses insights along this second pathway.

In contemplating Maria Alice Campos Freire's words about concentrating on wellness as an essential part of the response to illness, I decided to renew my focus on what I understand to be "well" at this pivotal moment in history: What *is* "healthy?" For me, working as an artist with a background in environmental studies, addressing this question has meant focusing on how to express the beauty, wonder, and intelligence of nature in order to explore a new Earth-honoring narrative in contemporary society. The balance, elegance, and sustainability inherent in the "natural laws" of the Earth have much to teach us about essential well-being, especially when we consider that what these laws govern—all life on the planet—has been evolving over 4.5 billion years. Imagine the sophistication and workability of any project given that much research and development time! Imagine the folly of ignoring the finely tuned ecological systems of this long-enduring project.

One of the most vital capacities in initiating a new worldview and the cultural transformation we now need is participating in a deeper kind of listening to the living Earth. When we are in the presence of this natural environment and we listen with our whole selves, we have the possibility to remember the balance inherent within the natural systems of our Earth and our interconnected relationship to the community of our living planet. Carson writes, "It has come to me very clearly . . . that people everywhere are desperately eager for whatever will lift them out of themselves and allow them to believe in the future. I am sure that such release from tension can come through the contemplation of the beauties and mysterious rhythms of the natural world."[5]

While I don't think that reconnecting with the natural world will solve all of our daunting problems, I am proposing that reviving our intimacy with the Earth is an essential and irreplaceable component in turning from our destructive course.

The feeling of belonging to the Earth and the joy and inner peace that many people experience when walking alongside an ocean or in a forest is essential to both our well-being and our impulse to care for our home planet. Along a river or in the mountains, we can reinvigorate ourselves and find the necessary energy to meet the challenges ahead. Taking time to appreciate our Earth's wonder and beauty allows us to deepen our comprehension of the majesty of life and to find renewed personal meaning. After decades of listening to false claims that consumerism—things—will fill our lives with the meaning we seek, it is time we draw upon a different kind of wealth.

Moreover, there is a treasury of knowledge and wisdom in the natural world that beckons us and summons our attention. Here is one inspiring example: In recent years, scientists and designers have turned to Mother Nature's "ideas" to find energy-efficient technology solutions that are non-harmful to the environment. In Harare, Zimbabwe, where temperatures fluctuate between 37 and 107 degrees Fahrenheit, architects of the Eastgate Building (an office complex) designed an air-conditioning system modeled on the self-cooling mounds of termites. Yes, termites! The complex is using 90 percent less energy for ventilation than conventional buildings its size.

My thesis is this: whether we seek to renew our inner world or search for solutions to meet our human needs in the outer world, the potential for living in a state of natural good conduct with the

Earth is greatly magnified through contemplative listening and thoughtful encounters with nature. I like to call this special presence with the natural world "listening to the Big Quiet."

⸻

In light of this great need to be attuned to our living landscape, it is important to note that over half of the world's population is living in urban environments, mostly disconnected from the natural world. This escalation of urban living is due, in part, to severe environmental and economic pressures in rural regions that have forced country people into cities, as well as an increase in worldwide population. As humanity has become increasingly immersed in an industrial society, so has it become exceedingly difficult to focus on the Earth and regain a sense of the Big Quiet. This is not the sole cause of our environmental crisis; yet, the lack of direct connection with and knowledge of local forests, watersheds, and wildlife have certainly been a hindrance to their protection. Equally harmful is the way this feeling of distance from nature, with which we are inseparably connected (whether we are conscious of it or not), can create an internal distance from our personal goals, dreams, and sense of wellness. Early ecologists led by biologist Edward O. Wilson formed the Biophilia Hypothesis, which states that people deprived of contact with nature decline in well-being.[6]

In developing this idea further, Richard Louv in his book *Last Child in the Woods* makes a powerful case for why our children must have time in nature for their overall health: "As the young spend less and less of their lives in natural surroundings, their senses narrow, physiologically and psychologically, and this reduces the richness of human experience. Yet, at the very moment that the bond is breaking between the young and the natural world, a growing body of research links our mental, physical and spiritual health directly to our associations with nature—in positive ways."[7]

So, although it might seem peculiar to begin a book—necessarily expressed through the hum and whir of nouns, modifiers, and verbs—with an invocation to Quiet itself, we have a primary and pressing need to explore a certain kind of stillness at this time. In the roar of modern civilization, with its contrasting beneficial and destructive elements, many of us sense a yearning for this spacious quietness in nature and in our inner nature.

In approaching the complexity of our current cultural and ecological conundrum and pondering the new path we need to travel, I turned to wise storyteller Frank Waters for some welcomed insight about quietness from the Pueblo people of the southwest United States. More than ever, the knowledge and wisdom of Indigenous people who have remained intact with their ancestral ways and their relationship to the land is crucial to finding our way forward. It is prudent for us to listen. In the opening to Waters' 1942 book, *The Man Who Killed the Deer*, I see a reflection of the Big Quiet.

The main figure in the story, a young Pueblo Indian named Martiniano, is forced by the federal government to attend "away-school." When he finally returns home, Martiniano has great difficulty reintegrating with his people and faces great economic challenges. Needing food for his family, he kills a deer out of season, thus breaking the laws of both the Anglo world and the Pueblo. From his own tradition, he has not done the killing with proper permission from the deer spirit or with the required ritual afterward.

Following the illegal hunt, Martiniano is arrested by a federal officer but escapes. He is shot in the process and left for dead in the mountains above Taos, New Mexico. A tribal friend senses a disturbance in the mountains and uncannily rescues him. When they both return to the Pueblo, a Council meeting is convened to consider both tribal and governmental issues of the unlawful hunt and Martiniano's arrest. Although the deer killing is the main issue, the situation is actually far more complex and reveals intertwined historical and spiritual conflicts. In the Council meeting, we are introduced to the elders' sophisticated ways of approaching the problem.

The Council Chiefs, wrapped in ceremonial blankets, gather in the evening. For a long time no one speaks; only the crackling fire punctuates their shared quiet. One Chief finally opens the discussion. "Well then, let us consider it fully and calmly ... let us move evenly together." After each of the young men involved in the trouble has an opportunity to address the Council, there is more long, brimming silence.

Waters writes:

A Council meeting is a strange thing ... when the guttural Indian voice finally stops there is silence. A silence so heavy and profound that it squashes the kernel of truth out of the words, and leaves the meaningless husks mercilessly exposed. And still no man speaks. Each waits courteously for another. And the silence grows round the walls, handed from one to another, until all the silence is one silence, and that silence has the meaning of all.... A Council meeting is one-half talk and one-half silence. The silence has more weight, more meanings, more intonations than the talk.[8]

Waters then narrates the intricate dilemmas of the Pueblo and the Anglo, from considering how the land was originally Pueblo land to Martiniano's failure of protocol on both accounts and how the government will respond. In the end, it is the silence that speaks the loudest. "There is something else to consider," one Chief says. "The deer. It is dead. In the old days we all remember, we did not go out on a hunt lightly ... this deer's permission was not obtained. What have we done to this deer, our brother? What have we done to ourselves? For we are all bound together, and our touch upon one travels through all to return to us again. Let us not forget the deer."

After the Chiefs contemplate the words listened for in the whole of the silence together, "The meeting of the Council was over. They were one body, one mind, and one heart. They moved together evenly."

To not reduce further this deeply perceptive story, let me just say that the recounting of the Council meeting gives us an opportunity to feel the power and presence of intentional silence. This kind of contemplative quietude also reminds me of Henry David Thoreau's insight about silence: "In human intercourse the tragedy begins, not when there is misunderstanding about words, but when silence is not understood."[9]

In this kind of silence, the Big Quiet, there is knowledge, beauty, and the remembering of our deeper life-dream, all of which can truly influence our conduct and self-governance if we can but listen deeply enough to hear its meaning.

⌁

The Big Quiet can be found in numerous ways; mine is most often and easily found through experiencing wild land. Ultimately a very personal awareness of our living planet, the Big Quiet is that place where your inner geography provides an open meadow or other unfettered interior place, like a rippling lakeshore of your mind, where you can listen to the outer landscape expressing itself in long-known natural sounds and vibrations, some audible, some not—for the Big Quiet also encompasses a sensibility. In this attuned stillness, we can listen not only to the Earth but also to our human story within the unfolding of the Earth's long history. This is the subtle work of re-imagining and rejuvenating our relationship with both nature and culture. This deeper reflection and intimacy allows the natural world to inform culture, and as many land-based peoples have demonstrated over time, acting in accordance with the natural laws of the Earth establishes living with a viable ecological footprint. A culture or civilization bereft of its connection to nature will not be sustainable—the past decades have clearly shown us this. We will need to reconnect with the rhythms of the natural world to generate inner and outer resilience and to move through the challenging times ahead. At our urgent crossroads, this kind of reconnecting and renewal involves transitioning from an essentially destructive, over-competitive industrial society to a more sustainable and cooperative global community.

The Big Quiet can be encountered in the tapping and thrumming of raindrops gently falling on the lake, and from within this watery rhyme subtle thoughts may come to us about our own particular watershed and the realization that our own bodies are made primarily of water, water that we keenly want to spring from an unspoiled source. Quiet breathes through us when we listen to leaves purling in the wind, singing their "shi-shiiii" song, which then may speak to us of air unsullied by factory smoke. We then think about our children, and by extension, all oxygen-dependent beings, having the chance—the right—to breathe from unpolluted skies. The Big Quiet echoes in distant thunderclaps that make us stand still for a moment, reverberating with the power of a winter storm. We are reminded that each season is alive with its own moods and that we are, remarkably, in orbit around the sun, which causes the seasonal changes. As we watch a sunset over the ocean, it takes a certain inner quiet to grasp that we are on a sphere moving about 67,000 miles per hour around our home star. In the mystery of this dynamic system, we don't even feel the transit.

The Big Quiet invites us to be present with ourselves and our place, wherever we are, and to include the entire Earth community, down to the smallest of plants and animals, in our conversation. This is not a "romantic" concept; on the contrary, it is one of vital importance to our survival as a species.

⌁

A new science called biomimicry is based entirely upon learning from nature as model. Biomimicry is a discipline that studies nature's designs and then emulates these processes and forms for sustainable solutions to human problems. Researchers at the Biomimicry Guild and Biomimicry Institute in Montana learn, for example, how desert beetles collect water from fog and mist. They then emulate the beetles by designing synthetic sheets to do the same. They also study how a lotus leaf with a creviced surface that repels liquid can teach us to design paints that self-clean, reducing the need for chemical cleaning on the sides of buildings and homes. Of immediate concern to our mounting energy problems, scientists are working to create more advanced solar cells that mimic the photosynthesis of leaves in order to design more cost-effective solar power. Janine Benyus, the biologist who named this emerging science, tells us, "The more our world functions like the natural world, the more likely we are to endure on this home that is ours, but not ours alone."[10]

One of the most valuable insights gained from nature that concerns us right now on a societal basis is the inherent quality of diversity. When we walk through a wild forest, we may see native oak, madrone, and fir trees populating a hillside with equal grace, displaying sophisticated relationships with soil, water, and sunlight. When we deeply listen to the language of the natural world, we experience that the oak tree is not a better tree than the madrone or the fir. Together these trees equally comprise a healthy forest, and their diversity of form and function, their glistening broad leaves and needled branches, maroon and striped bark, acorns and seed pods, all may stir us to think in a new and yet more ancient way.

We learn in this natural setting that diversity does not mean hierarchy, but rather a circle of interdependence or a healthy tolerance. In our typical social constructs, diversity of any kind—from color of skin, gender, and age to religion, financial status, and nationality—is often manipulated into a pyramidal hierarchy. Those who rule and claim the top then discriminate against the many below them. While certainly there have been significant societal improvements over the past decades, and in some cases centuries, as we work to dismantle these inequitable and ultimately counterproductive constructs, we are far from completing a widespread cultural transformation to an egalitarian framework. In a time when domination models of society and thinking have long ruled the day, it is judicious to note that a healthy biosphere operates in spirals and circles of interdependence and not so much in pyramids and hierarchies of dominance. Together, as a global citizenry facing climate destabilization, working in domination or isolation models is no longer an option. Instead, we can learn from nature's model of symbiosis and co-existence, collaboration and cooperation.

One of the most devastating consequences of our dominator model of society is that for more than two thousand years the female half of humanity has been ranked below the other.[11] The result: women worldwide have been subjected to every kind of discrimination and violence imaginable, and we as a whole species have been operating at half capacity. Fortunately, the tide is changing with women's empowerment improving worldwide (although to varying degrees), and this is no small consideration as we look to a better future. Beyond the morality of women's equality, United Nations studies, among others, demonstrate that women's empowerment is critical and in some cases the defining factor in changing many serious problems we face today: from ending wars and stabilizing populations to lifting communities out of poverty.[12] Women's equality and leadership is an invaluable key to social and environmental justice and is a resource that governments, organizations, and businesses worldwide are just beginning to recognize on a broad scale. Looking again to our living planet, nature models to us that male and female aspects of creation work in partnership to generate ecological balance and sustainability.

—•—

As the challenges of the twenty-first century confront us and citizens around the world discuss the need for a new social paradigm, we frequently hear the idea that, "Problems cannot be solved by the same level of thinking that created them" (that quote attributed to Albert Einstein). I believe a significant factor in moving beyond this same level of thinking likely to send us down the superhighway to disaster in Carson's warning is a revitalized kinship with the natural world through personal and direct experiences with the Earth.

Einstein, who spent a great deal of time studying and listening to the natural world, wrote, "Look deep into nature, and then you will understand everything better."[13] Throughout the ages, the quietude and grandeur of the natural world has informed and profoundly inspired scientists, religious teachers, artists, and world leaders. Spiritual traditions, philosophical disciplines, and many scientific truths around the globe were first revealed through experiences in nature.

Newton watched an apple fall and came to the concept of gravity, and Thoreau's *Civil Disobedience* was birthed from contemplations at Walden Pond. Beatrix Potter's illustrations and contributions to land conservation were conceived while living in England's rural Lake District, and more recently, Green Belt Movement founder and Nobel Peace Prize winner Wangari Maathai has been listening to trees, planting them, and so changing the world. These are just a few of the rich and abundant examples.

In the Big Quiet, amongst mountains and streams, we have the chance to alter our perception and transform. This special stillness allows us to explore our inner world. In the full-bodied silence, we can create a larger space within for disparate parts to coexist. And, as in a great poem, our inner mythological world can be set free. Here, we can move beyond perceived limitations and learn new ways of knowing. Our hands touch wild stones and tumbling rivers; our feet sink into tree loam and meadow grasses. We breathe slow and down low. In this vibrant quietude, held within the beauty and mystery of nature, we come to more intimately know ourselves, for this is a very personal journey.

Here, there is room for the complexity and contradictions we face in our work places, our homes, and ourselves. There is space for our imaginations to ponder and wrestle with bewildering personal and global problems. Concern for our children's futures as we read the daily news might merge with bereavement for people in war-torn countries, forests clear-cut or dying from acid rains, beautiful wild species gone, oceans and shores poisoned with oil, and ice caps melting. Yes, we all know of these fears and losses and how we sense them particularly in our solitary moments. In the Big Quiet we can be still, feel great comfort, and listen inwardly for right comportment. There is knowledge resting in this subtle, undisturbed terrain of quietude; older cultures know of it, and we can each begin to renew this sensibility today.

Where can we find the entrance to nature's secret passage? The opening to the Big Quiet is right here, when we stop and listen. Portals of insightful quietude are in the garden, on a mountain trail, in the park, by the sea, out our window, in the closing of our eyes, or wherever we might be in an attentive repose that allows for at least a moment of true deep listening to the Earth within.

The reflections in this book weave together cultural explorations, ecology, art, and ethics in an endeavor to approach deeper real- izations generated from moments of stillness. Each chapter is an invitation to you, dear reader, to explore various landscapes of the Big Quiet in urban areas, in valley and forest, in the wisdom of land-based knowledge from different cultures, in the Earth close to home, and in our histories.

Our industrial age has generated—for certain groups only— beneficial technological advances and opulent material wealth. It has also generated—for everyone—terrific ecological disturbances and global heartbreak. Consequently, we are now compelled to further a necessary conversation about using good manners where the Earth is concerned, as well as with each other. While walking down the less-traveled road and listening to the land, I wish to explore with you reflections on a contemporary "Earth etiquette." The use of the word "etiquette" by poet and environmentalist

Gary Snyder sits well with me. I have thus adopted the word and asked it kindly to go to work for me in expressing an ancient memory of humans living gracefully with all of creation.

What would an Earth etiquette look like? Many people all over the world are now asking this sort of question in a variety of ways. For instance, what if human communities and other-than-human communities shared the same rights and protections? What if we understood that it is no longer possible to separate human rights and environmental concerns, like the right to clean water? What if we stopped forcing rivers and creeks into underground pipes for real-estate developments and, instead, let them run freely so we could have beautiful and functional waterways in our cities? What if we stopped using words like "resources" or "commodities," which only distances us further from intimacy with our living Earth when we speak about our forests, water, and minerals?

The exploration of an Earth etiquette is a complement to the brilliant land ethics, philosophies, and practices expressed over the past years by ecologists and environmentalists Aldo Leopold, Vandana Shiva, John Muir, Maria Cherkasova, and many others. It is offered here as a complement to legal action on behalf of both the environment and social issues. Dr. Martin Luther King Jr. said, "Judicial decrees may not change the heart, but they can restrain the heartless."[14] Legislation is surely necessary for protection, but to care sustainably and enduringly for our lands and peoples we need to generate an essential feeling of well-being and appropriateness that only arises from our innate sense of right living. This will mean creating a new cultural narrative that includes nature and a respect for all people and all species. It necessitates an end to outmoded and dangerous beliefs in a mechanistic view of the natural world, which posits that the Earth is nothing more than dead matter and that nature is to be dominated, exploited, and controlled. Instead, it requires engaging in a regenerated worldview that remembers its origins in a living universe.

We can see tangible societal changes toward a new Earth etiquette through online databases like WiserEarth, a community directory that lists people who are transforming the world by addressing the main issues of our day: climate change, poverty, peace, water, hunger, social justice, conservation, and human rights. With more than one-hundred thousand organizations in the directory and representing millions of people worldwide, there is clearly a fast-growing interest for a more integrated approach to person-planet issues and a great desire for meaningful and sustainable living. As Maathai says, "Within a few decades ... the relation between the environment, resources and conflict may seem almost as obvious as the connection we see today between human rights, democracy and peace."[15]

At the center of an Earth etiquette is deep, respectful listening; knowing what to do comes from the listening. When we listen to the Big Quiet and feel the rhythm of our home planet, we become mindful that our survival is completely intertwined, people and planet. When we take a deep breath and allow for it, listening becomes, again, a part of our very nature, one that connects us with greater Nature.

In our day, educators and psychologists, artists and activists, elders and leaders, have all asserted that at the core of our global societal and environmental crises is a need to change our fundamental personal values and what we uphold as meaningful in our lives. Personal transformation is critical to mitigating our global crises. While we teeter on a precipice without knowing the outcome, it's encouraging to remember that unprecedented changes have occurred throughout history, positive shifts that at one time seemed impossible. Many of us have drawn upon examples of these shifts for inspiration: From the abolishment of slavery to women's suffrage, from the end of Apartheid in South Africa to the fall of the Berlin Wall, from unchecked industrial pollution to the restorative Clean Air and Clean Water Acts, from green technology moving from a fringe venture to a critical and fast-growing contribution. And although each of these changes still face ongoing struggles, we can see and experience the worldwide benefits of these paradigm shifts as they occur. Yet, these changes came about in our human realm only because the root cause of the problem, the suffering or imbalance, was first recognized by individual people who changed their own minds, thus changing the world around them.

I simply wish to point out that the outer geography of our human presence on Earth will change on a larger scale only when our internal geography changes, and not before. We require a new cultural story and societal dream for this new approach to be realized and in order to formulate Earth-honoring choices as we journey down this road less traveled.

Berry articulates this in his landmark book, *The Dream of the Earth*: "It's all a question of story. We are in trouble just now because we do not have a good story. We are in between stories. The old story, the account of how the world came to be and how we fit into it, is no longer effective. Yet we have not learned the new story."[16]

To find new cultural and personal stories, and to learn from their subtle sensibilities, is to first hear them. Through deeper listening we can become present to an alive world, one in which we can learn something new. Maybe we can find something we have been searching for, something that comes to us because we have been listening to the stories of woodlands and creeks, glaciers and deserts, polar bears and honeybees.

One night on the Northern California coast by a small lake, under billions of stars glittering in the Milky Way, a red-throated loon treated me to an evening concert. Usually much further north during courtship time, the loon startled me with its sudden, majestic wild song whose long, tremolo notes evoke divinity itself and an echo of the birth of stars. It seemed fitting that the loon's midnight-black feathers were adorned with white star-markings. In between these calls, lifting up from the lake's deep pools, frogs filled the night with mysterious riddles woven between the steady and comforting rhythm of their song. I could not actually see any of these singers, the loon or the frogs. They were hidden in the darkness but beckoned me most assuredly into an enchanted listening. It was the spaces left hollow after their wild and haunting music, between the melodies, that beguiled me into deep thought.

As I listened in, I was surprised to think how this open space of quietude can occur not only in the auditorium of wild nature, but also in human-made concert halls. There is no substitute for the stillness and sacredness of wild nature—in fact, I believe we cannot live without it; hence, the well-known words of Thoreau resonate with many of us: "In wildness is the preservation of the world." Yet, by the lake that night, I questioned how we might more consciously recognize and nurture integration points between modern civilization and the natural world, and music certainly seemed a noble candidate for this exploration.

Musicians the world over have granted us many inspirational encounters with listening. Here is one impression: During symphony performances conductors often utilize grand, sustained silences between important structural junctures or movements. These are golden moments, especially those silences directly after the endnote has cast its final echo, right before the audience bursts into applause. Conductors hold the numinous silence in their outstretched hands as long as possible, as if reaching for something we all sense and wish to know, then drop their arms like graceful birds pulling in their wings after long flight, signaling to the audience it is now their time. No one really wants this golden moment to end; it has been earned throughout the concert as the musicians offer their euphonic talents. The hall is reverberating with poetic harmonics, blazing chords, and spacious melodic reveries; the atmosphere itself is illuminated. This breathless, short silence is so richly imbued with aliveness that it can attune listeners to their extraordinary place in the community of the universe. I was reminded again, through the creativity and open space generated by the musicians, that humanity has a remarkable capacity to live beautifully and with grace, and to contribute life-enhancing wonders to the world instead of life-destroying exploits. This is part of our essence as a species. Again, I turn to Carson: "The human race is challenged more than ever before to demonstrate our mastery—not over nature but of ourselves."[17]

In our psyches, there are things found, envisioned, reconciled, and healed in golden moments of quietude, whether experienced in the concert hall or the great halls of wild Nature.

With this book, I offer you a collection of ideas "found" through listening. The reflections are personal in nature and mythopoeic in style. I wish for them to illustrate, as with a hologram, a micro-cosmic part of the larger emergent new story and render glimpses into an unfolding Earth etiquette. I offer them simply as entry points because each of us has something enlivening and useful to discover and share in the timeless soundings of the Big Quiet. Surely, we will need all of our hard-won findings to transition from the perilous course we are now on to a sustainable and Earth-honoring global culture.

2 Of Redwoods and Whales, Jewel Baskets and Roots

I wondered what would happen if I kept walking north. I let my imagination drift to another time beyond this one because, in actuality, I knew exactly where this wild Californian beach met with roadways and towns to the north and south. With my mind free from any particular map or century, I could wander as a nomad through place and time, walking these black sand shores into an endless wilderness extending all the way to Canada. I think many of us who love wild land imagine that if we just keep walking hard and strong in a place that has been allowed to remain itself, its boundaries will mysteriously keep expanding beyond our footfalls.

Walking on sand with a forty-pound pack involves the art of "footing." If you step very lightly and quickly, your feet do not sink so deep, as if defying gravity. It is the motion similar to that of water striders—you move each foot with just enough speed to catch the next step, skimming the top layer of sand and stones without stopping.

Along the Pacific Rim, on the Northern California coast, the roaring pull of the great ocean reverberates like thunder and does not stop, sometimes drowning out old, habitual thoughts and sometimes inspiring new ones. Whether eliciting deep contemplations or simple joys, the powerful sea is always turning our imaginings over and over, in circles and spirals, like shells rolling in the surf. I wanted my thoughts to be transformed into polished shells, naturally shaped by surf and sand—solidified mental saunterings that would glisten in the tide, made better for having been given to salt and sea.

Beginning at Black Sands Beach and meandering twenty-five miles north to the mouth of the Mattole River is a unique stretch of coastal wilderness. This extended area is called the Lost Coast and includes the King Range National Conservation Area and the Sinkyone Wilderness State Park. The coastal mountain range comes jutting down in a descending array of magnificent natural pyramids right to the shore. So rugged are the peaks that the workers who built Highway 1 could not strike through here, and the roadway was forced some miles inland. I like to think that this majestic coast protects itself for all time through its commanding form, making way for deer and bear, bobcat and raccoon to continue their timeless migrations to the ocean's edge unchanged. Fellow wanderer Skip White once told me that on one of his sojourns to this beach he saw three bucks swimming in the ocean. Early one spring morning, he was watching the sun touch the sea as it rose. Suddenly he noticed antlers emerging from behind an incoming wave, then the full heads of several deer. Ocean-going bucks—it still delights my imagination.

I have been coming to these wild shores all my life. It is my annual pilgrimage to the heart of Earth: the one I know best, each time a coming-home, each time a deep listening. I grew up slightly south of the Lost Coast in the small littoral town of Mendocino, and I ask, respectfully, when I visit this wild beach, that these lands again claim me as their own. Like others along these shores, I belong to Pacific Ocean, Coastal Redwood, Coho Salmon, and Gray Whale.

As I walk the northern shore along the lace of white foam, I carry with me questions and riddles, hopes and concerns that surface with the rhythm of long-distance walking. These stirring inquiries are weightless yet sometimes feel heavier than all my camping supplies combined. How does it really feel to be present with rolling waves, pelicans, sea lions, whales, sunsets, morning fog, seagulls, and crabs? In my everyday life in our technologically rich culture, the natural world is so often marginalized. What does it mean to care about open space, wildlife, and wild land as modern-day citizens? I have been told at times that my approach to life is too "romantic" for our contemporary age, and so I wrestle, once again, to brush off what I consider cynicism and continue my inward contemplations. How can I offer something of dignity and authenticity to the Earth? The Earth is gifting me with life, I am asking how to gift back. Entire cultures have been anchored to this concept of giving, and I ponder the lack of this exchange in our world. I remind myself that this is a pilgrimage to my holy place and not an escape from my life, not a running-away but instead a walking-toward. I come here to walk into myself and so meet the land with not just my feet but my whole self; I do it not to avoid but to contemplate.

Rainer Maria Rilke wrote:

> There is only one single, urgent task: to attach oneself someplace to nature, to that which is strong, striving and bright with unreserved readiness, and then to move forward in one's efforts without any calculation or guile, even when engaged in the most trivial and mundane activities. Each time we thus reach out with joy, each time we cast our view toward distances that have not yet been touched, we transform not only the present moment and the one following but also alter the past within us, weave it into the pattern of our existence, and dissolve the foreign body of pain whose exact composition we ultimately do not know. Just as we do not know how much vital energy this foreign body, once it has been thus dissolved, might impart to our bloodstream![1]

Like other Americans, I am an offshoot in this country's large and diverse cultural garden. I sometimes see myself as a new branch growing on an ancient tree, the roots of which are deeply anchored in the original people of this land and the spiritual soil of this beautiful and complex country.

I am originally a city person. Until the age of eight, when my mother moved my sister and me to rural Mendocino, I lived in San Francisco among concrete walkways, paved streets, and tall buildings. Once we moved to the country, I began to learn to live with the land and the seasons. Initially this was not a welcomed experience, as I was unaccustomed to walking to school in mud boots during rainy winters or navigating my every step as I hiked through rattlesnake territory in summer. However, in time there was an unexplainable reversal, a breach in my perception of what is "civilized," and I soon came to know and passionately love the nearby wilderness areas, many of which were already struggling.

It was then that I began to question the lack of respect most people, including myself, had for our living planet. It seemed to me that one of the biggest reasons people had not been respecting nature was because they had not been directly experiencing the Earth's beauty and natural wisdom. This sense of separation from the natural world, of which we are most essentially a part, can cause a great deal of imbalance and isolation. I recall the words of Thomas Berry: "The human venture depends absolutely on this quality of awe and reverence and joy in the Earth and all that lives and grows upon the Earth. As soon as we isolate ourselves from these currents of life and from the profound mood that these engender within us, then our basic life-satisfactions are diminished. None of our machine-made products, none of our computer-based achievements can evoke that total commitment to life."[2]

Consequently, in my late teenage years and into my twenties I started to lead small treks of personal discovery to different wilderness areas in California. This is how I discovered the Lost Coast. Through many excursions and conversations with wilderness companions, I learned that I was not alone in my longing for a deep connection to the wild. We all found solace in our rootedness in the physical world and a sense of home within the context of our time. It seemed clear that we desired to belong not only to family and culture, but also to place—a place beneath the pavement of modernity's disregard for wild nature.

I began to search for answers in the wisdom and legacy of our ancestors from different traditions that honored the Earth. I say "our ancestors" because no matter where we may live presently, we are all descendants of ancestral people who lived intimately with the land. All of us have the potential to recognize and ex-perience ourselves once again as aboriginals of the Earth with a sophisticated kinship with nature, even if it is an effort to reclaim these roots. It involves a courageous inner exploration, but I think it is a worthy endeavor and one that vitally contributes to the well-being of both ourselves and our ability to care for our planet, whether we are city or country dwellers. It may take some genera-tions to learn the language of the land once again, both its more hidden urban vernacular and its more accessible rural dialect, but ecological elocution is essential.

Before I lose my footing on these shifting sands, let me say that this idea is not meant to disregard or usurp the great need we have to honor and learn from the present-time Indigenous people of each continent. Their precious voices and knowledge need to be revered and protected, especially after so many years of violent discrimination and often outright annihilation. Wade Davis, noted anthropologist and National Geographic Explorer-in-Residence, relates in his books and speeches his fervid concern about the rate of loss of Indigenous cultures and languages:

> The key indicator is language loss. There are at present some 6,000 languages. But of these fully half are not being taught to children. Which means that effectively, unless something changes, these languages are already dead.... A language is not merely a body of vocabulary or a set of gram-matical rules. It is a flash of the human spirit, the means by which the soul of each particular culture reaches into the

material world. Every language is an old growth forest of the mind, a watershed thought, an entire ecosystem of spiritual possibilities.[3]

Shifting the pack on my back, I slow my pace to savor a moment in the warming sun. Now that I have hiked six miles, the untamed shore opens up before me. A graceful pelican flies low over the waves in search of fish. Like a dancer anticipating a partner's every move, I marvel at the bird's effortless skill in tracking the rise and fall of the water. This is an animated language of flight and navigation, which the pelican teaches us. There is pure and unencumbered beauty and knowledge everywhere here. A mist-filled breeze lifts off the tops of the waves, sprinkling my face with saltwater. The seashore seems to embrace me, and I feel as though this place has not known human brutality, that these shores are still a place of natural balance and timeless rhyme. I take in a long breath, close my eyes, and listen. The heartbeat of the Earth is here if one just takes the time to be quiet enough to hear it.

Many people of many tribes have migrated and intermarried over the eons; nevertheless, every one of us can trace our heritage back to a place or places where our forebears once lived closely to and respectfully with the Earth. The potential for each of us to discover, heal, and nurture our modern-day aboriginal natures, our "nativeness," in a new way is one of our most important attributes.

What, exactly, is in need of healing? It is our loss of meaningful, well-rooted identity with a land-based ancestry, as well as with our present-day dwelling place. No matter our urban lifestyles, we still belong to the ground, and forgetting or ignoring this fact of existence leaves a sad hollow in our soul. On a larger societal scale, feeling uprooted and disconnected can cause a desire to conquer or dominate others in order to establish self-worth and regain a sense of belonging. This includes attempting to dominate the physical world by over-consuming material goods in an attempt to fill a personal and cultural emptiness generated when we lose a meaningful and fulfilling kinship with the Earth and each other.

Most Americans today are both beneficiaries of conquest and descendents of displaced and conquered people. These are challenging lineages to reconcile. Restoration and living relationally can be accomplished once again by learning to fully embrace the places where we live, by coming to know the Earth right around us and the history of the people of our regions. We can gradually diminish and begin to reverse the effects of conquest (both internally and externally) through honest, in-depth history and natural science education. This scholarship, and its telling, is part of the new cultural story we need to enliven in our era, right in our own communities and homes. Part of this process for me, besides looking east to my European and Ukrainian history, has been the discovery of the cultural and natural history of Mendocino County. I am still listening to and learning from the original Northern Californians and their land as much as I can.

Stories of our Earth-honoring ancestors worldwide are important to all of us for the wisdom they share and the sense of belonging they offer. One of the many things the original people of Mendocino County did so elegantly was to live with the land in a balanced manner, a way now called ecologically sustainable. The point of story sharing is not to look nostalgically to the past and pretend to re-live what once was or to feel that contemporary life is hopelessly lacking, but rather to resourcefully examine beneficial "keys" of information that were and still are at the heart of place-based people. Just as in harvesting a mature garden, we find that the seeds of the past hold fruitful knowledge about survival for the future. It seems wise to step back occasionally from the everyday and look through a wider lens to view most appropriately our human continuum. We can then better appreciate that whatever has already happened informs us and that whatever is occurring now and appearing on the horizon can potentially offer the best of life experiences—even those we might beg to end at the time. Sometimes the experiences we want to escape the most are also those that teach us the most.

Like a lot of young people in America at the time, I grew up hearing about the settlers and "how the West was won." This is a common phrase found in school textbooks and films of all kinds. I began to wonder about this "winning," these "settlers." What was so unsettled before?

I imagined that before the land we call the Northern California Coast was "settled" there was quite a harmonious "unsettledness" here. The Yurok, Pomo, Sinkyone, Wailaki, Mattole, Miwok, Wyot, and many other peoples were living contentedly in a land of plenty. They were not always at peace with one another (there were raiding and disputes over territory among tribes to be sure), but there was a general, peaceful, and highly sustainable way of life that followed a natural ebb and flow.

As Malcolm Margolin tells us in his book, *The Ohlone Way*, when the Spaniards first came to California they recorded in their journals that there was such an abundance of salmon a person could reach into a stream and pull out any number of fish, that fox were not frightened by humans and commonly ran underfoot, that ducks were so plentiful a hunter could often bring down several birds with a single shot. One could hardly call taking down a deer "hunting" as we think of it today, because there was really no tracking involved. Deer, rabbits, and quail—a less-wary wildlife—lived closer with their human kin in those days. The graceful relationship between American Indian people and their homeland hardly seemed to need any more settling.

Indians have lived throughout Mendocino (and adjacent Humboldt) County for more than ten thousand years and, it is important to say, they still do. I frequently meet people who are surprised upon hearing this. Different tribal people live throughout this region, including those on the Round Valley Indian Reservation in Covelo and more than fourteen Rancherias.

One summer I worked on the Round Valley reservation building wilderness trails with Indian youth. One of the mothers,

Rosemarie, who lived in Covelo, remarked, "Yes, I want people to know we're still here!"

Some of the tribes here are the Pomo, Yurok, Wailaki, Sinkyone, Yuki, Concow Maidu, Nomlaki, Cahto, and Pit River, yet few if any of these people were really a singular "tribe" or called themselves by these names. Originally, each of these groupings was made up of several dozen different tribelets, not united, each a nation, each one a government unto itself, each with its own language. Many of the groups lived a few miles inland from the coast (near, but not in, the redwoods) or in the warmer valleys, journeying once a year to the ocean during certain months to harvest salt, kelp, and seafood.

It was not until my high school years that I learned of the Pomo people of Mendocino. I was not looking to find them. Nor was I, unfortunately, taught anything about their existence in school.

One day a friend's mother took us on an outing to the historic Sun House in Ukiah (this was before it officially became part of the Grace Hudson Museum in 1986). An elder woman walked us through the unusual redwood structure, and there on a table, a very small Pomo Indian basket caught my eye. It was tiny, not more than an inch-and-a-half across and covered in bright green mallard duck feathers and finely crafted abalone shells that reflected the light of not only the room, but seemingly, the light of the mind of the basket maker, who I could only dimly imagine even so. The exquisite little basket gleamed with aliveness, and I remember thinking I had never seen anything that small constructed so perfectly. I later learned that such a piece is called a jewel basket—a gift basket. I also learned that basket weaving was sometimes said by the women to be the weaving of the long hairs of Grandmother Grass. Hearing that dazzled my imagination.

Slender willow shoots form the main part of many Pomo baskets, and each willow branch is carefully peeled and cured. The threads woven into and through the willows are of many colors and textures and collected from different roots, grasses, and shrubs. One of the most important roots is that of the familiar sedge, used as a lacing material. Sometimes, the weavers used stripped and dried redbud bark to create a beautiful red accent. The Pomo lived within the cycles of collecting basket materials on a daily basis. At one time the people of this region were called Digger Indians, not because of the gathering of tubers for food, but because they were observed continuously collecting roots and grasses for their magnificent baskets. Pomo baskets display such subtle and complex designs, each with a unique shape and exhibiting patterns perfected over centuries. They are some of the most intricate and decorative in the world—also among the most coveted by collectors.

The Pomo had baskets for almost every aspect of life: holding seeds, grinding acorns, collecting roots, snaring woodpeckers, carrying fire wood, ladling acorn mush, and even for carrying babies. Newborns were soon nestled in portable "papoose" baskets. Other baskets were so tightly woven they could hold water for drinking and cooking. Stones were heated in a fire and then carefully placed in a basket with water and food and stirred in such a way that the stones cooked the food evenly but did not burn the basket. The Pomo lived in a culture inseparable from baskets, and when they died, their baskets were often placed on the funeral pyre to accompany them in the next world. I tried to picture what it would be like to live in a world of such spiritual elegance and artistic sophistication.

Many years later after my first encounter with a Pomo basket, in the summer of 2008, director of the Grace Hudson Museum Sherrie Smith-Ferri generously took the time to further explain to me some of the extraordinary culture of basketry. Sherrie, who grew up in a Pomo and Miwok family, described basket making as a living art that is at the heart of Pomo culture. She told me that to understand the essence of an individual basket was to understand the time period and circumstances of its making: how the basket was made and what it was made for is always very specific.

She spoke eloquently about the immense diversity of techniques and designs of the baskets and how the collecting of the materials was an integral part of the basket crafter's decision-making.

I asked Sherrie about the jewel basket I had seen years ago. She revealed to me that these kinds of baskets are also called treasure baskets and are the highest expression of skill. Most often, they are the very ones that are placed on funeral pyres. Because of their great artistic beauty and value they are a tangible symbol of grief, and when they are given to the fire, they demonstrate the great loss that is felt when a loved one dies. They help people to mourn and express their love, she told me.

Speaking to Sherrie and reading ethnoecologist M. Kat Anderson's book *Tending the Wild*, I was again reminded of the intricate relationship the Indians had, prior to European arrival, with the natural landscape and management of California's ecology. The basketry craft is a poignant example of how the indigenous people were involved in the caretaking of the plants of their region. The baskets literally began by the tending of the native plants that would eventually be the converted materials for weaving them. Much of the soil of "wild" sedge beds, for example, was actually continuously aerated and cleaned of debris by weavers selecting and collecting the sedge rhizomes generation after generation. Anderson notes that given the huge quantities of plants cultivated for basketry, the line between gathering and agriculture is not distinct. In a larger sense, to deeply understand the ecosystem of California, and to re-learn good conduct here, is to learn how the original people lived with the plants and animals.

Anderson writes:

> The California landscapes that early explorers, settlers and missionaries found so remarkably rich were in part shaped, and regularly renewed, by the land management practices employed by native peoples. Many of the biologically richest of California's habitats were not climax communities at the time of Euro-Americans' arrival but instead were mosaics of

various stages of ecological succession, or fire subclimaxes, intensified and perpetuated by seasonally burning. In a very real sense, some of the most productive and carefully managed habitats were in fact Indian artifacts. In many cases these landscapes experienced far greater degrees of managerial care and ecologically sophisticated manipulation than are found today.[4]

Mihilakawna Pomo elder Lucy Smith was Sherrie's grandmother and the person who taught Sherrie how to make baskets. When she was interviewed by Anderson, Lucy Smith put it this way (relating what her mother taught her about caring for all her relatives):

> (She said) we had many relatives and … we all had to live together, so we'd better learn how to get along with each other. She said it wasn't too hard to do. It was just like taking care of your younger brother or sister. You got to know them, find out what they liked and what made them cry, so you'd know what to do. If you took good care of them you didn't have to work so hard. When that baby gets to be a man or woman they're going to help you out. You know, I thought she was talking about us Indians and how we are supposed to get along. I found out later from my older sister that mother wasn't just talking about Indians, but the plants, animals and birds—everything on this earth. They are our relatives and we better know how to act around them or they'll get after us.[5]

There are not many traditional basket makers anymore, Sherrie explained, but she was also hopeful that the art would be renewed because of a slow but increasing interest of new basket makers. In thanking Sherrie for her words with me, I mentioned how special it was to see the baskets in Ukiah—instead of a museum on the east coast or such—in the region where the plants were collected, where the baskets were made, and where the basket makers actually lived. We were silent for a moment and then simultaneously laughed as Sherrie said what was clearly on both of our minds, "The baskets are happier here."

It did not escape my attention that each of these brilliantly woven baskets required hours and hours of work. An everyday working basket might have as many as twenty-five thousand little stitches, each made with a refined bone awl. Thus, it could take the creator more than a week to complete a single cooking vessel.

⤙

Another question emerges as I step further along the beach: How can I, and we collectively, gracefully integrate "high" technology with the sphere of the wild, which is often mistaken for a "low" realm? In these electronic times, how do we integrate our need to stay connected to simple naturalness and (keeping the Pomo baskets in mind) the authenticity of handmade things, the real digital technologies? I ponder this as I recall leaving my car, cell phone, sound system, and computer behind, admittedly some of my favorite devices. I am convinced we do not need to force the question of technology vs. nature so much as we need to proceed with attention to purpose-of-use and ask ourselves: What would truly improve the quality of our lives and the sustainability of the Earth's ecosystems?

In 2006, I attended an international conference of leaders in the field of mediation and happened to be present for a discussion between a university professor and two American Indian women from New Mexico about the relevance of indigenous knowledge to our contemporary systems of governance. At one point the sincere professor became agitated, exclaiming with frustration that the entire idea of listening to older indigenous cultures, employing nature awareness, and going "back to the Earth" was, in fact, passé and demonstrated a useless "post-modern sentimentalism." We are in a new time, he declared, one of advanced technology, high-definition television, and new democratic ideas and practices developing on the Internet. We nodded our heads in agreement and were excited about the new technological advances and acknowledged them in a positive and inclusive manner (social media was just exploding at that time and was/is a thrilling example of how the Internet is enabling advances in democracy and innovative collaborations). But, I thought it was important to remind him that all these activities, inventions, and technological developments were still taking place right here on Earth. In this sense, I could hardly consider the entire living ecosystem of the planet "passé" or "post modern," especially if we still consider eating plants and animals, drinking water, breathing air, and manufacturing our daily needs from natural resources essential human activities.

In thinking further about the question of technology, I realized that as much as I depend upon and seriously enjoy my computer, cell phone, and other clever, helpful devices, I would always cherish and desire handmade things. There is no aesthetic substitute for those things fashioned simply by the direct movement of skilled, working hands.

⟶

On one of my excursions to Black Sands when I was around sixteen years old, I visited Mr. Turner, who was skilled in the use of handmade tools. These were hard years for me, and I went to the coast to soothe my unquenchable loneliness and try to remedy my endless searching for something beyond my everyday life. I had studied literature of different cultures, from Buddhist to American Indian, which reflected upon the nature of loneliness; it seemed to be the thing that all humans had in common. Knowing of this shared loneliness was, oddly enough, something comforting to me. I felt I finally belonged to something, even if it was just the collective isolated lonely.

Mr. Turner was a fisherman who lived along my route from Mendocino to the wilderness beach north of it. The summer sun and ocean wind had sculpted his leathery, exposed skin into a textured relief map. I could almost make out the continent of North America on his high-boned cheeks. We had seen each other over the course of several years, and though we rarely spoke, there was a sense of understanding between us. On this particular trip on my way to the Lost Coast, the old man was sitting outside his cabin carving a small whale from driftwood. I felt as if he had known I was coming.

When I walked near, he stood up, quietly greeted me, and offered me some of his homemade dried fish, already wrapped in paper for my hiking trip. When he handed me the gift, I realized it was the first time I had ever looked directly into his gentle eyes, and I suddenly found myself crying. When I quieted, he told me this story:

> I am told my ancestors were here over ten thousand years ago. We called our ancestors The People Of Whom We Are Born. They touched all the Earth with the old dances. These dances traveled up the coast on the rivers. There was the Jumping Dance. The dancers would sing and dance in boats all the way across the river. The boats were not paddled but moved by the leaping of the dancers. The dance lasted many days and the people traveled up the river until they came to the mountains, and there the dance ended with a big feast. This was the time of renewal for the people and the land. All the people dearly loved this land here as they do today. The forests and rivers were happy. We remember it, and it will be that way again.

His words deeply touched me, but later, my heart sank as I discovered over the next few years more about what had happened to the Indian people in this region. Tragically, it is the same sad story that is told throughout the Americas, a story that still wounds us today. When the European settlers claimed the land along the coast, the indigenous people did not uphold the settlers' concept of private property and so dangerous conflicts arose as the original inhabitants were no longer able to travel freely their traditional migratory paths between valley and coast. European settlers along the Mendocino coast insisted that the Indians were a threat to their safety. Within a short time, many Indians had been brutally assaulted, displaced, or murdered by these white interlopers, all in the name of civilization. The federal government made an effort to deal with the "Indian problem" by rounding up several thousand native inhabitants. In 1857, the government established a coastal reservation with a central garrison: Fort Bragg. The reservation only lasted ten years because of poor crops, misappropriation of funds, and the greed of those running the reservation. The settlers also wanted more of the reservation-allotted land. In essence, the entire production was a calamity: disease and predation greatly reduced the Indian population. Many of the survivors escaped the compounds and the area; others were forced into the Round Valley Reservation.

I read further about the plight of the Indians in Robert Winn's essay published in the 1986 *Mendocino Historical Review*:

> Around 1859 relations between the settlers and the Indians in Round Valley took an ugly turn. Driven by hunger and a desire to discourage the settlers and drive them away, the Indians had begun to kill stock. In retaliation, the stockowners killed Indians. ...Volunteers conducted a campaign of extermination, attacking Rancherias indiscriminately and slaughtering the innocent along with the guilty. Reports of these brutal raids made their way to San Francisco and Sacramento, and in 1860 a joint committee of the state legislature was appointed to investigate the 'Mendocino War,' as it came to be called. The committee went to Round Valley, interviewed ranchers, Indian agents, and soldiers, and confirmed the reports: 'Accounts are daily coming in from the counties on the Coast Range, of sickening atrocities and wholesale slaughter of great numbers of defenseless Indians in that region of country. Within the last four months, more Indians have been killed by our people than during the century of Spanish and Mexican domination.'⁶

I do not want to forsake this critical part of my coastal account because the story of the original people is still here, still alive. I feel it is held in the folds and valleys of Mendocino and Humboldt Counties. The trees and creeks, the stones and the hills, intimately know the tears and howls of grief shed amongst them just as they also remember the dances, the crafting, the dreaming, and the prayers of beauty still told for them. The proud descendents of these original people are still here, and they remember. I, too, want to remember. Perhaps then the precious little jewel basket that glinted at me from across the Sun House in Ukiah—that basket created so lovingly by the hands of a woman who knew where every grass and root grew in her neighborhood—cannot be mistaken for a cute trinket, but instead be revered affectionately in a place of honor set aside for those things made with natural loveliness, ancestral value, and deep-rootedness. I want to know where I walk and who has walked before me; otherwise, I will be just another tourist in my own dwelling place, never truly at home.

Today there are glimpses of renewal and respect for the original peoples of the land in the region. Since 1986, a consortium of ten sovereign tribes from Northern California has created the Inter-Tribal Sinkyone Wilderness Council, which has worked to return indigenous stewardship to lands that were violently taken from the Indian people more than a hundred years ago. The Council founded the 3,845-acre InterTribal Sinkyone Wilderness, the first of this kind of wilderness area in the nation, to ensure permanent conservation and stewardship of land that has great cultural significance to these tribes. Re-establishing indigenous stewardship to Sinkyone has been a community process and one that successfully arrested clear-cut logging in Sinkyone's rainforests, and the InterTribal Sinkyone Wilderness now serves as an inspiring model for other regions to support Indian people renewing and reclaiming their traditional land stewardship.

However we might understand the word "settle," many of us have assembled at the westernmost edge of the North American continent, and so it seems far past time to consider the current direction of this longstanding westward motion. California is now the most populous state in the country.

After thousands of years of migration from Asia east to the Americas, people from Europe and beyond have continued for centuries to march west with migrations and conquests—a movement that has displaced countless Indigenous generations and forced many people into slavery—in truth, a bloody superhighway running in the path of the setting sun. As I stood on the shores of the Lost Coast, I humbly realized, as thinkers have articulated with great eloquence before me, Western civilization has come to the end of its westward run. It is time to stop displacing people and plundering the land; there is not much choice. The road carved out from east to west has been paved with broken hearts and bodies, unacknowledged ignorance, and unquenched spiritual needs that churn beneath the surface of our cultural psyche. At some point, some of us are drawn to engage our collectively restless and suppressed questions about how to inhabit this land, now "ours," intelligently. How, in this way, can we fulfill our deeper longings to restore honor to the Earth we stand upon?

Just as the sea pulls back from the shore during low tide each day, revealing hidden tide pools with treasures not before seen, this is potentially a profound moment of opportunity. We can choose to transform this outward movement westward, of "manifest destiny" in the minds of the explorers, to an inward one, a journey within the internal landscape of our humanity. The next "expansion" could be, instead of conquest and domination, one of justice and sustainability, creativity and community. In this new motion, maybe—just maybe—something new and wonderful could happen. At the edge of the Pacific, we can experience the natural border between the land and the sea as a way to pause and view our own reflection. The tide pools are mirrors asking us to ask ourselves, how can we see things differently and inhabit a place well? Moreover, if we do, will this stop the incessant need for destructive empire building and conquest? Can we transform and heal our collective habit of displacing others, enslaving others, and excessively consuming material goods in a drive to find identity and meaning, and to fulfill a false sense of progress? It is time to draw upon a different kind of wealth and fulfillment, which can be fostered through intimacy with our Earth community.

Maybe if we stood still *well*, we could hear the Earth, hear our names in the wind, and realize that we are already home. It is now time to deeply know and care for this place, our planet, that gives us life and sustains us, despite our ignorance and assumptions that the latest financial reports and consumer products are more interesting than the stories that come exquisitely out of the land. If we are wise and creative, we can have both.

As I stand at the water's edge, my toes now wet with tide pool secrets, I feel compelled to explore further who I am living with. Isn't this part of being home, knowing with whom you share your corner of the world?

I looked to two of the most ancient beings of this coast: one that migrates well—the Gray Whale (*Eschrichtius robustus*)—and one that stands well in one place—the Coastal Redwood (*Sequoia sempervirens*).

Twice each year there is cause for great wonder and celebration as we coastal inhabitants and travelers enthusiastically gather at the headlands to watch the migration of the Gray Whales. No matter how young or old we may be, we cannot help but shout out with glee as the whales surface to breathe, sending their great white-water prayer flags skyward as unmistakable testimony to an enduring promise that fantastic life will prevail despite the odds, a basic faith greater than we can fathom. The whales give many of us a simple but profound feeling of hope, and the rhythmic passing of the whales by the shore each year signifies that something is still right with the world.

There are two populations of Gray Whales: the Korean, or Western Pacific, and the Californian, or Eastern Pacific. The migration of the Californian Gray Whales is massive, 16,000—22,000 kilometers round trip, from their summering home north of Alaska in the Bering and Chukchi Seas to their winter breeding grounds in the warm waters of Baja California in Mexico. They follow the sunlight because their main food source, the tiny plankton, amphipods, and other small creatures grow best in ample sunlight—more light means more food, which beckons them on their seasonal migrations.

With the approach of autumn, when the waters turn cold with less sunlight, and consequently, less food, the whales journey to the lagoons of Baja to calve and mate. In December and January, Gray Whales can be seen traveling south, passing off the Northern California coast, and then seen again returning in March and April on their route north with their newborns in tow. Amazingly, the whales swim continuously day and night, even while they are sleeping. That's some cruise control.

The Californian Gray Whale has the longest yearly migration of any mammal, and as I watch them, I find myself contemplating the obvious: although theirs is a vast movement, they leave no trail of destruction or displacement of others in their wake. What can we learn from these leviathans? They remind us of ancient mysteries and bring biological news from the bottom of the sea and the far ends of our world, yet they travel on through as peaceful diplomats without portfolios, touching so many disparate places and, by extension, the people who live there.

Even with all their tremendous strength and mammoth presence, the whales are fighting for their lives. The Californian (Eastern Pacific) population has fought their way back from near-extinction twice within the last hundred years. In 1857, the breeding grounds of the Californian Gray Whales were discovered, and they were almost hunted to extinction. When their numbers slowly increased, the hunting resumed, but soon again, their population was reduced to just a few hundred. Alarmed that the world could actually lose the last of the whales, people all over the globe made huge efforts, and legal protection was finally achieved. Since 1949, the International Whaling Commission has granted the Gray Whales protection from commercial hunting on a large scale. Since then the whales along the Asian Pacific Rim have made a significant recovery, with a population now between 20,000 and 22,000. However, the continuation of this rebound depends upon vigilance and the constant monitoring of other obstacles to the whales' survival, including pollution, the military sonar that disorients them, and the consequences of global warming.

The other population of Gray Whales, the Korean, has not fared as well, with their numbers dwindling to just 300. I try to take in this information and put it somewhere that makes sense, but I find myself unable to do so. I pause on my long, sandy walk north to remember how many of the world's beautiful creatures are going extinct each day due to human activities. Some scientists estimate this to be as many as one hundred to one thousand times greater than the natural phenomenon of extinction that occurs normally in nature over time. Biologists Phillip and Donald Levine estimate that every twenty minutes, an extinction happens somewhere on Earth. We are losing a startling thirty thousand species a year.[7] Yes, I think to myself, it does matter to attempt to comprehend this sorrowful reality.

It is not easy to grasp the size of these whales, who are up to forty-five feet in length, and then realize that although distant cousins, they are in fact mammals, relatives. Maybe if we remember them as family members, we would find the right comportment with them. We all know from school that whales evolved from land creatures that returned to the sea an estimated fifty million years ago. Their bodies transformed in this process: they lost their insulating fur and instead acquired protective blubber, eventually lost their hind limbs, and reconfigured their breathing apparatus, among other changes.

Although the Gray Whale is not the largest of all the whale species, there is nevertheless something extraordinary about seeing an animal so large in comparison to our own human bodies. It's not just the physical grandeur that is striking to behold, but also the greatness of intelligence and the blockbuster enchantment that comes with the whale's presence.

I once invited a small group of junior high school students on a whale-watching field trip. These young people had never before seen whales migrating, and there was a palpable excitement as we drove to the Mendocino coast to discover them at last. There was also a challenge. The date had been set and much planning had gone into the outing, so there was no chance of changing to a nicer day for whale watching. That morning the sky was bright and clear, but a furious wild wind was causing a frenzy of whitecaps all the way to the horizon. It was beautiful to behold but made it very difficult to discern white water from spouting whales. Filled with enthusiasm and undeterred, the group sat bundled in woolen scarves and thick coats right at the edge of the headlands, binoculars at the ready. We watched, waited, and wondered what we were actually seeing. I remembered thinking, after a wind-whipped hour, "Wouldn't it be incredibly rewarding for the students to really see the size of these whales and to experience a clear sighting?"

Just then, I lowered my binoculars from scanning the sea about a mile out and was shocked to see a Gray Whale just forty feet directly in front of us.

I hollered above the wind, exhorting everyone to immediately drop their binoculars. It took an immeasurably but marvelously long time for the entire body of the whale to pass its full arc above the surface of the ocean as it dove right before us. Then, to finish, the whale "waved" its fluke. The kids and I will never forget the thrill. This is the sort of first-hand experience that makes a child a friend, rather than a stranger, to Nature for life.

I had read several accounts of "friendly whales" in Baja, those who actually swim close to the tour boats, allowing visitors to touch them and admire their giant babies. With our very own Mendocino whale so near, the students jumped up and down in delight, though not too close to the edge of the cliffs, to be sure. I was dazzled, of course, and yet quiet inside, feeling touched with the privilege to experience the mystical dimension of whale "communication."

Along the coast, there are other gigantic denizens that command our attention, ancient ones who reach back far in time, some more than a thousand years. When you look up, you cannot see the top of these titans; that is how tall and expansive the Coastal Redwoods are.

On an excursion to the Lost Coast, I ventured to one of the few old-growth redwood forests still standing just north of Garberville, the Avenue of the Giants, to meet Mary Anne Kenney, an elderly woman and a dear friend.

Thin rays of light streamed through the feathered needles of the forest. The palatial trees filled the entire sky, allowing only small shafts of sunlight through the treetops like ribbons of molten glass. The shimmering sunrays reached downward to the cool bed of the forest floor, glancing off the top of my head as a warm greeting.

What is illuminated in a redwood forest is only what the upper branches reveal at any given time of day. Beyond this, there is only a blue glow within the ancient groves that seems to come directly from the trees themselves, as well as a deep quiet that arrests all outer and inner chatter.

One redwood must have felt the footsteps of a familiar friend who had been to the forest many times before. I watched as Mary Anne placed her hands in the folds of the deep furrows of the tree trunk. The stately woman leaned her body forward, looking up the column, eyes searching for the hidden firmament above. I marveled at how my friend's finely wrinkled face and hands blended with the crevices and woven strands of the fibrous bark. For a moment, human and tree became one. Time is stilled in these old groves, and the mind lifts and tunes itself to the hum of the ages.

These Coastal Redwoods are the tallest trees on Earth and have survived here for more than seventy-five million years. Individuals can grow up to three hundred and sixty feet tall and can live longer than two thousand years. The oldest recorded tree was a Coastal Redwood named Eon in Humboldt County, which fell in 1977 and was estimated to be a startling 6,200 years of age.

While these very old trees have much to teach us about survival and endurance, they now exist only as a miniscule living museum in small corridors along the north coast after more than a century of timber cutting. The journey to the California redwoods is bittersweet: the trees are still there, which is cause for celebration; yet, the old-growth forests have been mostly exterminated.

The ribbon of Coastal Redwoods in California typically extends about twenty miles inland, but in Mendocino County it reaches about forty miles east because of rivers and valleys that allow the fog, the key maritime climatic requirement for these trees, to drift further. These remarkable titans are so tall that ground water cannot make its way past the capillary-action limit of three hundred feet to the upper branches, so the top is watered through the upper flat needles by osmosis with the fog. In addition, during the long, rainless summers in this region, these top feathery leaves, perfectly designed to capture water droplets from the misty coastal air, provide water to the roots as it drips to the ground. Redwoods can also generate their own fog using huge amounts of transpiring moisture condensed at night above the cool valley groves.

Redwoods are also known for their special bark. This fibrous red bark is very thick and contains no resin, making the trees remarkably fire resistant and resilient. It is also a surprise to learn that these tallest of trees do not have deep-anchored roots, but rather shallow ones, reaching down only some six or eight feet. The secret to their upright strength is in the intertwining and actual joining of their massive roots, which radiate out horizontally several hundred feet. These interconnected roots stabilize the trees in flood conditions and high winds, and they can also share water through this extensive root system. In addition to the conjoined roots, during big winter storms the arms of the trees literally swim in the wind, as if treading water, to keep the trees upright.

Each time I pick up a redwood seed cone from the forest floor I am startled at its size, which is about the same as a grape's, and the seed itself, which is roughly the size of a rice grain. How can such a tiny seed grow into the tallest tree in the world? I wonder, is it possible that the smallest seeds we carry in the quiet of our hopeful hearts can grow into the very greatest and most noble things?

These trees are also unique because, besides the germination of seeds, they can also reproduce by sprouting from a root burl, creating a ring of smaller trees. Sometimes you can see several generations of trees growing around one central hollow where the parent tree once existed. It's a family circle of sorts, and it is thought that some redwoods actually contain the identical genetic codes of trees millions of years old—that is, a redwood of today can be birthed from a prehistoric one.

Sadly, only about 4 percent of the redwoods that grew along the Pacific coast before logging still exist, which has caused ongoing battles up and down the region as people have put their very lives on the line to save the last of these grand keepers of time. There are legendary women from this area who have risked life and limb because of their dedication to these trees, notably Judi Bari and Julia Butterfly Hill, and I remember them each time I visit the forest. Starting at the age of seventeen, I worked on a campaign to protect the redwoods along the Big River Watershed, which skirts the southern end of the town of Mendocino. During that time, the many biologists and environmentalists who fought for the trees were my champions (and they still are). I have learned that these redwood battles are always complex, but no matter what opinion or inclination a person might have toward the future of these forests, one thing is certain: no one with any sensitivity can be in the presence of these ancients without experiencing enormous inspiration and a tremendous feeling of awe. More than once I have seen men with tears in their eyes along these backwoods trails.

Hans Christian Andersen wrote in 1861 of the future and promise of poetry in his work *The New Century's Goddess*. This literary piece, in which Andersen elaborates on his hope for new freedom of thought, posits a few places as the possible origin of this New Goddess of poesy, and one of them is the stately redwood forest of California.

From Andersen:

The New Century's Goddess—whom our great-grandchildren or perhaps a still later generation will know, but we shall not—when and how does she reveal herself? What does she look like? What is the theme of her song? Whose heartstrings will she touch? To what heights will she lift her century?

Each century, each thousand years, one might even say, has its chief expression in its poetry. Born in the passing era, it comes forth and reigns in the new, succeeding era. When begins the New Age of Poesy? When will the Goddess be known? When will she be heard?

Will she come from the newfound land of Columbus, the land of freedom, where the native is hunted and the African is a beast of burden, the land from where we heard *The Song of Hiawatha*? Or from the antipodes, that golden nugget in the southern sea, the land of opposites, where our nighttime is their daytime, and where the black swans sing in mossy forests? Or maybe from the land where Memnon's pillar rings but we never understood the song of the Sphinx in the desert from the isle of the coalpit, where, since the age of the great Elizabeth, Shakespeare has reigned? Or from Tycho Brahe's home, where he wasn't wanted; or from California's fairyland, where the redwood holds high its crown as king of the earth's forests?

Greetings, you Goddess of the New Century![8]

Walking in these forests, "California's fairyland," I ponder Andersen's words and wonder how we are doing in regard to his salutation sent down to us through time and heard beyond "the clatter of engines, the screams of locomotives, the thunder of quarry blasts"[9] of his day. From my place in the Coastal Redwoods, I am attempting to greet this New Century's Goddess by holding a lantern up for her appreciation and emancipation. The promise of her freedom is rooted in America's soil, the Indigenous people of this land, and the hearts of all people learning to be at home here from their various places of origin.

As I continue my sojourn north along the coastal sands toward the Mattole River, I remember that places of origin have always remained important to people here and everywhere. Whenever we meet travelers on the road or in another country, it is only moments before we inquire or are asked, "Where are you from?"

I have wondered how to answer this question with integrity, because simply naming a place seems complacent and far too discourteous. An alive, vibrant, breathing homeland cannot be described by a street address or the name of a state or province. Perhaps a better answer would be to quote from Herman Melville's *Moby-Dick*: "It is not down in any map; true places never are."[10] My home is a true place; and I am attempting to learn everything about it—on and off the map.

One distinguished, traditional marker of a place of origin that has always intrigued me is the omphalos stone common to many old cultures. Omphalos is the Greek transliteration of the Latin *umbilicus* or the navel of the world. Indigenous people worldwide have recognized and marked sacred places or places of origin with omphalos stones. This navel stone indicates the center of the Earth, the source of all life. These are not human-designated places so much as natural forces of the land recognized by humans.

An image of a large omphalos stone is with me as I awake from dreams my last morning along the wilderness coast. The nights have been filled with the elliptical rhythm of the ocean waves, lulling me to sleep and washing my dreams. On this final day of my trek, my mind wanders back to the beginning mile along the beach, where I pay homage to my imagined navel stone, the stone of my morning dream. Approximately one mile up the first gentle curve of the Black Sands shore, a large boulder marks the entryway to the wild coast. I have secretly held that this magnificent mass of rock is my navel stone of the western strand, perhaps stretching the traditional definition in so doing, but this is what I can touch with what I have.

Most omphalos stones are egg-shaped and can indicate both the spiritual center of a people and their geographical place of origin. In this dual sense, there are navel stones in locations the world over, as they are the center of the Earth for the different peoples.

The ancient Greeks had several important omphalos stones, the most well-known of which is located at the temple at Delphi. Another can be found on the island of Crete. Zeus had designated these regions when he sent out two eagles to fly around the Earth and meet at its center. Delphi was famous for the oracle and Crete was known as the umbilical cord of Zeus, which fell to Earth after his birth.

All throughout Europe there are many navel stones. In Uisnech, Ireland, there is the omphalos known as the Stone of Divisions where the archdruid Midhe, at the beginning of each year, lit a fire that was then carried across the land to light all the hearth fires. Uisnech was regarded as the center of the country and specifically the middle point of the five regions of ancient Eire. Another navel stone is located at Glastonbury Abbey in Somerset, England. This site is also considered the land of the legendary King Arthur and his Camelot, as well as a deeply mystical area fraught with land-based symbols and important ancient cultural artifacts.

In the North American southwest, the Hopi spiritual center is the Sipapu, which is an ancient geyser (not a stone) that spouts up from the bottom of the Grand Canyon. From this place, the ancestors of the Hopi crawled from the last world into this one. Like omphalos stones, the Sipapu has the form of an egg.

The honoring of the middle point, or center, of the world appears to be universal. China was known as the Middle Kingdom, and Midgard of old Scandinavia was the Middle Earth. The ancient Japanese called Japan the Middle Kingdom of Earth. Bethel, or dwelling place of the deity, was the name for this center place for the Hebrew people, and a Susa king of 700 BCE declared the Susan land to be the center of humanity. The Romans called the sea at the center of their empire the Mediterranean, literally meaning the middle earth sea.

For many people, Jerusalem was and is the honored center of the Earth, and in ancient times, Mount Gerizim, in Samaria, was referred to in the Old Testament as the Navel of the Earth. Consequently, Alexander the Great commissioned a temple to be built on Mount Gerizim in the fourth century BCE.

Places of origin, places of honor, have a long-standing history for a reason. These special places offer people a way to directly connect with the land and their undisputed belonging.

One time I stopped for a full morning at the large boulder at the entrance to the Lost Coast, my chosen navel stone along Black Sands Beach. I wanted to give this place something meaningful and remembered Mr. Turner's carving. I rolled my pack off my back and sat down to carve a whale out of a weathered piece of driftwood.

After a few moments, I suddenly heard the loud cry of a sea lion. I quickly made my way to the water's edge to see a sea lion mother rapidly swimming back and forth parallel to the beach, her calls sounding out high above the crashing waves. I looked where she was looking and saw a newborn baby sea lion attempting to get through the strong breakers back to its mother, further out to sea. Each time the babe swam out, the waves thrust it rolling back to shore. I watched for some time at a slight distance, not wanting to interfere, but then something changed. The baby lay very quietly on the sand and had stopped entering the water. I decided I was there for a reason and quickly found two smooth driftwood sticks and cautiously approached the whelp. With the mother's eyes intently upon me, her cries now quieted, I gently lifted up the little one, walked into the surf up to my knees, and then with great hope threw the babe as far past the breakers as I could. After a few nervous moments, I saw the little sea lion's head pop up, just past the big waves, and mother and newborn were reunited. The mother attended to her young one and then looked up right at me. Perceived accurately or not, I felt love, simple and pure, as the mother blinked her soft shining eyes as they looked directly into mine. With the familiar aroma of the sea's salty perfume around me, and the intimate connection to this mother sea lion, I felt surely home.

It is with this sense of belonging to place that I walk the final five-mile stretch of the wild beach to meet the river's mouth. Wherever our feet touch the ground, we can ask: Who lives here? What can those who have lived here before, and live here now, teach us about living in this place well?

3

Reshaping Interior and Exterior Landscapes

Part One: Earth and Sky

Our origins are of the earth. And so there is in us
a deeply seated response to the natural universe,
which is part of our humanity.
−RACHEL CARSON

If the success or failure of this planet, and of human
beings, depended on how I am and what I do,
how would I be? What would I do?
−R. BUCKMINSTER FULLER

Late morning sun, and with it a shadow cast from a miniature
geodesic dome, is creating a hieroglyph on my studio wall.
The little dome, fashioned after Buckminster Fuller's design,
is quite old, made from recycled chopsticks I carved and glued
together many years ago. Firmly taped into one of the triangles is a
black and white photograph of the celebrated Japanese-American
artist Ruth Asawa. Several of Ruth's elaborate wire sculptures sur-
round her, each one revealing magnificent structural properties
found in Earth's mysterious house of natural forms. The dome

and photograph stand out even though they share a crowded shelf space with twenty or so seashells, mostly cockles and clams, placed like stepping stones leading to a large chunk of obsidian I collected in northern Italy and with great and ridiculous effort, carted home in the summer of 1994. These are only a few of the various cherished collections piled high, though not without care, in every nook of my studio. With a quick glance, my eyes take in the peculiar and comforting chaos.

The "arrangement" of bent wire, rough sketches, curled leaves, torn paper, and loosely formed clay shapes are graphic notes, and they all now stand in firm defiance, not to be moved as I attempt to "clean up." Perhaps these are unpleasing compositions when compared to, say, a traditional Japanese garden, with its thoughtfully positioned stones in finely raked sand, designed to bring forth a meditative state of mind. In comparison to such a refined space, my studio is a rather wild, knobby sort of topographical map, one that no one else would likely be able to navigate. Yet, the scattered bits are each important entrances to my imagination, a trail to an interior landscape that is courted and shaped into being.

These markers of clay and fiber, stone and bone, feather and leaf, are directly speaking to me from an otherworld where things that are still invisible look with yearning toward my outstretched hands to cast them into the realm of the visible. These artworks yet to be created "ask" to emerge in such a way that their mystical other-worldliness is maintained, a state that cannot—and should not—ever be fully captured, thus keeping the resultant art durably resplendent with mystery, aliveness, wonder, and enchantment. No, I dare not move a thing lest a sequence is lost or an entire design disappears. The angled copper, knotted wool yarn, and polished stones are precious links to the living, breathing, vaulted firmament of Earth and Sky, where many artists reach for their inspirations and designs.

These creative passages to the universe are, in fact, at the heart of the matter because, for me, art has always been about how we are to nourish and pay homage to the world and thus also nurture ourselves. In this age, I ask myself continually what is needed from the realm of the Muse, from the creativity of artists. What is the Earth asking to be told or re-storied, to be, in essence, re-stored, revered, and thus brought anew into our present consciousness?

Whether we artists are shaping images, sounds, or words, we have the possibility in our searching to bring more beauty and meaning into the world. We have the opportunity to remind ourselves and others about our place in the larger story of life and in the grander mythological time known by geological seasons—yes, a time known by layered rocks. Whether with success or failure, we can certainly make the attempt and offer the energy of our impassioned effort. In the wild garden of my studio, I invite those things that most openly and willingly come forth to state their case.

Since the modeling of my first sculpture at the age of twenty, the Buckminster Fuller geodesic dome and the Ruth Asawa photograph have always been with me. They stand as both points of origin and current signposts along the trail that opened my mind to the idea of "shaping in the world." I recall sitting at the long kitchen table at Ruth's house in San Francisco. Her children, my parents, my sister, and I were all listening to Fuller talk enthusiastically about the number nine. He brilliantly engaged each of us, youngest to oldest, with tales of the magical mathematical properties of this number. There was a visceral sensation of tingling at the top of my head, and I felt something wonderful racing like a galloping horse through my mind. New thoughts actually do expand our inner geography—neuroscientists have proven that neural pathways in our brain are literally, not just virtually, opened when we think new thoughts—and this horse, running with mathematical equations, made fast pace along new trails in my mind. Numbers were never dull after this experience with such a lively teacher as Fuller.

My mother learned to draw and paint with Ruth Asawa as

her mentor, and they became lifelong friends; consequently, our families often were in each other's homes. Both my mother's and Ruth's studios fascinated me, as well as the drawings of Ruth's well-known architect husband, Albert Lanier. When I was eight years old, he remodeled our house in San Francisco, and that is when I became enthralled with the knowledge that you could tear down walls and build new "made-up" spaces in an existing structure. This atmosphere of simultaneously shaping the world and observing the shape *of* the world certainly created a lasting imprint in my young psyche, a territory from which I have never really returned.

Ruth and Albert met at Black Mountain College, a unique experimental interdisciplinary art college that had a fiery and powerful, if not long, life. Located in the rural hills near Asheville, North Carolina, Black Mountain existed from 1933 to 1957. Fuller, a true Renaissance Man with ideas and projects blending knowledge of philosophy, architecture, engineering, and history, was a teacher at Black Mountain College during the summers of 1948 and 1949.

This legendary college also hosted other leading-edge thinkers, artists, and writers, including Josef and Anni Albers, John Cage, Merce Cunningham, Albert Einstein, Bernard Rudofsky, Richard Lippold, and William Carlos Williams. The school was a focal point for many avant-garde "Black Mountain poets," such as Denise Levertov and Allen Ginsberg, who later became part of the Beat Movement. Many credit the college as the fountainhead of artistic and cultural perspectives of the 1960s.

You could say, then, that I was a sprout of parents who were of the flower-child generation. Through our parents, my sister and I deeply experienced the horror and sorrow of the Vietnam War and the shock, anger, and bottomless grief after the assassinations of John F. Kennedy, Martin Luther King Jr., and Robert Kennedy. Somehow, we remember these things within our bodies; I still become breathless upon thinking of their names.

I believe we come from several generations that have not yet healed from the trauma of assassinations and revolts. As children, we knew something was very wrong, even if the words were not spoken. Only through external, societal experiences are we taught to mistrust this inner guidance from childhood that simply "knows." Nevertheless, as many of us who have held on tightly to our incurable optimism have learned, the good news is this: the inner knowing never really leaves us, but we need to take the time to listen inwardly in order to keep it alive.

In the vibrant tumult of the 1960s in San Francisco, my mother made fabulous etchings while Ruth made her amazing wire sculptures, and they talked about changing the world as we kids went with them to the Fillmore and the first Human Be-ins to hear Country Joe and the Fish, Jefferson Airplane, Janis Joplin, Jimi Hendrix, and other musical luminaries.

One time at Ruth and Albert's house, I remember Fuller relating a story to us about bees. He stood up suddenly and began teaching us about the life of a bumblebee and a flower. Transforming his arms into wings by tucking them tightly to his sides and flapping wildly, he danced his story to us. Only years later, when he happened to give a lecture sponsored by the college I attended in Portland, Oregon, did I fully comprehend the meaning of the marvelous bee dance.

I learned then that I had been given my first lesson in what Fuller called "precessional effects," which take place in nature at 90-degree angles to one another and produce both intended and inadvertent results. Fuller described it this way: "Precession is the effect of bodies in motion on other bodies in motion."[1]

What captured my attention then was that his concept of precession is an early description of how humanity could live in a sustainable, balanced, evolutionary relationship with the natural world. Fuller developed this idea in 1927 and thus was one of the first Western thinkers who brought ecological thinking to the forefront of the conversation about human activity. While dipping in and out of giant imaginary flowers, Fuller spiraled around the university lecture hall with his arms fluttering, demonstrating to us how the bee dance expresses perfectly the idea of precession.

The nature of honeybees is to enter flowers in search of honey-making material. Simultaneously the bee's bottom is layered with pollen. Then, on its mission for more honey-making material to collect, the bee enters another flower and "inadvertently" fertilizes this flower. These events create mutually beneficial effects for both the bee and its colony and the flower and its plant.

Another good example of precession is the seeding of forests by birds, squirrels, and other animals. They eat seeds, fruits, and nuts, and their seed-filled excrement provides the perfect conditions for new trees to germinate and grow.

I acquired a great deal of hope for the future by listening to Fuller convey how humans could participate consciously in precession by listening wisely to nature. If we followed our own human passions to love, to belong, and to live our lives in a meaningful way—respecting our own true natures—we could live well and long on "Spaceship Earth," as he called it.

Here is a valuable application of precession in Fuller's words:

Humans, as honey-money-seeking bees, do many of nature's required tasks only inadvertently. They initially produce swords with metal-forging-developed capability, which capability is later used to make steel into farm plows. Humans —in politically organized, group-fear-mandated acquisition of weaponry—have inadvertently developed so-much-more-performance-with-so-much-less material, effort, and time investment per each technological task accomplished as now inadvertently to have established a level of technological capability which, if applied exclusively to peaceful purposes, can provide a sustainable high standard of living for all humanity, which accomplished fact makes war and all weaponry obsolete.[2]

Fuller had an ability to see into the greater movements of society by following unique paths of inquiry. He quested all his life long, asking, "Does humanity have a chance to survive lastingly and successfully on planet Earth, and if so, how?"

Fuller also made popular the venerable word "synergy." For him this meant, "behavior of whole systems unpredicted by the behavior of its parts considered separately."[3] He applied this word to concepts in every field from cellular biology and geometry to politics, architecture, and economics. With this whole-systems view, he explored principles of energy and material efficiency. Thus, Fuller came to agree with prominent oil geologist Francois de Chardenedes' claim that the production of petroleum had cost nature far more than its worth, if we considered petroleum replacement costs. They both concluded that the petroleum used to transport people back and forth to work each day actually creates a giant net loss in comparison to what these workers could actually earn in terms of Gross National Product (GNP).[4]

What remains a resounding theme in Fuller's work is his appreciation and exploration of what he considered the most brilliant and beautifully patterned technology. It had for millennia already shown its viability, balanced dynamics, interconnected benefits, and functional imperatives: the technology inherent in the natural laws of the Earth and greater universe.

To Fuller, if humans are part of nature (and they obviously are) then the technologies of humans could not be separate from nature. The optimistic Fuller saw the current industrial technological age as a phase that humanity could transition out of into an era of human communities living in more optimum efficiency with nature and the Earth.

Given our current state of affairs globally, it is also important to stress that Fuller saw this era as the pivotal moment of humanity's survival, hence the title of his last publication, *Critical Path*. He opens the book with four reasons for writing it. One is his "driving conviction that all of humanity is in peril of extinction if each of us does not dare, now and henceforth, always to tell the truth, and all the truth, and to do so, promptly—right now."

—

As a sculptor, I was taught to look for what belongs to the "underneath" of things, to peer beyond edges of visibility and perception into how things are constructed. When modeling a sculpture out of clay or wax, there is often some sort of armature, a framework fashioned from wire or wood, upon which the modeling material is built up. Although in the final artwork, whether cast bronze or another medium, this armature is not seen, it is, in many respects, the most vital element of the piece. Similar to the infrastructure of a building or the wooden framing of a house, whatever lines and measurements exist in the armature will decide the sculpture's outcome. After many experiments and errors, I eventually learned that the framework, the skeletal bones, of a creative project matter hugely to the end result. This is a valuable, if initially difficult to grasp, life lesson. It is difficult mostly because we humans want results fast at any cost, even failure, until we see that such methods just don't work. As I have learned over time, the hidden, underneath of things needs to be thoughtfully measured and nurtured in an unhurried manner.

Beyond the measured calculations in a sculpture's armature, there is an organic magic, a creative dynamic that slips in through the language of our hands. Our fingers and thumbs in motion seem to know things about the peculiar curves of beauty, the bent angles of grief, the fierce edges of freedom, and the contours of dignity. There is sophisticated animal knowledge in our hands that knows how to position an armature with emotions and grace. Our sensible hands, after tens of thousands of years of embodiment, know how to form these hidden bones. Thus, I have found it wise in art to let these ancient hands of mine wander free when I first shape a new design.

The exploration of "what lies beneath" also includes striving to see and perceive what is underneath the structural design of society—to look into, as it were, our societal precession. I believe artists and designers have the task of getting to the bottom of things and attempting to comprehend intrinsic movements and patterns in our human story. With this in mind, I began to ask myself: What are the specific cultural stories, perceptions, and images encoded in our everyday lives? What are the bones of our collective stories, myths, and symbols? How are these stories and imaginings guiding and affecting us now? I will address just a few components of this historical story-armature by exploring some of the visual embodiments and symbols found in our cities. What cities portray physically is a direct mirror of what human beings are thinking about, imagining, dreaming, and choosing as their cultural life-story.

—⁀—

Specifically, the architecture and public art of a city describes the relationship between a particular location, the citizens who dwell there, and the *zeitgeist*. The designs of our cities, which often guide how we build and live in our communities, conveys our civilization's values, ethics, worldviews, and philosophies. In essence, the architecture and art of any city demonstrates the primary thrust of the metaphoric and moral narrative of the inhabitants. I say "primary" because there are people and groups in each region and era who do not feel that their city is identifying and expressing their core values or views. It is important to include these marginalized citizens' opinions because they are often the ones who bring about transformation. For example, the "green" building movement began in the margins and is steadily moving toward the center, both as a concept and in the real world of urban change on the ground. Many cities around the world are now fully engaged in sustainability planning, from developing green rooftops to implementing Smart Grids. A successful strategy that's now an example for other cities is the revolutionary work in ecological sustainability demonstrated by the city of Curitiba in Brazil, through imaginative transportation systems, innovative recycling, and environmental education. Brazil also already produces over 50 percent of its energy from renewable resources.

As more of the Earth's populations are living in urban environments, it has become a great challenge for people to connect with the natural world. Yet, even with the increase of urban sprawl (with sustainable planning or not), the inner hunger for wild nature still tugs beneath the surface of our psyches—like the desire to fully recall a dream of which we only catch glimpses just before awakening. Many architects, urban planners, and city designers are becoming aware that the citizenry is yearning not just for ecologically balanced developments, but also for more green spaces, parks, city gardens, green trails, and nature-themed art and architecture to address the deep spiritual and psychological need to reconnect with the Earth. This longing is wedded to the idea that we must build in a manner that both mirrors nature's design and causes no harm.

The simple fact is this: we are animals, and as such, inhabit actual bodies and locations on this planet. The reality of our existence drives (consciously or unconsciously) our need to sense and know our physical embodiment and the living landscape around us in order to maintain our personal welfare. This natural "compulsion" can cause us to feel at odds with ourselves right now because many of us may spend countless hours indoors, in a virtual world with the ubiquitous presence of computers and technology in our everyday workplaces and homes. All too often, forgotten beneath the crosshatches of city streets and pavement, shopping malls and parking lots, there is a living, breathing planet. Hidden by high-rise buildings that eclipse sun, moon, cloud, and star, there is a sky that reaches into expansive realms where our hearts and minds also need to wander. In our modern urban context, it is imperative that we increasingly find ways to remember, more often and more joyously, that we are very much a part of, not apart from, our living terrain, our boundless universe.

Transforming our cities into livable, Earth-welcoming spaces is vital because it is not practical or realistic for most of the world's population to return to an agrarian or rural lifestyle to renew itself with nature. I also believe that cities are not inherently "bad" or that wild nature is the only "good." Both environments have their import to us, and for thousands of years humans have inhabited both. There were large cosmopolitan centers in the ancient past, while simultaneously, nomadic populations were living in rustic yet elegant structures fashioned from reeds and grasses, animal hides, tree bark, and felt—as remains true today. My question here is about the significant symbolic, contextual, and sensorial differences in the cities of antiquity from our contemporary urban centers.

Reflected in the architecture and art of most ancient cities is a clear and present demonstration of an alive and powerful human-nature relationship—one that did not create a sense of separation between people and the land, but rather enriched a meaningful understanding between human inhabitants, their immediate environment, and the greater universe.

I am not suggesting that the ancient metropolises of, say, North Africa, Southeast Asia, or Mesoamerica were utopias, because each of them had their own serious societal and environmental challenges; what I am proposing is that we approach the study of these old cites in an inquisitive fashion to see what can be learned about how, within the everyday rush of life, the designs and symbolic components of these (and any) cities might help their citizens maintain a rootedness in the land. Maybe we can learn something from a time when people had less distance, both outwardly and inwardly, from wild nature and held worldviews that supported and prospered from significant kinship with the Earth upon which they stood.

The design of many ancient cities was founded upon an alignment with and orientation to features that specifically connected the city structurally and geographically to the land and cosmological features. By cosmology here, I mean all that exists in the worldly realms of the watersheds, mountains, valleys, forests, plants, and animals, as well as the sky with its sun, moon, stars, and beyond—what is usually called "the firmament" of old.

The Quiché Maya, like many of our nature-minded ancestors, did not separate sky and earth. Their word for the universe (transliterated to "Cahuleu") literally means "Sky-Earth." In this Quiché Maya articulation we get an immediate comprehension of connecting the land with the heavens—the universe is not "out there" somewhere as an abstract concept "universe," but the ground directly under us in relationship to the sky above us.

We now live within a multi-generational consciousness of humanity seeing photographs of Earth from space. We have online tools like Google Earth™ that allow us to "fly" around the world, viewing three-dimensional representations of our planet on our computer screens. We are at the point where it is time to take responsibility for this visceral imagining of our home planet, allowing the pictures to move well past our eyes, through our minds, and into the chambers of our caring hearts. The idea of designing a home, village, or city to best express our interconnectedness to each other and the greater universe is part of our collective heritage and one vitally worth resurrecting; clearly, the loss of this knowledge has been only to our peril.

The measure and perspective provided by daily "Earth-awareness" could deeply affect how we think and act. The question is, "How do we design an alive, cosmologically aware city for a contemporary citizenry?" This is not an esoteric exercise but rather a simple and direct call for city planners to explore design that enhances a relationship to the living, breathing Earth for more harmonious living, a harmony that includes other species. It is an exploration in which some forward-thinking architects, city planners, artists, and local municipalities are already deeply immersed and have begun to incorporate into urban spaces all over the world. These are inspiring ventures that will be useful as we strive to transition to healthier communities, especially in urban areas that have been particularly ignored and injured by pollution and blight—often neighborhoods inhabited by historically marginalized people of color and the economically disenfranchised. It is here that the undeniable relationship between environmental and social justice issues becomes glaringly clear. There is much work to do to heal these socio-environmental landscapes and to respect their residents, while simultaneously creating spaces that reconnect the citizenry with the natural world. One of the most inspiring new leaders working to transform these kinds of cityscapes is Majora Carter. As the director of the Majora Carter Group, she works in city planning by creating a connection between ecological, economic, and social concerns. In one of her signature projects, she developed a greenway along the once-degraded South Bronx waterfront, which has brought walking paths, open space, and areas for economic development into the neighborhood. Her motto: "Green the ghetto!"

Innovative designers are increasingly utilizing environmentally sustainable "green" architecture and technology, as well as considering the deeper symbolic and contextual questions of urban design. These explorations bear fruit in more general "livability" features such as central plazas, extensive walking and bike paths, garden rooftops, parks with lakes, and large open spaces within city limits. City administrators worldwide are beginning to acknowledge the mounting evidence that people truly need to feel a connection to nature. Studies have shown that where there are more parks and green space in downtown areas, there is a marked decrease in violence.[5] In hospitals, the recovery rate for patients who have a window facing trees or a park is faster than those with no view of nature. Yes, we want and need a taste of authentic wild places even in the inner city. We yearn for spaces still open to the unpredictable, spaces on the threshold of flying away with clouds and birds, spaces in which it is still possible to discover mushrooms under trees and tadpoles in tiny streambeds.

One of the most significant resources we have in this research is the previous efforts of our ancestors. Significant place-making was essential to ancient peoples worldwide, and they have left us many architectural and artistic examples that still stand as dazzling monuments to urban ecology, connecting us to Earth and Sky. We can draw upon these models because, throughout most of human-ity's history, no matter our origins, we have been people of the land, and we actually have been acutely aware of our place in the larger universe until recently. The aromas, images, stories, and sounds of the wild Earth still linger in us. Can we remember enough to regenerate that vital experience and again build upon it?

The old Chinese word for cosmos, *yu-zhou*, was understood to mean a kind of great house for human beings while also convey-ing the meaning of the greater universe, of heaven plus earth. Thus in ancient China, the development of municipalities and villages was interpreted as "a city or house of cosmic order," and the purpose of the built environment was to create with skill a harmonious relationship between the universe, the physical land, and the human. Utilizing a holistic, interconnected approach, a city, building, or homestead was consciously oriented to the natural world; most often this was accomplished by an orientation with the cardinal directions. The ancient Chinese considered the world to be divided into four quadrants representing north, south, east, and west, respectively: *Xuan-wu* (Black Turtle), *Zhu-que* (Red Phoenix), *Qin-long* (Azure Dragon), and *Bai-hu* (White Tiger). Almost every city, village, and home was designed to celebrate these sacred directions. That being so, the built environment directly enhanced the symbolic understanding of knowing one's relationship to the larger world through local orientation.

These relational concepts were employed in ancient cities throughout the Americas, as well as those in the Old World. The ancient Inca Empire in Peru revered Cuzco as its central capital. Cuzco in the ancient native Quechua language means "navel of the Earth." The entire empire radiating out from the central city was called *Tahuantinsuyu*, which means "the Land of Four Quarters." Politically and geographically, the region was oriented to the four directions and, within these quarters, different structures were oriented to astronomical or topographical directions. For instance, the Temple of the Sun in Cuzco, paramount to Incan spiritual life, was aligned with the summer and winter solstices. In this manner, the city inhabitants were living in a structural design that directly expressed connectivity to the procession of the seasons with the seasonal precession of Earth's axis.

The municipal design in classic Mayan cities like Tik'al and Palenque (Bàak' in modern Maya) included many large, open spaces where people gathered. Broad avenues burgeoning with flowering trees connected monumental pyramid structures and platforms surrounded by great plazas. The cities and their principal structures were oriented to a cardinal direction and often to a certain feature in the natural landscape, such as a mountain, river, or lake. The directional orientations, sprawling plazas, and grand pyramids echoing and displaying planetary movements created a living, cosmologically integrated urban center.

In central Mexico, about twenty-five miles from the current-day mega-metropolis Mexico City, is the site of the ancient city Teotihuacán, regarded by the Aztec people as the origin-place of civilization and the birthplace of the cosmic order. The Aztec believed they inherited the city from older cultures. Most historians seem to agree that the Olmec people directly influenced the culture and architecture of Teotihuacán. Known throughout the modern world for their stunning sculptural artworks, such as the colossal stone heads found in the jungles of the Yucatán Peninsula, the Olmec are regarded as the "mother civilization" of Mesoamerica. In this mysterious ancient city of Teotihuacán, two huge structures mark the urban focal point: the pyramids of the sun and the moon. Various cultures that inhabited the city over time shared recognition of the cosmos.

Another important city for the Aztecs was their ancient

capital, Tenochtitlan, the ruins of which are located in and under current-day Mexico City.

This city was divided by four great avenues that originated at a central pyramid. Both of these metropolises, Teotihuacán and Tenochtitlan, had many complex geometrical and cosmological expressions that have intrigued architects, archeologists, and astronomers for centuries. As scholars tabulate additional information, more mysteries continue to unfold. Such studies demonstrate the highly sophisticated celestial knowledge of the Aztecs, Olmecs, and other early Mesoamerican cultures and how their cities were developed to enhance a seamless connection between humanity and the vast landscape of the greater universe.

Anyone who has had the opportunity to walk the voluminous avenues of these time-honored cities or climb their mountainous pyramids knows that it is impossible to resist sensations of a deep, rich kinship to something larger than the human realm. Whenever I have visited these grand ancient metropolises I feel plunged into a mythic sphere where all epochs spiral back in on themselves and the giant old stones, placed hundreds and hundreds of years ago, still speak vividly and tenaciously of our human existence held within the wide girth of sky and land, time and space.

Across the globe in North Ossetia Alania in the Caucasus Mountains are the people known as the Ossetians, descendents of the ancient Sarmatians (a remarkable coalition of nomadic Persians) and, before that, the great nomadic tribe of the Scythians. From ancient times until the early twentieth century the Ossetians maintained a particular location in their villages from which to observe and utilize distinct, clearly defined horizon calendars, which are quite accurate and were in widespread use throughout the ancient world. Very simply, they require a designated spot from which to watch the sunset each evening and an observer who notes where the sun sets on specific landmarks in the west. All the holidays and pragmatic events were determined with this method of timekeeping. The horizon calendar was embedded into the community's landscape; the people, village, time, and space were all united into a living environmental and cultural ecology.

In Mesopotamia, inhabitants of Akkadian, Sumerian, Babylonian, and Assyrian cities built ziggurats to architecturally portray relationships between various aspects of the natural world. These massive human-made brick and clay "mountains" were named to reflect cosmic interconnections: House of the Storm, Bond between Heaven and Earth, House of the Mountain. The designers likened the gigantic steps of a ziggurat to a ladder or stairway linking Earth to Sky.

The pyramids in Egypt are better-known testimony to cosmological alignments in ancient architecture. The Great Pyramid of Giza was built over several decades concluding around 2560 BCE. The four sides of the Great Pyramid are oriented to the four cardinal points, and the mathematics of the pyramid reflect vast knowledge of and reverence for cosmic events and planetary geometry.

The city of Knossos in Crete, built by the Minoans—a remarkable Bronze Age civilization—was designed with particular sensitivity to the natural shape and lay of the land. The city center was positioned to be framed by a mountain rift with double peaks, or "horns," symbolically honoring the Cretan spiritual relationship with horned animals, particularly the bull. These horns and their symbology are reflected in ritual activities in which dancers jumped through bulls' horns in ancient Minoan ceremonies, as pictured in murals and on ceramics uncovered in excavations of the city site. Here, topography and cosmology unite in aesthetically advanced urban design to create a site-specific and elegant intimacy between the people, their spiritual life, and the land.

Not only did the urban designers incorporate the skies and broader landscape into the designs of ancient cities but also the local flora. Many of the wide streets and promenades were lined with flowering and fruiting trees that provided not only shelter from the sun but also food and beauty throughout the city centers, an idea we ought to utilize more fully today to revitalize our urban cores.

Over time, as my thoughts have traveled these ancient roads, I have explored ways to reconnect with these place-making ways. I have taken to marking the four directions just outside my studio with colorful ribbons that festoon branches in trees to the east, west, south, and north. One year I stood nearly every day at sunset on my studio deck and marked the path of the disappearing sun from summer to winter solstice. I cut little notches on the wooden handrail that corresponded to the location on the horizon where the sun vanished each evening. The magnitude of this seasonal planetary movement struck me when, just after midway between solstices, the tilt of the season was so extensive that, instead of notching the handrail, I was forced off the deck to line up little sticks on the ground in order to continue this marking of days. The small notches and row of pegs could hardly match the majesty of a Mayan calendar pyramid—grandly erected to salute the stars and planets, the curvature of eons. Nevertheless, directly experiencing such a large sweep of celestial movement, demonstrated by my little markings, had a tremendous impact on me, and I humbly lost all false perception that time is isolated from space or the great motion of the Earth.

Clearly, the design legacy of these ancient cities demonstrates a kind of intimacy and affinity with the land and each other that we can seek again in this current era of ecological and cultural renewal.

For Indigenous people, this relational understanding of living in balance with the surrounding natural world and designing structures accordingly has also been honored in individual dwellings. While enrolled in an environmental studies program in college, I read John Neihardt's book *Black Elk Speaks: Being the Story of a Holy Man of the Oglala Sioux*. Black Elk sadly recounts how the conquering Wasichus (white man) had devastated his people by forcing them out of their indigenous dwellings into square homes or "little gray houses," as he called them.

Black Elk:

You have noticed that everything an Indian does is in a circle, and that is because the Power of the World always works in circles, and everything tries to be round. ... Everything the Power of the World does is done in a circle.

The sky is round, and I have heard that the earth is round like a ball, and so are all the stars. The wind, in its greatest power, whirls. Birds make their nests in circles, for theirs is the same religion as ours.

The sun comes forth and goes down again in a circle. The moon does the same, and both are round. Even the seasons form a great circle in their changing, and always come back again to where they were.

Our teepees were round like the nests of birds, and these were always set in a circle, the nations' hoop, a nest of many nests, where the Great Spirit meant for us to hatch our children.[6]

The round has great import as well to the nomadic Mongolian people of the steppe regions who dwell in circular homes called yurts or "gheer." These round houses, made primarily of felt, are extremely practical for the nomadic life, easy to disassemble and transport, and well-suited for the harsh landscape. Simultaneously these structures embody the spiritual views of their inhabitants.

The door of the yurt always faces south so that the central circular opening in the roof (the smoke hole) works as an astronomical clock. Time is kept according to the position of the sun as it shines through the spokes of the roof hole. The yurt is understood to be a mirror of the greater macrocosm, with the central hearth representing the Earth, the circular ceiling the sky, and the central hole in the roof the eye of the universe through which light enters the home and illuminates the souls within.

The Mongolian yurt is a predecessor to the dome of Hadrian's Pantheon in Rome. This spectacular circular building, reconstructed in the second century CE after burning down a century before, opens to the sky with a round portal in the ceiling, the oculus—the Great Eye.

Another example of Indigenous people expressing a highly relational lifestyle and worldview can be found in the recounting of author and educator Martín Prechtel, who lived among the Tzutujil Mayans in a small Guatemalan village near Lake Atitlán. Prechtel became a part of their village life, finally ascending to the rank of leader. The following is an excerpt from Prechtel in a 2001 interview with author Derrick Jensen:

> In the village, people used to build their houses out of traditional materials, using no iron or lumber or nails, but the houses were magnificent. Many were sewn together out of bark and fiber. Like the house of the body, the house that a person sleeps in must be very beautiful and sturdy, but not so sturdy that it won't fall apart after a while. If your house doesn't fall apart, then there will be no reason to renew it. And it is this renewability that makes something valuable. The maintenance gives it meaning.
>
> The secret of village togetherness and happiness has always been the generosity of the people, but the key to that generosity is inefficiency and decay. Because our village huts were not built to last very long, they had to be regularly renewed. To do this, villagers came together, at least once a year, to work on somebody's hut. When your house was falling down, you invited all the folks over. The little kids ran around messing up what everybody was doing. The young women brought the water. The young men carried the stones. The older men told everybody what to do, and the older women told the older men that they weren't doing it right. Once the house was back together again, everyone ate together, praised the house, laughed, and cried. In a few days, they moved on to the next house. In this way, each family's place in the village was reestablished and remembered. This is how it always was.[7]

Innovative, forward-thinking architects also have much to offer in understanding a more Earth-connected shaping of our homes and buildings. World-renowned contemporary designer William McDonough says:

> But what if buildings were alive? What if our homes and workplaces were like trees, living organisms participating productively in their surroundings? Imagine a building, enmeshed in the landscape, that harvests the energy of the sun, sequesters carbon and makes oxygen. Imagine on-site wetlands and botanical gardens recovering nutrients from circulating water. Fresh air, flowering plants, and daylight everywhere. Beauty and comfort for every inhabitant. A roof covered in soil and sedum to absorb the falling rain. Birds nesting and feeding in the building's verdant footprint. In short, a life-support system in harmony with energy flows, human souls, and other living things. Hardly a machine at all.
>
> This is not science fiction. Buildings like trees, though few in number, already exist. So when we survey the future—the prospects for buildings and cities, settled and unsettled lands—we see a new sensibility emerging, one in which inhabiting a place becomes a mindful, delightful participation in landscape. This perspective is both rigorous and poetic. It is built on design principles inspired by nature's laws. It is enacted by immersing oneself in the life of a place to discover the most fitting and beautiful materials and forms. It is a design aesthetic that draws equally on the poetics of science and the poetics of space. We hope it is the design strategy of the future.[8]

As we reflect upon ancient civilizations and indigenous and "green" architectural ways of designing, we can see that there is a wellspring of place-based knowledge invaluable to contemporary society, particularly as we embark upon a new Earth-honoring, relational co-habitation with our home planet and each other.

Yet the question still lingers: how can we more fully experience a breathing, alive, sensate world?

⤙

Before continuing, I want to say something about senses, beginning with fragrances and sounds and their importance in our surroundings. Just as our acoustical sense can transform our immediate experience when we listen to music or the cry of a seabird, our sense of smell, too, can take us to alternate realms. For many years, I have kept unusually scented flowers in my workspace for a helpful reminder of wild or unknown places.

When I inhale the elegant perfume of a gardenia, my body is flooded with subtle, positive emotions. The fragrance is sensual, and I travel to faraway lands. The creamy-white blooms offer an unflinching scent, which weaves into a continuum of time because the flowers are descendants of seeds borne of plants going back thousands of generations in Asia. In China, gardenias are called the Zhi Zi flower, and their seeds are often used in traditional herbal preparations. Their petals are like delicate, luminous wings that seem to fly upward to flutter in the sun streaming through my studio window.

Steeped in this untamed flowery world, I begin to imagine. Part of designing and creating for me involves synesthesia, that peculiar blending of the senses in which, say, a poem may be inextricably perceived as the color blue in the mind's eye, or an aroma awakens another body sense or cognitive pathway. When I breathe in the intoxicating fragrance of the gardenia, I inhale sunshine in the form of a flower; this aroma, floating freely in the atmosphere, is unrestrained and sets my mind free to create.

It also happens when I immerse my hands in sculptor's wax that I've left in the sun to warm and soften. Upon first touch, I immediately "hear" epic poetry of the Earth and an arpeggio of old-time myths that petition to be shaped and forged.

In the early morning just outside my countryside studio, the

Madrone trees are warming in sunlight, and mist rises off the dew-moistened branches, creating a dancing puppet show of evaporating cloud-dolls. I wonder what the trees in this little forest are sensing. I imagine that I hear the Madrone trees quietly telling me what they love—like the rain watering them deep at the root, the winds caressing their limbs while birds nest high in their upper reaches, bees tickling and pollinating their flowers, squirrels rambling about, and children climbing on their smooth lower limbs. When it comes right down to it, I must feel and sense, then consult with, the land and its inhabitants before I can create anything.

A classic rhetorical question goes: If a tree falls in the forest, and no one is there to hear it, does it make a sound? This question seems to come from the old school of thinking that does not promote our inherent kinship with the living, breathing world. It suggests a human-centric world in which an event somehow does not exist if humans are not present to experience it. What if we were to ask instead, "If we are in a city, staring into our computers, forty flights up in a high-rise building, do we even remember the trees?" How can we know about the sounds, sights, and smells of the forest and care for the health of the woodland ecosystem if we have limited or no contact?

I am concerned: What happens to us, to our children, in our urban centers when we experience primarily the smells of industry, smog, petroleum, and chemicals? What happens to our native ears when left only with the sounds of cars, telephones, freeways, and mechanization? What happens when our hands and eyes rest only upon human made things? Because our senses directly and immediately transport us into our living world, what if we cannot see or touch a real tree? What is it exactly that we are connecting to with our senses? What, indeed, are we sensing?

Our human experience is dependent upon what influences our daily lives, and we are only beginning to take into account the consequences of depriving our children of direct communion with the Earth and all the plant life and creatures. Our planet offers so much more than the inventions of a fairly recent industrial society. Beyond shopping malls and computers, there are marvels everywhere to discover. I further ask: How will we come to care for our particular bioregion upon which the local mall sits if we have no relationship to it?

———

Having walked some avenues of critical urban thought—as well as thoughtfully critiqued urbanity—let me attest here that there are many marvelous modern cities with buildings and parks that are truly great works of art and honorable places of habitation. What I am suggesting here, as are many people now in the field of design, is that we need to broaden our urban scope to make room for discovery, to develop an intimate relationship with the Earth as an essential part of our nature. The city cannot and will never emulate untouched wilderness, but certainly we can invite a bit of the wild to shine its undomesticated light upon us and give our eyes a glimpse of native trees and local flowers at the city's center or a building's edge. Innovative architecture, city planning, and public art with feet on the ground and eyes aloft can open us to this possibility.

With our capacity for boundless human imagination and our innate love of nature, we might pause to question how it came to be that so many of our cities primarily feature a financial district in their urban centers. While trade, exchange, and business are important human experiences, do we wish to over-emphasize consumerism and moneymaking at the center of our cities, the habitat of millions?

Our metropolitan hubs have ample literal and symbolic statements of economical and political awareness via our financial and civic centers, yet very little if any orientation to the broader landscape of Earth and Sky. As we move about the city, we easily relate to street addresses, markets, malls, and offices. We understand that we live in an urban location situated in a county, inside a state, within a country, yet do we question exactly where this urban location is in the context of a living, spinning planet?

Earth is not a street address. Are we aware that the spot we inhabit is part and particle of the living landscape? Are we so overwhelmed—or underwhelmed—that we have no remaining capacity to embrace this awareness? Or do we simply conform to the designs painted in front of our eyes, designs mostly intended merely to stimulate our appetites to consume?

This brings us to the question of what symbols and images are portrayed in our cities through public art. What cultural story are we telling ourselves through public artworks and symbols? Not surprisingly, given the values of our modern society, the majority of public statues and monuments are dedicated almost solely to the human world—to people, usually males, who founded or conquered a city, to war heroes, to political leaders, or, on rarer occasions, to significant cultural figures. While it is certainly important to honor our service men and women and remember historic human events (although significantly there are far more statues honoring wars and warriors than peace and peace makers), we have very little imagery or symbolism in public art and monuments to connect our communities to the beauty and wonder of the natural world and to our larger relationship to the awe-inspiring greater universe. Symbols are the very stuff of culture and deeply affect our psyches, and so are very relevant to social transformation. Advertisers know this potency all too well.

How do we create contemporary public artworks that rejuvenate our intimacy with the land? How do we demonstrate in our designs that our planet is not a commodity but a life sustainer, that the soil and water, the air and sunlight are important beyond their utilitarian purposes? These are pressing and exciting questions from which I think civic artworks need to take form.

Thomas Berry tells us in his book *The Great Work*: "No effective restoration of a viable mode of human presence on the planet will take place until such intimate human rapport with the Earth community and the entire functioning of the universe is reestablished on an extensive scale. Until this is done the alienation of the human will continue despite the heroic efforts being made toward a more benign mode of human activity in relation to the Earth. The present is not a time for desperation but for hopeful activity."[9]

In light of our daunting multiple crises, it is essential that we reconnect with the Earth community rather immediately, and do so, as Berry says, with hopeful activity. It is time for our deft and wise hands, hearts, and minds creatively to bring forth new ideas, designs, and images for a revived era that weaves land-based knowledge into a contemporary framework. This is an interactive encounter: the more we see and experience Earth-honoring symbols, images, designs, and architecture in our immediate environment, the more we will internalize this invaluable perspective. Likewise, the more Earth reverence we internalize, the more we will emulate natural designs and thus strengthen the process of shifting from harming the world to living in a mutually enhancing manner.

It is important that we not underestimate the power of symbols, art, cultural stories, and physical context to enhance any society's move toward more sustainable lifestyles. We can, as in sculpture work, build a new armature and reshape the bones of our assumed societal narratives and dreams. This is particularly necessary for the long road ahead as we navigate the dire results of climate change, water shortages, and many spiraling calamities. We will need a new kind of aesthetic for deep inspiration and cultural renewal, one that can keep us steady and strong through what scientist Edward O. Wilson calls "the bottleneck," the small passageway defining our current environmental and societal challenges (more on this in Chapter 10).

I would like to say here that, although the passage itself will be (and already is) quite difficult, I remain basically hopeful that so-called modern civilization is in fact in transit from a major cultural story of dominion over Nature to one of a more respectful and reverent relationship. The concern is how quickly this change will occur. The once-guiding words of seventeenth-century philosopher René Descartes who said that in order to understand a complex scientific problem, it is best to reduce it and to "make ourselves the masters and possessors of nature," and those of John Locke who stated that "the negation of nature is the road to happiness," no longer loftily resound within our society as profound truths. Instead, they rather rudely clang to the floor because they hurt our post-industrial, ecologically sensitized ears and sensibilities. Descartes and Locke made extremely valuable contributions to the world; my point here is that our perspectives concerning the natural world fortunately and necessarily have been changing since their time. Some of these changes have been made by choice and others involuntarily because we have been forced to learn that it is not possible to dominate or control Nature. Think climate change, floods, droughts, and oil spills.

There are countless ways in which we need to reshape our current deleterious habits and worldviews. In the arena of consciousness change toward an Earth-caring presence, two important efforts that could help usher in this transformation are 1) a more embellished and celebrated cosmological orientation of our communities that connects us to the rhythms of nature, and 2) more Earth-driven symbolic content of our public cultural images to connect us to our local bioregions.

No matter if we are city or country dwellers, further opening our minds to an alive, relational presence with our surroundings and to the beauty and wonder of our region's bounty will imbue our actions with the possibility of proper care and right living. This kind of new, yet very old, in-depth regionalism may also give rise naturally to a more universal affection for other species, other places, other ways of life, which we are connected to and interdependent with whether we recognize it or not.

Indigenous people around the world have said in a myriad of ways that when we listen to the natural rhythm and songs of the land, we will know how to live and what to do. Along with steps toward sustainability, such as sun- and wind-powered energy systems, supporting local farmers, recycling, reducing, and the design of renewable products, we urgently need to address our intuitive and emotional listening to our living planet. As Berry states, we need to revive an "intimate human rapport with the Earth community."[10]

One of the most direct actions we can apply toward this intimacy is the immediate reclaiming of watersheds, plants, and animals in our own communities. Literally getting to know the names and ways of the trees, flowers, grasses, and birds of our area and what they like and how they live is a good place to begin. This familiarity with place not only protects the region environmentally as denizens become more informed about their surroundings, it also fills a deep spiritual vacuum often created when television, computers, frantic work habits, or consumerism substitute for meaning.

We may have an intellectual concept about where we live, but this is a far cry from actually walking outside and meeting the land and learning that our community is not only people but also goldfinches and bluebirds, eight different oaks, three species of firs, burrowing native bees, temperature-dependent lizards, migrating monarch butterflies—and that each of these extraordinary creatures has a story and a place in the community as much as or more than we do.

It is strange to think that we have come to the point at which walking out our front door, *on purpose to be outside*, might be considered a "non-consequential" action. Hawken remarks that the average person can recognize more than a thousand corporate brand names and logos but fewer than ten local plants.[11]

Learning what is on our street has unknown potential. My horticulturist friend Bonnie has gardened in an urban landscape in her backyard for many years, and in so doing has kept close watch on the hillsides around her Northern California home. She was the first person in her neighborhood to see the signs of Sudden Oak Death disease, *Phytophthora ramorum*, which, since the 1990s, has plagued areas of California, Oregon, and Europe. Through early detection, organically treating the trees with calcium and azomite soil amendments, and feeding nutrients through the bark, Bonnie was able to save many of them. By interacting with the local flora and making the garden her place in the world, she has created a mutually enhancing relationship with her region. As Snyder posits, "Find your place on the planet. Dig in, and take responsibility from there."[12]

Within this listening to place is the opportunity to learn from the narratives borne of local mountain ridges and riverbeds, forested slopes or desert plateaus, even if we can only see these places from a distance or sense them under the sidewalks or freeways. It will take some labor to recover these living-landscape narratives. Stories birthed from not just physical but also spiritual intimacy with a bioregion lie forgotten as paved streets and our leveled imaginations—disconnected from an alive world—attempt to destroy their life-affirming tracks and alternative worldviews.

Old-time land-based stories carefully charted and kept over the years by Indigenous people, oral historians, and ancient poets are not typically offered as coursework in traditional educational institutions. Yet, the regeneration of these stories is an essential part of revitalizing our society. Most often, these stories come from peoples who have lived in one place for many generations. The emotional, physical, intellectual, and spiritual knowledge acquired from inhabiting a region for a long time, conveyed in the old-time tales, is irreplaceable as we seek to reestablish resilient and sustainable local communities. Fortunately, such insightful narratives are beginning to be retraced (in the case that there are no longer living carriers of the stories) and more openly respected (in the case that there are current indigenous carriers) by cross-disciplinary ecologists, cultural historians, biologists, and other scholars. In the coming years it will be critical to a new cultural narrative to weave these wisdom-filled stories into a modern context, while respecting and preserving the original roots.

In the unfolding of this new and old land-based narrative, some wonderful fragments can appear in their most innocent form in our offspring, such as when a child speaks to us of a discovery while digging in the ground or after scampering up from a riverbed or asks about a local legend or what the name of a town might mean. It is one of these stories, shaped by the land and my own memory, to which I now turn.

⤙

Enclosed in a soft, blue cloud: this is how I recall the fluffy feel of the goose-down snowsuit I wore as a child during the winter in Germany. My father, in service to the American military, was stationed in Germany for two years in 1961, and our family lived near Munich. While my parents traveled on short trips around Europe, Lena, a German woman from Augsburg, cared for my sister and me in the small town of Westheim. Lena became quite adept at packing me into my favorite blue snowsuit. Her duties as a nanny were those to be expected of someone caring for two young children: cooking and cleaning, bathing us, and ensuring our safety. Yet, beyond these responsibilities, Lena took it upon herself whenever I was alone with her to educate me about "real secrets," as she described them. She explained to me that whenever I took off my shoes at the front door it was essential that I always place them side-by-side, left to right, or my feet would grow crooked, and empathically that I should never eat standing up or my legs would get fat. Yet, beyond some of these strange and sometimes dire warnings, her revelations were often captivating fairytales and stories collected from rural folklore.

The first winter snows, as all German children learn, come

from Frau Holle shaking out her feather bed. Very much liking this story, when I shook my winter bedding with Lena's help, I did it with extreme enthusiasm to help Frau Holle bring more snow. I later learned that Frau Holle was the maker of not just snow but all weather—the rains, sunshine, clouds, and wind.

One night at story time, I asked Lena where Frau Holle lived, and she described to me a big, snowy mountain. Fire also came from this same mountain and was brought to the houses in winter. She also told me the tale about the two sisters who visited Frau Holle. One sister was lazy in her wool spinning and the other was quite industrious; when the latter ended her stay with Frau Holle she was rewarded with a rain of gold that covered her all the way home, and the lazy sister was sent home covered in pitch. At the time I had no idea what pitch was, only that it was something very undesirable. Lena utilized just the proper tonality in her voice and a stern eye to make it clear this was not "just" a story. Again, this tale and versions of it were well-known to most German children. Lena enjoyed telling me many Frau Holle fairytales, so it was not surprising that much later, when I returned to Germany as an adult for one of my art exhibits, I again became curious about this Frau Holle of the snows.

The wintry trails of fable eventually led me on an excursion to the Hessen region in middle Germany, which most of my research indicated as the origin-place of Frau Holle. I wanted to learn if the so-called fairytales contained recognizable knowledge and lore of the region, since it is not uncommon that information and customs about the land from pre-Christian times were protected and remembered by cleverly tucking them into children's rhymes or fairytales for safekeeping.

I drove with a German colleague of mine to the Naturpark Meissner-Kaufunger Wald, which cradles the Hoher Meissner, the mountainous home of Frau Holle. What was remarkable as we approached the area was not the height of the Hoher Meissner (although relative to the surroundings it is a sizable mountain at some 750 meters tall), but that, in the midst of a mostly low terrain of lush and thickly forested hills, the mountain virtually jumps out of the landscape with its high plateau.

The residents of the region explained to me that the first winter snows fall exclusively on the Hoher Meissner. The snow also lasts on this high plateau longer than anywhere else and well into spring. Another fact quickly attracted my attention: The original name of the mountain was Wissener, as documented in 1195 at the nearby Germarode cloister. There are various interpretations of this word, but all of them add to the poetic and informed unfolding of the Frau Holle folktale. The word *wissener* can mean the wise person or the knowing person, and Frau Holle was a symbol of wisdom to the ancient people of northern Europe who recognized her as a Goddess of the land. Weissager, another of her monikers, means truth teller, as *weise* means wise; *weiss* means white. In this sense, an interpretation is *weismacher*, which is both the wise maker and the white maker (or snow maker), clear to all who look toward the Hoher Meissner when the winter season approaches.

Over the years, researchers have found that, due to the height of this mountain area compared to the bordering terrain, there is a unique climate atop Hoher Meissner. The mountain rises above the Werra Valley nearly 600 meters, and at the top, the slopes rise quite steeply, adding to a powerful climate system that is more similar to that of northern Sweden than to the prevailing local conditions. From the valley below it appears that the mountain is in its own weather realm, creating its own weather patterns. Indeed, it seems the unique, often fast-changing climate of Frau Holle's mountain supports the idea of her as the keeper of weather—rain, sun, and snow.

Because there is such a very different average temperature and climate on Hoher Meissner, several kinds of plants and animals that have all but disappeared in this part of Europe since the last ice age still live there.

Another notable distinction of this northern European massif is that in the Tertiary period, the region was blanketed with dense forests that, over many millennia, formed large lignite layers. Particular to this lignite deposit is that it is covered with a massive stratum of basalt. This geologic component created intriguing hexagonal stone formations where the volcanic flow that birthed the mountain originated. Sadly, starting in 1949, huge strip-mining operations almost decimated these Hessen Mountains. The top layer of basalt was aggressively removed to get to the lignite, as the lignite-coal was used for industry fuel and at the power station in the city of Kassel. The destructive operations at the Hoher Meissner were finally halted in 1974, but there remains undeniable damage to the mountain. Furthermore, other mining operations, mostly for granite, are still gnawing at the Hoher Meissner from the northeastern side at the Bransrode.

At one time, many hundreds of years ago, the population of the Werra Valley was gentler on the land. There is a local tale cited by Johann Praetorius, a German writer of the 1600s, about the village of Hirschberg, where a glass blower was running out of wood to feed the fire oven for his glasswork. The local Count had forbidden him from going into the forest to cut trees (a law in place to protect the sacred woodlands). The glass blower, now distraught, meets Frau Holle, who shows him how to use lignite. He, in turn, teaches this to his entire village. The villagers dug not from the top of the mountain, but rather from the side, and created small, undamaging tunnels on the hillside underneath the basalt layer to collect the coveted fire-makings. They were careful to not create too many tunnels or to dig too deep. I could not help but remember the tale that Lena shared with me so many years ago, relating how Frau Holle and her mountain provided for the people of the region. Somehow, I am certain this tale did not originally include the removal of the entire mountaintop!

I reflect again upon the folk legend about the two sisters. Frau Holle showered the considerate and industrious one with gold.

The other sister, the lazy one, was sent by her greedy mother to get what she could from Frau Holle and ended up covered in pitch. If the mining continues, the mountain itself, hollowed out by blinding short-term industrial demands, will disappear. It will not be gold for the region, but pitch—a sign of our modern laziness in not caring for the land or in creating a plan for real, long-lasting wealth that is mutually enhancing for the people and the place.

Frau Holle, of course, is the subject of many other legends, some associated with the underworld as her name indicates: Holle is related to Hohle, meaning cave in German. Some of her other names are Hulda, Holda, Helle, and Hel. The passage to and from the underworld in many mythologies represents the cycles of life and death and the seasonal changes of growth and dormancy from spring and summer to autumn and winter and back again each year. It is likely that the reference to Frau Holle as a Goddess of the weather is also due to the seasonal changes that her associated tales indicate. When the girls in the fairytale visit her they must go underground into a well, only to return later when their chores with Frau Holle are complete. This entering and returning from the underworld can refer to the spring return of life after the long winter—a change in both weather and season. In this sense, Frau Holle is a much older and many-faceted deity than her modern-day German persona would first imply.

It is fortunate for us today that the Brothers Grimm dedicated their lives to chronicling folklore and legends throughout Germany, and it is to them we owe thanks for recording the Frau Holle oral tradition. Beyond the important Grimm and Praetorius collections, many old tales have been passed down through the generations and still circulate all across Europe. These stories are often dismissed as merely children's fairytales, quaint rhymes, superstitious lore, and the like. No doubt, many of these tales have been altered and hybridized over time or the suspect stalks of their original meaning ripped from the ground, yet beneath the surface there often remain rootlets to the authentic land-based knowledge and hidden seeds for a deeper kinship with place. Much of the local vitality and instruction about how to live well in a specific region are conveyed in these old-time tales. It behooves us not to dismiss them, especially as we seek to develop a contemporary renewal with the Earth that integrates culture, technology, ecology, history, art, sustainable practices, and our own inner well-being.

As I mentioned earlier, in universities as well as with individual scholarship, research is underway to revive and decipher the meaning of these old stories, and I think they will be understood best and become more revealed when these tales are not only recovered and re-examined, but also accurately mapped to their points of origin. A story from a particular place has all the components of ecological intimacy and timeless mystery. At the deepest strata of culture, the regeneration of these stories will not, as some of my European colleagues have expressed concern, lead to some sort of misbegotten nationalism, but rather will stimulate a renewed contemporary "Earthalism," a way to foster togetherness between place and people in a story that weaves past and present times.

Human/nature kinship can also be revitalized through attention to old-time language rooted in the landscape: During a tour for one of my public monument projects, I stayed in Prague long enough to become intrigued by the Czech language, with its compelling zh sounds and rolled r's that almost always confounded my tongue. Through my good friend Milan, a dentist and painter, I learned that the Czech names of the months were still close to the older Slavic root and not based on Roman or Latin translations used in most European languages.

What excited me about the Czech names is that each of them portrays a physical description, often poetic, of the actual local goings-on of that month. They are an entrance, an invitation, to recognize and see the land and weather in an alive and interactive relationship:

January: Leden (Ice)

February: U'nor (Hibernation or Ice Lowers)

March: Brezen (Birch or Sap)

April: Duben (Oak)

May: Kveten (Blossom or Flower)

June: Cerven (Red)

July: Cervenec (Redder or Ripen)

August: Srpen (Sickle)

September: Zari (Blazing or Glowing Sun)

October: Njen (Rutting)

November: Listopad (Leaves Falling)

December: Prosinec (Slaughter of the Pig or, as it was inter-preted by Milan, Ask for Something to be Given)

The naming of months according to the cycles of nature is widely practiced by indigenous people throughout the world. In the book *The Sixth Grandfather*, we learn the month names that Black Elk taught to John Neihardt. Each title can immediately give us a glimpse into a relational, sensate experience with the integrated place and lifestyle of the Plains Indians and their landscape:

January: The Moon of Frost in the Tipi

February: The Moon of Dark Red Calf

March: The Moon of Snow Blind

April: The Moon of Red Grass Appearing

May: The Moon When Ponies Shed

June: The Moon of the Blooming Turnip or Making Fat

July: The Moon of Red Cherries

August: The Moon of Black Cherries

September: The Moon When Calf Grows Hair

October: The Moon of Changing Season

November: The Moon of Falling Leaves

December: The Moon of Popping Trees [13]

A colleague of mine from Hawaii explained that, in her tradition, she was taught that each phase and day of the moon cycle has a specific name that is coded with knowledge about when to fish and what to fish for, when to collect medicinal herbs, and when to plant specific seeds. She said, "As the traditional elders have taught me, I know what to do by knowing which month it is and then looking into the face of the moon."

There are, of course, thousands of deeply powerful stories and place and time names throughout the Americas. But these stories and names are for the keepers of them, the First Nations people, to decide when and how they are best shared (if at all), for they were the people who listened to the Earth community and learned the many songs. We can be grateful for what stories and knowledge have already been passed on to us by our ancestral hosts. They have helped generations of Europeans and others from around the world who arrived in America. Without this deep generosity on the part of indigenous people, often unwarranted and unreciprocated, our lives would not be as meaningful today, and certainly many of our forebears would have perished before having the opportunity to have and sustain families, finally resulting in us.

When the old stories, in a rejuvenated form, return to our speech through knowing sunrise, sparrow, shoreline, and stream, it is possible that villages, towns, and cities will have a chance to be re-membered again in tribal concert with the other creatures of the Earth in a likewise remembered universe. Let us not wait any longer or lose one more trace of the wild Earth and sheltering Sky.

4 Reshaping Interior and Exterior Landscapes

Part Two: Honor the Women

The day will come when man will recognize woman as his peer, not only at the fireside, but in councils of the nation. Then, and not until then, will there be the perfect comradeship, the ideal union between the sexes that shall result in the highest development of the race.
−SUSAN B. ANTHONY

I mages of women are plentiful in my art studio, women from many cultures and historical periods: Golden-skinned women from Mexico dressed in rainbow-colored dresses, women from Africa sitting in a council circle, young girls running through the streets of Sardinia on a festival day, women in Iraq huddled in grief over their dead, women in parliaments intent on changing the world, a woman—a mother—nursing her babe. The women's faces remind me that their stories have just begun to be told.

Uncovering our cultural story, the armature of our society and foundation for our future dreams and direction, requires not only searching for what common themes appear but also courageously taking a penetrating look into our collective narratives that have been misunderstood, omitted, or suppressed.

Just as a natural ecosystem is in continuous motion toward balance and a healthy equilibrium, our collective soul longs to reclaim a healthy societal narrative for the sake of wholeness and wellness. In a time when the larger story of freedom and equality wishes to break apart old beliefs and fears—as a hammer cracks open a geode to reveal an enchanted interior—stories of women, their history, and their empowerment are central to this timely and essential work of reclamation.

There is an old saying that our tears are hidden laughter and our laughter is hidden tears. I understood both when I let out a woeful laugh after learning the history of the only statue dedicated to women suffragist leaders in our nation's capital.

Along with many women concerned with the ongoing struggle for women's equality, I have recognized a disproportionately abundant number of statues and memorials dedicated to male leaders, in stark contrast to those that memorialize historically important women. This is true not only in the United States but worldwide. As of 2008, the National Women's History Museum (NWHM) recorded that, of the 210 statues in the United States Capitol, only 9 are of female leaders. Nationwide, less than 5 percent of the 2,400 national historic landmarks chronicle women's achievements.

The story of the suffragist statue in the Capitol Rotunda exemplifies the challenge women still face.

Karen Staser, founder of the NWHM, made a presentation at the 1998 meeting of the President's Commission on the Celebration of Women in American History held in New Mexico. Staser recounted the history of artist Adelaide Johnson's suffragist statue, which features three significant leaders: Susan B. Anthony, Elizabeth Cady Stanton, and Lucretia Mott.

From the public archives of this meeting:

> In 1993 her (Karen Staser's) family moved to Washington D.C. and she realized that women's history was virtually missing from the nation's capital. She noted that at the time the only women represented in the Capitol Rotunda were

Pocahontas, Martha Washington looking down on George, and two bare-breasted Native American women cowering in fear of Christopher Columbus.

Ms. Staser and a number of other women came together to develop a three day celebration in Washington D.C. to celebrate the passage of the 19th amendment. A major goal of the group was to return to the nation's capital a statue of Susan B. Anthony, Elizabeth Cady Stanton, and Lucretia Mott that had been displaced since 1921.

Ms. Staser described the history of the statue. American women had commissioned, paid for, and given the statue to Congress, but Congress refused to accept it. Ms. Staser said that the women shamed them into accepting it by dragging the thirteen-ton statue to the steps of the capital where the press began to take pictures. After its dedication, within the next twenty-four hours, the all male congress took the statue to an underground storage room and scraped off the inscription. Ms. Staser then said that in 1995 Congress had said that the statue wasn't worth the money required to move it, they were not sure the women's contributions had been significant enough, and that the women were too unattractive and too old.

Ms. Staser made the representation of women in the Rotunda her focal point. On June 25, 1995, with private funds totaling $125,000, the statue was returned to the Rotunda and remains there today.[1]

There had been three earlier attempts to bring the statue, officially called the Portrait Monument, back to the Rotunda. So, all told, it took just about as long—seventy-six years—to return the 26,000-pound statue (chiseled from Carrara Italian marble) back into the public sphere as the seventy-two years it took women to gain the vote in the United States.

It is also important to mention that, since the statue's return, several organizations began efforts to add a sculpture of the renowned African-American leader Sojourner Truth to this grouping of acclaimed suffragists. After a ten-year-long struggle initiated by Dr. C. Delores Tucker, co-founder and former chair of the National Congress of Black Women, a bust memorializing suffragist and abolitionist Sojourner Truth was unveiled in the Emancipation Hall of the Capitol on April 28, 2009.

Part of the 210 statues in the Capitol consists of an array of prominent sculptures called the National Statuary Hall Collection, which is a series of statues donated by the fifty states to honor historically significant people from their region. Each state has the opportunity to donate two statues, and the final collection of one hundred is located in and extends beyond the Rotunda. As of 2008, only eight women were represented in this collection.

Memorials and statuary are certainly not the only indicator of women's significance or equality. However, with the increased numbers of female leaders in the United States and around the world, historical women of the past and prominent women of the present also need to gain visibility in the sphere of public art, thus being honored and reaping due praise, not to mention offering public testimony to the power of visible role models. This is vital to the renewal of positive symbols in our cities, especially concerning transforming our one-sided cultural story to one of gender equity.

A full story of human history that equally reveres both genders is crucial for a sustainable and just society. History enables us to learn who we are and opens the door of possibilities and imaginings. Where we come from, our personal and societal origins, has a large influence on our lives and outlook on life. When the recounting of our cultural past is severely edited and the female half is in large part excised or distorted, so, too, are our viable choices and our dreams as a people, a civilization, equally diminished.

In conventional history textbooks for high school and college levels we can observe that, although women's history has garnered more presence since the 1980s, it still constitutes far less than half.

In 2007 when I spoke with Joan Wages, current president of the NWHM, she informed me that her organization conducted a survey of eighteen commonly used history textbooks and found that only 3 percent of the text was dedicated to women. This alarming number demonstrates the chasm between the story of what women have actually accomplished and the story that has been made readily available. It is the omissions from written history and in educational institutions that create a false picture—and it is these omissions that concern me and need to be remedied.

We know that women have led countries and armies, women such as Catherine the Great of Russia and Cleopatra of Alexandria. Women have died for the cause of their countries, like Boudicca of ancient Britain, Joan of Arc of France, and Benazir Bhutto of Pakistan. They have been influential and prolific authors: Mercy Otis Warren, Mary Wollstonecraft, Alice Walker, Ada Deer, Simone de Beauvoir, and Maya Angelou. They have been world-renowned scientists: Marie Curie, Rachel Carson, Jane Goodall, and Lise Meitner. They have been politicians and diplomats, such as Pocahontas, Indira Gandhi, Mary Robinson, Angela Merkel, Golda Meir, and Margaret Thatcher. They have been singular agents of change, like Mother Teresa, Margaret Fuller, Florence Nightingale, Wangari Maathai, Vandana Shiva, Tz'u Hsi, Sojourner Truth, Rose Schneiderman, Aung San Suu Kyi, Rigoberta Menchú Tum, and Aleksandra Mikhailovna Kollontai. Even when not famous, they have been mothers or teachers who have educated the children, humanity's future, and have been significant members of every other profession known.

To share the story of women is to share a story of great beauty, dignity, courage, and power. Yet, after so many years of oppression and silencing, many of these accounts are also very frustrating and painful to hear, such as reports telling us about the significantly lower wages for women in equivalent positions to their male counterparts, or the U.S. Department of Justice reporting that a woman is raped every two minutes in America, or when we learn about the worldwide increase in the trafficking, disappearance, and forced prostitution of women. In 2008, United Nations studies estimated that two million women are forced each year into the worldwide sex industry.[2] They are controlled through violent beatings, isolation, and drug and alcohol dependencies, amongst other horrors. The U.S. government estimates that fifty thousand people, mostly women and children, are trafficked each year into this country, mainly from Southeast Asia, Latin America, and countries of the former Soviet Union.[3]

These accounts, no matter how heartbreaking or uncomfortable to hear, need to be brought to daylight, for in the telling there is the possibility of awareness, justice, transformation, and healing.

When we bypass conventional history telling and diligently research and listen, we can hear women's voices rise through the ages—from the poetic words of Sappho to the battle cry of Boudicca, from the anguished echoes of inquisition-era women to the protests of brave suffragists. In women's daily stories, we can hear the exhilarating trills of Ukrainian singers and the enduring, endearing lullabies of mothers everywhere. We can hear women leading their countries, as well as their families.

As sculptors will tell you, complete works of art are already alive inside untouched rocks and boulders, images already animate in the very terrain. Awake within unchiseled marble, alabaster, limestone, or jade, women's stories have always been there, calling to be revealed, emerging from wild stones, intact and vital. The world over, women are delivered and sculpted from contrasting terrains of society—both uplifting and tumultuous—and within these multifaceted topographies, women lead glorious and resolute lives, and their stories need to be acknowledged.

I think it is safe to say that the widespread telling and retelling of women's history will create an essential revolution in humanity's thinking, because knowing women's history will greatly transform how both women and men view and understand themselves and the world. We will not only get a wider understanding of women and women's lives and roles but also gain an integrated wholeness in society and within all of ourselves as full human beings.

In her groundbreaking book *The Chalice and the Blade*, cultural historian and sociologist Riane Eisler tells us:

> One result of re-examining human society from a gender-holistic perspective has been a new theory of cultural evolution. This theory, which I have called Cultural Transformation, proposes that underlying the great diversity of human culture are two basic models of society.
>
> The first, which I call the dominator model, is what is popularly termed either patriarchy or matriarchy—the ranking of one half of humanity over the other. The second, in whom social relations are primarily based on the principle of linking rather than ranking, may best be described as the partnership model. In this model—beginning with the most fundamental difference in species, between male and female—diversity is not equated with either inferiority or superiority.[4]

As many archeologists and anthropologists will tell you, equal respect for men and women was once known in many cultures of the ancient world. And, for many Indigenous people today, gender equality has never left their way of life.

Beyond the morality of women's equality and benefit to our individual personhood, women's empowerment is critical in changing one of the most serious problems we face today: the explosion of our human population. Scientists from around the world agree that the population issue of the past decades is now a global problem. The growth of our species has created a complex series of worldwide social and environmental crises. The demands on food supplies and fresh water alone are taxing the Earth's ecological balance and particularly hurting people in developing countries. International scientists in a 2001 United Nations study make it clear that while there is no real consensus for a definitive figure for the carrying capacity of the Earth (in this case meaning the size of the human population that the Earth can sustain in the long term) they give a median estimate of 10 billion people, depending on the values used in calculations.[5] Given that we are currently a population nearing 7 billion and quickly growing, it is clear that overpopulation is a critical driver of many of our planetary problems.

Women can make a huge difference in changing this course. A 1995 United Nations study on the relationship between female education and fertility reveals that women's education has long been identified as a crucial factor affecting reproductive decisions.[6] Many studies in the past decade have shown similar findings: with education and empowerment, women consistently want smaller families. Around the world, empowering girls and women has been a key component in stabilizing populations.

Women are essential in peace making, and in some cases, the main component in ending wars, whether through protests, negotiations, or voting. Women are also an important factor in stabilizing and further developing a community's economy when they are allowed to participate in an equal and independent manner. Studies from the World Bank, UNICEF, and the United Nations Development Program all demonstrate that women's empowerment improves economic productivity and contributes to better health and education for families.

Greg Mortenson, Director of the Central Asia Institute, has been building schools in the mountains of rural Pakistan and Afghanistan for the past fifteen years with a specific focus on educating girls. An important goal for this courageous humanitarian has been to build schools in al-Qaeda and Taliban regions to foster peace. "Young women are the developing world's greatest agents of progress…. Teaching girls to read and write reduces the ignorance and poverty that fuel religious extremism and lays groundwork for prosperity and peace," says Mortenson.[7]

His tremendous success has even penetrated the U.S. military: Authors Nicholas Kristof and Sheryl WuDunn reported that in 2008, the Joint Chiefs of Staff held meetings about girls' education in Pakistan and Afghanistan as a serious counterterrorism strategy.[8]

In my own work, I am exploring how women in particular can address climate change. Women as a constituency are a relatively untapped and potentially strategic force for helping to make the societal changes we need for a clean energy revolution and green living evolution. For instance, women now control over half of the wealth and are behind 80 percent of all consumer purchases in North America.[9] Women in the U.S. vote more, volunteer more, and give more to charities than men.[10] Imagine this force of power focused on addressing the climate crisis.

Moreover, women face a disproportionate burden from the impacts of climate change, especially in low-income communities and developing countries. Giving voice to these women will accelerate progress in these communities and guide best practices in mitigation and adaptation strategies.

Research by communication experts and authors Lisa Chen and Lisa Witter shows that foundations directed or primarily made up of women are particularly interested in the root causes of social and environmental problems. These studies show that women are willing to face issues directly and insist on change at a systemic level, not just settling for superficial or short-term solutions.[11] With the complexity of the climate crisis calling for unprecedented levels of collaboration and problem-solving skills to meet a deeply rooted dilemma, it seems to me that women in particular are poised to help solve and overcome this daunting challenge.

Clearly as we look at all of these studies, women's empowerment is necessary to the positive transformation of society, and it can be greatly enhanced and made long-lasting through the acknowledgment and increased visibility of women through reclaiming and honoring their stories.

We can imagine textbooks that dedicate an equal number of pages to both men and women, and once we do, we can write them. We can ensure that our educational institutions give equal attention to women's accomplishments and societal contributions as well as to men's. Knowing that women have attained great things, girls will look toward their futures with confidence, a sense of responsibility, and excitement. The full recounting of women's contributions to humanity will bring hope, dignity, and freedom to girls and women. For boys and men, it will provide spiritual health and respect for others, as well as self. It is important to say this is not a matter of putting men down, but rather of creating balance and partnership by lifting women up.

I am not attempting to make a convincing case for the obvious need for equal female leadership. The history of the past two thousand years of patriarchal rule (a conservative number) has already clarified the issue. I wish only to lament the terrific tragedy of humanity having experienced so many years of brutal hardship and loneliness, and the consequences to society and nature once bereft of women's equal council.

Let's take a look at the shape of it for a moment: Over the past several millennia, a difficult pyramid has been constructed from the labor of the ruled; this structure is not built to mark the movements of the sun, stars, planets, and revolutions of time. Rather, it is a dangerously hierarchical pyramid designed to oppress all the stones beneath, aiming only to hold up the small, angular top piece, which appears falsely to ascend by itself to the stars, as if a glorious but illusory floating mountaintop. Yet, a true sacred mountain peak with its grand vista can only truly be celebrated by remembering the journey to the top. The climber who has attained the peak recalls all the things that comprise the loft of the mountain, from the lush greenery of the forests at the base to the rivers cascading down the slopes to the layers of minerals, soils, and rocks that form the mount. It is the support at the bottom of the peak, the bottom stones and throughout, which allows the mountain or pyramid to stand and to be as grand as it is. In this new, or renewed, era of feminine equality, some pyramids of thought and design will need to be completely dismantled, and circles and spirals of networks will replace them. Other pyramids will need to be put in their proper place by remembering that a pyramid only exists because of collaboration, a collection of parts that form a greater whole.

I wish to honor the women who have fought, and those who died fighting against, tyranny in all its forms, personal and political. I wish to remember the women who were lost and lonely, and then went on anyway. What women have done, are doing now, and will do, despite hardships, needs to be lifted up into the light of our civilizations' awakening eyes for recognition and appreciation.

I have taken my sculpting chisel to these words to reveal what we could and should bring back into our body of knowledge. We need to be critical of what we have been trained to believe is worth noting. As social scientists and teachers of gender studies have cautioned, often the tasks in which women typically have been engaged are not valued highly because they are (even though essential and of great consequence) tasks that our culture considers routine, unremarkable, and less worthy of comment, like child rearing, health care, and running the family home, while their male partners are out doing things in the wider world.

Thankfully, in recent years, social activists, progressive historians, cultural commentators, and philosophers of both genders have been exploring and elucidating women's contributions beyond the staid norms and forms. In her book *The Real Wealth of Nations*, Riane Eisler points out that the value of women's unpaid work worldwide is an astounding $11 trillion per year according to a 1995 U.N. Human Development Report. Eisler also recounts that in Nordic countries, where women have held the highest political offices in the world, there are policies to acknowledge this (usually) unpaid "invisible" work of women. Countries like Norway, Sweden, Denmark, and Finland have initiated care-giving policies such as paid parental leave and government-supported childcare. These care-giving policies also have contributed to positive economic standing for everyone in these same countries.[12]

Thousands of years' worth of omissions and distortions will not be remedied overnight, but the labor of emancipation, restoration, preservation, and celebration of women and their stories is a valiant cause to which people across many disciplines worldwide are now dedicated. These public acknowledgments, especially in Western societies, must include women of color, who are too often ignored and debased under the double challenge of being other than white or male. Women's equal visibility, as well as visible equality, in tangible ways, is essential to a yet-unfulfilled dream of true democracy, a dream that grants as well as professes equality for all.

There are many ways to honor citizens of merit; and coming back to my original point, we as a society have chosen statuary as one of the most prominent forms. Given this, it only makes sense that we attempt equal female representation. There is certainly no lack of magnificent and significant women to commemorate in order to balance the equation. In fact, the list of women who deserve the prominence that a statue would afford in our nation's capitol is so long I shall name only a handful to open the conversation. Each of these women deserve (and, thankfully, some already do have) full-length biographies about their lives and deeds, including critical analyses of their work, which we would expect from any in-depth historical review. Naturally, it is controversial to name names since there is a plethora of opinions about who deserves honoring; but it is best to venture this much, no matter the difficulty, lest nothing progress. If the woman you hold most dear is not mentioned here due to my own ignorance or preferences, I beg your pardon and applaud your advocacy for her. In truth, after so many decades of women's achievements having gone unattended in public art, we ought to be writing beautiful epic poems in praise of notable women and printing them on grand ornamental silk banners that fly throughout our cities' libraries, civic centers, and educational facilities. Women from around the world need to be included on commemorative flags and, like the sacred roll calls of ancient times, the epics would tell of women's lineages and noted events in eloquent legendary style.

Here are nascent nominations of women who I believe are essential additions to the some 210 leaders, disproportionately male, currently memorialized in the Capitol, or, if not placed in the Capitol itself, then in significant sites in Washington, DC. I have focused on this one location for its obvious symbolic importance, but I encourage this discussion in government buildings and cities across this country and beyond.

I wish to honor:

AMERICAN INDIAN WOMEN

There are American Indian women represented in the Capitol, in the form of Pocahontas and Sarah Winnemucca. But I wish to further acknowledge Indian leaders who lived here on Turtle Island (an American Indian name for this continent) long before Europeans arrived on its shores and therefore not recognized or recorded by them. The proper historical representation of these women and their people is grossly missing from the capitol. This is not to ignore the great significance of the National Museum of the American Indian located on the National Mall, but rather to bring attention to specifically acknowledging Indian women leaders. The names of the women to be honored I suggest we leave to the First Nations people.

In this distinguished lineage of American Indian peoples, I also would wish to remember the Indigenous women who first welcomed European-American women leaders like Susan B. Anthony and Matilda Joslyn Gage and introduced them to a new understanding of women's freedoms and power in governance. The Indian women offered a worldview that white women had never before experienced, igniting in them a new sense of personal liberty that influenced an entire movement.

In her revealing book, *Sisters In Spirit*, historian Sally Roesch Wagner documents how Haudenosaunee (Iroquois) women shaped and inspired the revolutionary vision of early suffragists. Wagner's account opens with an introduction by Jeanne Shenandoah of the Onondaga Nation:

> We Haudenosaunee live within the traditional structure that we've always had, the structure of equality among members of our community. Women, men, and children have equal spiritual, human, and political rights. We have equal opportunity to voice opinions or objections to any situation within our community, and we know that our voice will be heard. And so, when we met these white women so long ago, I am sure that our women were probably shocked at the lack of human equality that these other women had to live under … how people who fled their homelands, for exactly the same reason, could appear here on our Turtle Island, our Mother Earth, and bring with them the exact oppressive behaviors that they had experienced. These women raised the children, gave them teachings and influenced them to be caring, respectful people—and still had energy to claim their place on earth, standing equal in all areas of life.[13]

MERCY OTIS WARREN (1728–1814)

Warren was not only a great wit but also an influential American writer who deserves credit for helping to arouse widespread courage in the war for independence. She was a key figure, and perhaps the most important woman, in prominent circles of revolutionary thinkers. It was in her home that many meetings were held to strategize for the American Revolution and form the Constitution of the United States.

Abigail Adams and Mercy Otis Warren cultivated an important friendship and frequently wrote to one another about the development of the new country and the conditions for women. Adams and Warren are the rightful feminist predecessors of Susan B. Anthony, Elizabeth Cady Stanton, and Matilda Joslyn Gage.

Warren wrote *The History of the American Revolution*, a recounting alive with personal reports because she witnessed it first-hand. She was best known for her satirical plays, particularly *The Adulateur*, a work that casts Governor Thomas Hutchinson of Massachusetts as "Rapatio," a villain bent on destroying the colony.

The Adulateur takes place in the fictional but undisguised land of "Upper Servia," in reference to her opinion of the colonies under British control. Circulated as a pamphlet, the play became an instant success, captivating the attention of many colonists and bestowing upon them the responsibility for the nation's future.

I had the opportunity to direct several high school students in a performance of the play, which was an assignment for their American history class. Even while Warren had us laughing at her parody, let there be no mistake—the play is startling in its clear portrayal of the extreme violence of the times.

As a woman, Warren wrote under enormous duress; in fact, she did not publish under her own name until she was in her early sixties, choosing instead anonymity, although it was widely known what she had authored. Her outspoken brother, the lawyer James Otis, is known for his words, "Taxation without representation is tyranny." He was severely beaten, almost to death, by British soldiers for his revolutionary views; she herself received threats and harassment. Despite the dangers, she continued to write her revolutionary works until independence was achieved.

The influence of Warren's work equaled or surpassed Thomas Paine's in contributing to the cause of the Revolution, and Samuel Adams remarked that her bold satire did more damage to the British Crown than any other public attack.

Warren's vision was also far reaching. As noted historian Doris Weatherford remarked, "More than most of the men of her era, she saw the American Revolution as having significance beyond its apparent economic and political welfare; instead, she foresaw a deep and permanent shift of Western ideology. At a time when even most Americans still thought of democracy as an impossible notion tainted by ignorant rabble, Mercy Otis Warren understood that the natural rights philosophy inherent in the Declaration of Independence would inevitably mean democracy and egalitarianism."[14]

Abigail Adams (1744–1818)

Although Abigail Adams lived too early to be claimed a suffragist, she was certainly instrumental in the battle for women's rights and women's place in a new country striving to become a free and more egalitarian society. Adams was passionate about women's education and brave in expressing the terrific neglect she saw in a culture that feared women becoming "too intelligent." In a letter to her husband, future president John Adams, she wrote: "You need not be told how much female education is neglected, nor how fashionable it has been to ridicule female learning."[15]

Before United States independence was even declared, Adams voiced her conviction about women gaining new rights in another letter: "I long to hear that you have declared an independency and by the way in the new Code of Laws which I suppose it will be necessary for you to make, I desire that you would Remember the Ladies, and be more generous and favorable to them than your ancestors. Do not put such unlimited power into the hands of the Husbands. Remember all Men would be tyrants if they could."[16]

Sojourner Truth (1797–1883)

Born into slavery in New York state, Sojourner Truth (born as Isabella Baumfree) was an African-American abolitionist and suffragist who boldly spoke out for social justice. Truth is best remembered for her famous "Ain't I a woman?" speech at the Ohio

Women's Rights Convention in 1851. She was the only woman of color at that gathering and single-handedly saved the meeting from the uproar of jeering men. Mr. Frances Gage, who helped steer the meeting (women were still gaining the confidence and independence to preside over their own public events), poignantly documented the atmosphere:

> There were very few women in those days who dared to 'speak in meeting'; and the august teachers of the people were seemingly getting the better of us, while the boys in the galleries, and the sneerers among the pews, were hugely enjoying the discomfiture, as they supposed, of the 'strong-minded.' Some of the tender-skinned friends were on the point of losing dignity, and the atmosphere betokened a storm. When, slowly from her seat in the corner rose So-journer Truth, who, till now, had scarcely lifted her head. 'Don't let her speak!' gasped half a dozen in my ear. She moved slowly and solemnly to the front, laid her old bonnet at her feet, and turned her great speaking eyes to me. There was a hissing sound of disapprobation above and below. I rose and announced 'Sojourner Truth,' and begged the audi-ence to keep silence for a few moments.
>
> The tumult subsided at once, and every eye was fixed on this almost Amazon form, which stood nearly six feet high, head erect, and eyes piercing the upper air like one in a dream. At her first word there was a profound hush. She spoke in deep tones, which, though not loud, reached every ear in the house, and away through the throng at the doors and windows.[17]

After her speech, Gage then commented, "Amid roars of ap-plause, she returned to her corner, leaving more than one of us with streaming eyes, and hearts beating with gratitude."

Here were her powerful closing remarks: "If the first woman God ever made was strong enough to turn the world upside down all alone, these women together ought to be able to turn it back, and get it right side up again! And now they is asking to do it. The men better let them. Obliged to you for hearing me, and now old Sojourner ain't got nothing more to say."[18]

Harriet Tubman (1820–1913)

An abolitionist, suffragist, and Union spy during the Civil War, Harriet Tubman is one of the most acclaimed African-American women. She was born into slavery in Maryland and experienced terrific violence throughout her childhood: she was severely beaten and suffered a head wound that caused her seizures all her life. Tubman escaped captivity in 1849 and returned to rescue her family soon thereafter. Risking her life many times, she continued to conduct rescue missions for other slaves, utilizing the Underground Railroad. Tubman worked for the Union Army as a scout and spy, and after the war was active as a suffragist. Her life of courage in the cause of freedom is the very essence of the struggle for the American ideal.

Matilda Joslyn Gage (1826–1898)

Ms. Gage (not related to Frances Gage) dedicated her life to the liberation of women in every sphere, socially, politically, spiritually, intellectually, and physically. She was an abolitionist (her childhood home was a station of the Underground Railroad), an activist for Native American rights, a brilliant thinker, and a prolific writer.

Along with Susan B. Anthony and Elizabeth Cady Stanton, Gage was one of the founders of the National Woman Suffrage Association, and, in my view, should have been included in the Rotunda Portrait Statue. In addition to her lifelong work on the behalf of women, she was also a strong advocate for ending violence against American Indians and for their fair treatment. Due to her work with and interest in indigenous people and their knowledge, she was officially adopted into the Mohawk Nation. Upon initiation into the Wolf Clan, Gage was given the name

Ka-ron-ien-ha-wi, which means She Who Holds the Sky, or Sky Carrier. This was a fitting name for a woman of such luminous vision. Ironically, the year of her naming and admittance to the Mohawk Council of Matrons, where she would be considered for full voting rights in the Mohawk Nation, she was arrested for voting in her local school board election.

Through her close ties to the American Indian world, she was deeply influenced by Indigenous understanding and the Mohawk model of governance and of women's rights and equal place in society.

In addition to co-editing *History of Woman's Suffrage* with Anthony and Stanton, Gage is most noted for her brilliant analysis in *Woman, Church and State*, in which she outlines her powerful views on the need for separation of church and state. Well-educated about women's historical struggles not only in America but also around the world, Gage's motto, engraved on her headstone, reads: "There is a word sweeter than Mother, Home or Heaven: that word is Liberty."

ELEANOR ROOSEVELT (1884–1962)

Indeed, a statue of Eleanor Roosevelt does stand in Washington, DC, yet only as a component of husband Franklin Delano Roosevelt's memorial. Eleanor Roosevelt was a political leader in her own right, utilizing her influence as First Lady during President Roosevelt's terms in office and even after his death. As a supporter of the New Deal, a suffragist promoting improvements for working women, a leader in the formation of the United Nations, and a founder of the United Nations Association in the United States, she continues to be a powerful example of women's leadership. Roosevelt chaired the committee of the United Nations general assembly in 1945, which created the Universal Declaration of Human Rights.

On my studio wall I posted the following Eleanor Roosevelt quote: Where … do universal human rights begin? In small places, close to home—so close and so small that they cannot be seen on any maps of the world.... Such are the places where every man, woman, and child seeks equal justice, equal opportunity, equal dignity without discrimination. Unless these rights have meaning there, they have little meaning anywhere."[19]

Alongside that quote rests this one from Nobel laureate Wangari Maathai: "It's the little things citizens do, that's what will make the difference. My little thing is planting trees."[20]

Rachel Carson (1907–1964)

A courageous biologist and elegant writer, Carson's research and books are widely recognized as the progenitors of the modern environmental movement. In 1962 her most influential book, *Silent Spring*, brought thunderous attention to the dangerous effects of synthetic pesticides. Carson made a brilliant case for humanity's interconnectedness with the natural world, while reminding us to respect this web of life or accept the perilous consequences. Although the scientific evidence presented in *Silent Spring* survived the rigors of peer review and was supported by many established scientists, Carson received fierce criticism, and her credibility as a scientist was severely attacked. Biochemist Robert White-Stevens described her as "a fanatic defender of the cult of the balance of nature."[21] Not deterred, Carson continued her work and toured the country with speeches and interviews, even though she was seriously ill with cancer. Her determination and meticulous scientific research withstood the storm of controversy. President Kennedy appointed a special review committee to examine Carson's findings, which resulted in Congressional hearings that further brought the issue into the limelight. This was a defining moment in the coming of age of public environmental awareness. Rachel Carson is lovingly remembered by generations for her evocative nature writing that so effectively yet poetically brings readers into a vital relationship with the living Earth. She said, "It is a wholesome and necessary thing for us to turn again to the earth and in the contemplation of her beauties to know of wonder and humility."[22]

In former Vice President and Nobel Laureate Al Gore's introduction to the 1994 reissue of *Silent Spring*, he wrote:

> Indeed, Rachel Carson was one of the reasons I became so conscious of the environment and so involved with environmental issues. ...Her picture hangs on my office wall among those of the political leaders, the presidents and the prime ministers. It has been there for years—and it belongs there. Carson has had as much or more effect on me than any of them, and perhaps than all of them together.
>
> Both a scientist and an idealist, Carson was also a loner who listened, something that those in places of power so often fail to do.[23]

ANNIE DODGE WAUNEKA (1910–1997)

A highly respected and influential Navajo (Diné) woman of the twentieth century, Annie Dodge Wauneka was the first woman member of the Navajo Tribal Council and was soon appointed to chair the Council's Health and Welfare Committee. She was active in this position, caring for the health and welfare of her people until 1956, when the Surgeon General of the United States invited her to become a member of the Federal Advisory Committee on Indian Health.

Wauneka is best known across the nation for her tireless and highly successful work battling tuberculosis. She also greatly influenced her tribe in countless ways, including in education and social justice issues. She received many awards for her remarkable work, including the Presidential Medal of Freedom in 1963.

GENERAL WILMA VAUGHT (B. 1930)

One of the most highly decorated military women in U.S. history, Vaught was the first female general in the Air Force. She was instrumental in the building and dedication of the Women in Military Service for America memorial in Washington, DC. Vaught retired in 1980 and went on to serve on the Committee on Women in the Armed Forces in NATO and as an influential member of the International Women's Forum.

Many others certainly belong on this honor roll call. I wish to acknowledge American labor organizer Mother Jones (Mary Harris Jones) for her brave and tireless fight for workers' rights and anti-child-labor laws. She and labor union leader Rose Schneiderman were major trailblazers in the battle for labor unions' claiming power and generating public awareness of the terrible hardship and violence inherent in workers' conditions. Patsy Mink, Fannie Lou Hamer, Lady Bird Johnson (Claudia Alta Taylor Johnson), Tsuyako "Sox" Kitashima, Lucy Stone, Elizabeth Wanamaker Peratrovich, Alice Paul, Jane Addams, Jody Williams, and Elinor Ostrom are also women we must never forget.

Thankfully, by a special act of Congress signed on December 1, 2005, a statue of the great civil rights activist Rosa Parks is to be commissioned and placed in the Capitol's National Statuary Hall. Known as the mother of the modern-day Civil Rights Movement, Rosa Parks' legacy, esteemed worldwide, has long deserved this proper acknowledgement. When she died in 2005, her body lay in the Capitol Rotunda for three days for public viewing, an honor never before accorded a woman.

I think we need to have a monument simply and significantly called "All Mothers" to honor the relentless and often thankless work of everyday women who raise the coming generations with tremendous love, courage, and sacrifice. The effort of mothers needs to be publicly recognized and elevated to a place of societal prominence and esteem.

Monuments to women and new textbooks, classes, and films ushering in an age of equal female visibility and leadership is imperative because the "dominator model" of society is now at a breaking point. With the dying of the old, there is room for the birth of the new, and we are in a cultural transition that demands equality and equilibrium between the genders. As the laws of nature demonstrate to us, equilibrium is an underlying force always in motion, seeking balance, for the health of all species and all natural systems.

We all, men and women alike, gain inspiration and confidence from learning about the important contributions of women. This knowledge and its visible portrayal in our cities and in our daily lives will add to the development of a healthy "partnership model" of leadership and society, and therefore a truer democracy, belonging to the people—all the people.

THE FEMININE PRINCIPLE

In addition to sculptures of historical women, there are female figurative statues in public art that belong to the realm of what could be called the "Feminine Principle."

Humans by nature are perpetual storytellers; since long ago and continuing into our day, statuary depictions have been a mode of conveyance for these stories. A considerable amount of public art is dedicated to both ancient and contemporary expressions of cultural stories, myths, legends, and sacred writings. Stories and parables from the Rig Veda, the Iliad and Odyssey, the Bhagavad-Gita, the Talmud, Bible, Qur'an, and the Popol Vuh—have all been central to the art and culture of many civilizations because they offer invaluable meaning and purpose to our individual lives, collective dreams, and societal storytelling. As the mythologist Joseph Campbell remarked, "Myths are clues to the spiritual potentialities of the human life."[24] He also tells us, "Essentially, mythologies are enormous poems that are renditions of insights, giving some sense of the marvel, the miracle and wonder of life."[25]

Since antiquity, many of these old stories have been wrought into dimensional form: chiseled in stone, forged in copper, cast in bronze, woven into tapestries, or painted upon pottery. A large portion of these artistic renderings are figurative images of both male and female characters who have been talking to us throughout the long ages through the media of metal, cloth, clay, and marble—and they creatively reveal our universal human journey.

Many of these figurative works are composed of allegorical images depicting human virtues, while others are expressions of cosmic divinities, Gods and Goddesses representing every aspect of life. Although the majority of these artworks are not from this modern age, there are contemporary artists who work with these timeless themes, and the transcendent symbols thus rendered still provide us with relevance and meaning. In our over-commercialized world, these archetypal artworks hewn from deep within the human psyche are certainly useful in addressing the larger dilemmas of humanity. I shudder to think what our common cultural life would devolve to without them.

In my teenage years, while poring over a book on Nordic mythology—a vintage publication that I still relish for its worn leather binding and antique illustrations—I came across a photograph of the Valkyrie statue that stands to this day in Denmark. At the time, I knew nothing of the mythological history or designated role of this figure. All I understood was that her image so fascinated me that I drew pictures of her in my notebook for weeks. Fearless, she rides her magnificent fiery horse bareback from the heavens, her long hair streaming, not behind her, but brilliantly forward, over the top of her head, to create enormous tension and fervent beauty in the bronze statue. Both she and her mount announce their arrival with mouths fully open, calling into the fierce wind that they themselves are inciting. Although the metal sculpture is silent, I could hear the Valkyrie's exuberant roar in my head.

I later learned that this twelve-foot-high statue, which graces Churchill Park in Copenhagen, was created in 1908 by the Norwegian-Danish sculptor Stephan Sinding. The Valkyries, in Norse mythology, are the female deities who govern the victors in battle and war. They also decide the bravest of the fighters who die in combat and then honor them in a Norse hero's heaven.

Here was a sculpture that pulled me from the inside; I wanted to touch the exquisite wild motion and force. Having only a photograph, I ran my fingers on the page, outlining the valiant warrioress. Of course, I knew she was not a "real" woman, but I grasped that she was majestic and powerful and, within this understanding, she was a role model, an ideal for me that evoked terrific personal energy and inspiration.

There were (and are) other so-called allegorical female figures that have captured my imagination from the moment I first saw them, such as the marble sculpture the *Winged Victory of Samothrace*, circa 190 BCE. One of the Louvre's finest masterpieces, *Victory*, or *Nike*, stands powerfully at the head of the expansive Daru stairs. Without head or arms, her motion and beguiling presence is not in the least deterred by these absences, and I could not leave her presence for an entire breathless hour.

I mention these sculptures because, as an artist who often works in the realm of symbolic figurative sculpture, various discourses, criticisms, and analyses have crossed my path concerning the importance, use, and meaning of allegorical statues in public artworks.

Specifically concerning female images, scholars in different disciplines have asked: Are these non-historic, symbolic women a hindrance and a substitute for honoring real women? Some cultural critics have been concerned that these allegorical women send the wrong message to society, telling us that the ideal is unattainable. Do these statues embody an unreachable female paragon?

When a city is lacking monuments to historical women as role models, then yes, I must agree—I can fully understand the apprehension. For example, it is important not to overlook the conditions for women when the Statue of Liberty in the United States and the statue of the Goddess Athena in ancient Greece were presented as public artworks. At the times when these two esteemed symbolic monuments were erected, women were not "liberated," did not have the right to vote, and were not treated as full citizens. It is all the more poignant because both ancient Greece and the United States were and are highly influential societies claiming creation and implementation of democratic governance. Therefore, yes, there is right cause for concern.

While we can see the contradiction here (i.e., the elevation of females as idealized symbols when actual women were disenfranchised) I think there is more to the story. My experience is that there is a need for representation of *both* historical and allegorical females. Many times, allegorical and mythological images serve the purpose of uplifting our awareness, helping us see what we are striving for in society, just as the power of ancient myths and teaching parables act as guidance for our spiritual understandings and discoveries. These images stand in the public square as dimensional, poetic bodies reminding us of our cultural armature. They remind us of our societal values and dreams, in which we are creative participants, even if they are not yet realized. In this sense, these images offer more good than not. As to design and style, I leave this to the artists who must struggle, as always, to manifest their work amidst the politics, trends, and funding difficulties of the day—matters of no small magnitude.

Evocative artistic expressions of the Feminine Principle have survived the ages despite different periods of religious and cultural suppression of the feminine and widespread efforts to singularly revere the male aspect of creation to the detriment and cultural diminution of the female. From small female figurines of clay dating back tens of thousands of years in the Paleolithic age to bronze and stone Goddess statues in Mesoamerica, Egypt, Greece, Europe, and China, there is a long tradition of symbolic female sculptural images providing guidance and inspiration for people of many nations and generations.

In the public sphere, female statues have represented and symbolized human virtues, nations, and divinities. As a virtue, she has been portrayed as Liberty, Justice, Hope, Peace, and Faith, to name a few. She represents a marvelous range of Goddesses: Kuan Yin statues adorn cities throughout Asia, and Mother Mary, Our Lady of Guadalupe, and Black Madonna statues appear in Westernized societies around the world. These artworks not only celebrate female spiritual imagery as embodied compassion, they also provide an unbroken connection to thousands of years of sculpture dedicated to the Great Earth Mother or Divine Mother that has been revered universally.

Although this connection survives, it is critical to remember that it has been severely attacked and scarred by patriarchal domination. Many feminist scholars and historians such as Riane Eisler and Maria Gimbutas have well documented the dismemberment of civilizations and Earth-based tribes that at one time revered the Great Mother.[26] Countless statues dedicated to the Feminine Principle were destroyed during these upheavals, and we might well consider what the loss of this once-ubiquitous Divine Earth Mother symbol has meant to the world. And, more importantly, we can ask what the return of the Great Mother would contribute to healing our currently impaired comprehension of the Earth as the sacred giver and sustainer of life. Thomas Berry emphasizes this point in his book, *The Great Work*:

> We might now recover our sense of the maternal aspect of the universe in the symbol of the Great Mother, especially in the Earth as that maternal principle out of which we are born and by which we are sustained. Once this symbol is recovered the dominion of the patriarchal that has brought such aggressive attitudes into our activities will be mitigated. If this is achieved then our relationship with the natural world would undergo one of the most radical readjustments since the origins of our civilization in classical antiquity.[27]

Eisler and Gimbutas have demonstrated that the effect of patriarchal rule dominating for more than five thousand years in Western civilization has continued to influence our modern societal constructs. Hand-in-hand with the establishment of patriarchal societies came the religious tenet that there could be only one God, and a male one at that. It was at this time that the understanding of balance between the Great Mother, or Creatress, and the Great Father, or Creator, was lost. Up until this point, many ancient societies observed a cosmology and science that described the world as a balance of female and male power, derived from skilled observation of the natural world around them.

The word for deity in older cultures usually referred to both male and female. The word "deity" derives from the Latin "dea," meaning goddess and "dues" meaning god, as well as from other Indo-European roots.

One example is Jehovah, the name of the Jewish God, which originally meant male and female, God and Goddess. According to oriental scholar Michael Angelo Lanci, the word *Jehovah* was pronounced Ho-Hi, meaning He-She, referring to Hebrew masculine and feminine pronouns.[28] Only much later was the word purposefully shifted in meaning to signify strictly the male God.

Deity refers to both the Feminine and Masculine Principle. In Norse mythology, there were the deities Freya and Freyr; Hellen and Helios from Greece; Hjuki and Bil, also from the Norse people and who later became Jack and Jill in nursery rhymes; and Belle and Balder from western Europe. The Japanese Creatress Mother and Creator Father are Izanagi and Izanami. In Egypt there are the deities Isis and Osiris, earlier known as Au Set and Au Sar. In ancient China the female and male twin deities are known as Fu Hsi and Nu Kua. In ancient Arabia the deities are Al-lah and Al-lat.

Today, many Indigenous people still maintain their reverence for both Mother Earth and Father Sky and a Creatress Mother and Creator Father. This understanding stems from honoring the natural laws of creation in which male and female are equally interdependent and a respect for the fact that all things are born from the female.

In our time of staggering inequality, uplifting the Feminine Principle is a move toward balance and sustainability. If the Male Principle were similarly cast down and disregarded, a move toward balance would be the restoration of the Male.

Fortunately, there are a few places where the Feminine Principle continues to hold its ground. The ancient link, although currently weakened, has not been broken completely. Today, the Feminine is still an honored emblem personifying the spirit of nations and people. Mother Sweden, or *Modern Sea*, is a national symbol of Sweden. "Mother Motherland" is a forty-foot-tall monument in Kiev City in the Ukraine. The female Britannia in England represents the spirit of Britain. In France, Marianne is the symbol of the French Republic, and although her image was suppressed under various governments, she is now widely revered as representing the spirit of the land. An article posted by the Department of the French Prime Ministry states, "The assimilation of the French Republic to La Marianne is now a fact. Marianne has survived five republics and the vicissitudes of history."[29]

What is remarkable is that throughout history, the Feminine Principle has never left our psyche, never left our deep, soulful affections. This dynamic Feminine Principle, with her many facets and long lineage, is a part of our human heritage and hope. When I ask people in cities around the world about their public female statues, whether the sculpture in question expresses a virtue, a nation, or a female divinity, only on rare occasions have I heard a cynical remark indicating the images are "old fashioned" or "too sentimental." By far the greater responses have been those of pride and enjoyment. The public monuments give rise to inspiration, direction, comfort, reflection, and hope, the people tell me. Though not without flaw or controversy, the essence of these statues can speak to us about what we value and seek to emphasize and ennoble in our transitioning civilization.

It was 1989, a year that was prismatic in sending a differentiated light into the world and in bringing about unforgettable moments, from the collapse of the Berlin Wall to the student-led Tiananmen Square democracy movement. There are two striking images from the Tiananmen Square protest that shall always be remembered worldwide: that of a young man, still carrying his shopping bags, standing in front of a column of military tanks to obstruct their forward motion and the ten-meter-tall Goddess of Democracy statue created by the students from the Central Academy of Fine Arts.

Journalists and social justice organizers declared that there were two critical moments of leadership that brought world attention to the students in their struggle: the hunger strike and the building of the statue. These two group events were the most significant symbolic acts that drew worldwide audiences. The Goddess of Democracy, constructed out of papier-mâché and Styrofoam, was destroyed when toppled by a tank in the horrifying violence of the closing days of the demonstrations. But the image of her lives on and continues to be a symbol in our international memory. Since 1989, the design of this Goddess of Democracy has been replicated many times in Hong Kong and throughout Europe, North America, and Asia. Where she stands with her torch raised high and her face brave and unwavering, she embodies hope and continues to bring global awareness to ongoing struggles for democracy and human rights. Her story extends beyond China and into the heart of every citizen of the world seeking justice and equality; in this sense, her elevated light of inquiry shines into the shadowed areas of the power structures of every country seeking or claiming democratic governance. The Goddess of Democracy confronts and uplifts us, having captured a moment in the evolution of the human quest for individual equality and freedom. She also asks us never to forget the bravery of our world's young people, willing to put their lives on the line for what they believe in.

As an American artist who has spent a fair amount of time and effort exploring the Feminine Principle in public art, it is only right, as well as an honor, that I proffer some words of homage to one of our country's most distinctive icons: the Statue of Liberty. She demonstrates not only an important feminine presence (a substantial 151 feet of presence!) but also the natural metamorphosis of this type of historic symbol's meaning.

One of the salient powers of allegorical symbols and ancient myths is that, when we take the time to engage them, they are breathing, evolving entities. These creative expressions of our human story are designed to be participatory as we seek to understand our society, the voyage of existence, and our inner life. Each time we allow ourselves to enter the mythopoetic realm in which these stories and symbols reside, they renew themselves according to time and place, and new interpretations emerge. The central truth or lessons of these narratives and symbols are tested and explored by each generation. We have the opportunity to dress the story armature anew in each generation. In this way, the stories and artistic symbols can stay alive with relevance; they can venture off the physical pedestal into our poetic imaginations, and there invigorate our passions as we embody their message.

The copper repoussé Statue of Liberty ascending from the eastern shores of our country, with her eyes focused out to sea and her gilded flame reflecting the sun's celestial light, asks each of us—as all cultural symbols and ancient myths do—that her message be renewed and her meaning regenerated. To vivify America's original essence and to honor a new American Dream appropriate for our era, we must look beneath the surface, into the bone marrow, for Liberty's story—especially as years of questionable wars and destructive environmental practices have dimmed her clear light.

Liberty is a big word, a rather spacious concept that far exceeds the size of the magnificent colossus at the entrance of New York's harbor. When we hear the resonant sound, "liberty," move across our lips, we evoke remembrances of our ancestral struggles to stand free.

To recall again the words of early American activist Matilda Joslyn Gage, "There is a word sweeter than Mother, Home or Heaven: that word is Liberty."

For the American revolutionaries who dedicated themselves and gave their lives to the cause of liberty and the end of tyranny, the concept of liberty meant entrance to a profound and newly found freedom—one unshackled from the oppression and servitude of Old World monarchs. Liberty was a great awakening deep in the heart and mind, a revolution of the soul, breaking the thrall of empire.

Thomas Jefferson and Thomas Paine were two of the most eloquent and influential writers to elucidate the new American understanding of liberty. Historian Lloyd S. Kramer connects and commends both of these prominent thinkers in their ability to articulate with great poignancy the grievances that engendered the logical reasons for America's right to independence. With their wisdom and fiery passion, they were able to see not only the righteousness of the American struggle for freedom and liberty, but to argue further for the rights that belong, by extension, to people everywhere in the world.

In the words of Thomas Jefferson: "Liberty is the great parent of science and of virtue; and a nation will be great in both in proportion as it is free." Says Thomas Paine: "We have it in our power to begin the world over again."

Paine's provocative pen was a sure force in this new beginning, and his contemporaries had high praise for his significant contributions. John Adams proclaimed, "History is to ascribe the American Revolution to Thomas Paine."

Although Paine is still not appropriately recognized as one of the "Founding Fathers" of our nation, his and Jefferson's thoughts have continued to breathe life into our young, yet to be mature, practice of democracy and expression of liberty.

In addition to the tremendous courage and vision we gain from Jefferson, who composed in the Declaration of Independence the famed words, "We hold these truths to be self-evident, that all men are created equal," we are also stung by an inconsistency in his personal life. He was himself a slave owner, and thus, we are forced headlong into the contradictions and flaws we see in our leaders and ourselves in this unfolding journey of freedom for all. As we see the grand Statue of Liberty stepping forward, trampling the chains of tyranny underfoot, it is important to reflect upon the heights of freedom we have witnessed and also the lows we have experienced—personally and as a country. These human faults, contradictions, and pieces of unfinished business must be accounted for as we look toward Liberty's flame. The contrast of shining light and shadowy cultural landscapes is a reminder that the health of liberty requires eternal vigilance through ongoing education, conversation, inward reflection, and engagement.

Embracing liberty, equality, and justice takes us through complex terrain, and I suggest that we invite the breadth of the dialogue and deliberation required to fairly traverse the landscape. Martin Luther King Jr. spoke to this point of complexity when he remarked:

> I have almost reached the regrettable conclusion that the Negro's great stumbling block in the stride toward freedom is not the White Citizen's Councilor or the Ku Klux Klanner, but the white moderate, who is more devoted to 'order' than to justice; who prefers a negative peace which is the absence of tension to a positive peace which is the presence of justice; who constantly says: 'I agree with you in the goal you seek, but I cannot agree with your methods of direct action;' who paternalistically believes he can set the timetable for someone else's freedom; who lives by a mythical concept

of time and who constantly advises the Negro to wait for a 'more convenient season.'[30]

The Statue of Liberty, with all her great promise, stirs a mixture of emotions and questions, which we need to ponder and act upon. When the grand colossus, a gift from liberty-seeking France, was unveiled in 1886, what kind of liberty was offered to women? American Indians? African Americans? Those of Mexican heritage? And, how far have we come today? These are inquiries the Lady with the Torch provocatively asks us as she stands upright in the portal harbor, representing our wish for a proud, free, and wise America.

The distinguished stateswoman Barbara Jordan, speaking about the unfolding of Liberty's journey and the dream of America, commented: "Let there be no illusions about the difficulty of forming this kind of a national community. It's tough, difficult, not easy. But a spirit of harmony will survive in America only if each of us remembers that we share a common destiny.[31]"

The historic election of President Barack Obama in 2008 opened a new door for the promise of a national community. Recognizing what seemed to be an inconceivable breakthrough, people across the country and worldwide celebrated in the streets. And though the road to our country's promise of equality and justice has more milestones to cross, Liberty's flame has surely been brightened by this historic achievement.

As we all learned in school, the Statue of Liberty was presented as a gift to America from France to commemorate the centennial of American independence, ten years after, in 1886. Yet, there is far more to the meaning than seen at first glance.

The idea for the Statue of Liberty was conceived in 1865 during a dinner party hosted by Édouard René Lefèbvre de Laboulaye, a French intellectual, lawyer, and chair of the anti-slavery society in France. Together with sculptor Frédéric Bartholdi,

Laboulaye launched the idea for the grand project after a discussion about an appropriate gift to send to America for her centennial birthday.

As historian Marvin Trachtenberg elucidates, Laboulaye's intent was not only to strengthen and honor the friendship between France and America, but also to explicitly sponsor a monument that would act as a political lever to influence the French government and society. At the time, France was struggling to emerge as a strong republic, but there were still those who desired to restore the old monarchy they had known under Napoleon III.

Here it is important to remember the full name of the statue: Liberty Enlightening the World. This was a symbol meant to celebrate America, but also to reach across oceans and nations.

While the design was underway—with Bartholdi deftly at the helm and citizens in France raising funds—Laboulaye gained position in the French government and successfully pushed through the parliament a call to establish what became the Third French Republic.

At this pivotal moment, the French envisioned the gift of the Statue of Liberty as a way to powerfully link the destiny of France with the ideals of the thriving American republic. America represented a radiant example of democracy, and Laboulaye, Bartholdi, and many others were keen to unite the two countries. The gift was meant to be a sign that the French Republic was in solidarity with the American Republic and with the concept of democratic governance.

Initially the statue was not understood and therefore difficult for Americans to embrace, but eventually the Great Lady began to "speak" to people, and funds from private American citizens primarily paid for her pedestal, the French having funded the statue herself. All told, it took twenty-one years from the inception of the idea to the arrival of the colossus in New York, when finally Bartholdi realized a lifelong dream.

Before the day of the monument's dedication, citizens were informed that, while some six hundred dignitaries would be present, no women would be allowed on Bedloe's Island during the unveiling ceremony. The irony was not lost on the New York State Women's Suffrage Association. They chartered a boat and, with megaphones in hand, circled the male-only festivities delivering protest speeches. Lillie Devereux Blake, then president of the Association, declared, "In erecting a Statue of Liberty embodied as a woman in a land where no woman has political liberty men have shown a delightful inconsistency…"[32]

The poem *The New Colossus*, inscribed on the statue's pedestal, was read during the opening event. Written some years earlier by the poet Emma Lazarus, the sonnet was solicited by William Maxwell Evarts in 1883 as a donation. Although the poem was originally intended to inspire the funding efforts to build the pedestal, it quickly added new meaning to Liberty's symbolism. The statue went from torchbearer of democracy to keeper of the hearth fire, welcoming the world's unwanted or endangered.

The New Colossus

Not like the brazen giant of Greek fame,

With conquering limbs astride from land to land;

Here at our sea-washed, sunset gates shall stand

A mighty woman with a torch, whose flame

Is the imprisoned lightning, and her name

Mother of Exiles. From her beacon-hand

Glows worldwide welcome; her mild eyes command

The air-bridged harbor that twin cities frame.

"Keep ancient lands, your storied pomp!" cries she

with silent lips. "Give me your tired, your poor,

Your huddled masses yearning to breathe free,

The wretched refuse of your teeming shore.

Send these, the homeless, tempest-tost to me,

I lift my lamp beside the golden door!"

We experience the metamorphosis of Liberty's message not in linear fashion, but rather in ever-enlarging, overlapping circles, like those created by tossing several stones into a pond simultaneously. The Statue of Liberty is at once a symbol of French and American alliance, the French uplifting their own democratic government, American independence, freedom and the downfall of tyranny, the end of slavery, and finally, grand Liberty—the Mother of Exiles, a beacon to immigrants around the world. (Alas, during these past decades, Liberty's lamp may have appeared fainter to many potential immigrants.)

This statue has a unique feature, upon which Marina Warner, along with other art critics, has remarked, one that does not exist in any other monument of Liberty's size. It is this: we have the ability to not only see the statue from the outside, but also to walk around inside of her. On the interior, as we observe the metal frame, we can witness the genius work of engineer Gustave Eiffel, who was commissioned to design the steel armature to which the three hundred copper sheets of "skin" owe their support.

With a walk into the skeletal interior of the statue, we can allow our minds to wander into our own interior contemplations. How do we enter the inner concept of liberty? What is our deepest understanding of freedom and liberty? What is liberty's embodiment in our daily lives? In our inner lives?

Of course, there is no single answer to any of these questions, but perhaps we can approach them more like koans. Teachers throughout the ages have taught that there can be many appropriate and insightful answers to the riddle-like koan, each different according to circumstances and personal realization. The Zen teachers also tell us that, while an answer might very well be true, it is not useful unless it is understood within us. The opportunity to see Liberty's sculptural armature is an invitation to inwardly reflect. By entering Liberty's interior, we can be part of shaping our country's emergent narrative and ask ourselves: What does liberty mean to me individually, to us as a country, and to me as a part of this country? As we climb the internal spiral staircase to Liberty's crown, now open again to the public after years of closure due to the aftermath of the 9/11 attacks, and look out from her gemlike observation windows, perhaps we can listen inwardly to the Great Lady's request. I hear her asking us to be torch bearers. She asks us to transform ourselves by holding a light aloft for others, especially future generations, while adding our individual lights to the room of the world.

In this hour, in this unique era of extreme environmental crises (most recently punctuated with the catastrophic oil spill in the Gulf of Mexico), I submit that we add a new radiance to Liberty's flame. We have gained remarkable and necessary civil liberties in this beloved country of ours, ones we must be vigilant to defend and expand in society, but what about nature's liberties? The rights of river and mountain, meadow and forest, ocean and desert? And with these, the rights of all nature's denizens?

In this time, Liberty is inquiring: How will you pass my torch to your children? In this unstable passage, this time of dire consequences, this question has to do not only with the human story of liberty but also with the liberty of the entire Earth community. We need a whole-systems liberty, and with it, a whole-systems democracy. All the world's people and the Earth together are participants in this ecology of liberation. All plants and trees, all of the wild creatures, all of the streams and woodlands, the seas and the atmosphere are party to the need for freedom from abuse, conscious or unconscious. Earth's liberties, nature's rights; this is the illumination of our generation, which older cultures already knew. Not only do we need to recognize the rights of nature but to look to the natural world for models of wise governance for people. At this time we must recognize that a whole-systems approach is irreplaceable. Thomas Paine recognized this long ago at the dawn of our country's birth, remarking, "All the great laws of society, are laws of nature." More recently Kenny Ausubel, co-founder of Bioneers, put it this way, "Taking care of nature means taking care of people—and taking care of people means taking care of nature."[33]

In the autumn of 2008, I attended a gathering hosted by the Pachamama Alliance, whose stated mission is "to preserve the Earth's tropical rainforests by empowering the indigenous people who are its natural custodians." The two dedicated co-founders of the organization, Lynne and Bill Twist, related their breakthrough work with Fundación Pachamama, an alliance of indigenous people in Ecuador. In their collaborative efforts, they have been exploring the relationship between the Collective Rights of Indigenous Peoples, as recognized in the Ecuadorian Constitution, and the by-laws of the Indigenous Federation. In a historic election in September 2008, the people of Ecuador voted to recognize nature as a rights-bearing entity, not just property, and now these rights, the inalienable rights belonging to ecosystems, are formally written into the new Ecuadorian constitution. Many environmentalists and ecologists have been seeking this liberation for nature for quite some time, including the pioneering American conservationist John Muir who, back in 1867, proposed respect for "the rights of all the rest of creation."

Ecological economists have been getting at this point, too, and a team led by Robert Costanza of the University of Maryland conducted studies on the economic importance of nature's benefits given "freely," such as the renewal of soil fertility, climate stabilization, and pollination. We need to further the idea of policy decisions that recognize and account for Earth's gift-giving, upon which we are totally dependent. With this in mind, it makes sense that nature deserves her rights and protections, the same as anyone. For this change to occur, we will need to liberate our minds from old beliefs and unquestioned assumptions that no longer address and promote the current and future well-being of the Earth upon which we must all live and depend.

Our world generation, those of us alive today and those soon here, has an unprecedented opportunity to shape and revive the essential meaning of Liberty's legacy, one that gives voice and recognition to the entire symphony of living beings within the village of the Earth. This is an Earth etiquette in action. Through revitalizing our relationship to nature, governance, and culture, Liberty's flame can light our path along a new sustainable and equitable road while also brightening our inner world as we face the many challenges ahead.

5 Reconnecting on Other Shores

Part One: Crazy Horse in the Soviet Union

The History of the world is none other than the
progress of the consciousness of Freedom.
–GEORG WILHELM FRIEDRICH HEGEL

I see a time when all the colors of mankind will gather
under the Sacred Tree of Life and the whole
Earth willbecome one circle again.
–CHIEF CRAZY HORSE

"Sailing to freedom's shores, with love from Aleksi."
Bending over the small hole in the ground, I softly
spoke these words to my only witnesses, the proud Black
Hills of South Dakota. In the palm of my hand, one last time, I
turned the brass ring Aleksi had made, and then quickly planted
it firmly in the earthen hollow. Over time, the ring had developed
a light green patina from natural oxidation, and I had spent the
evening before polishing it back to its original golden shimmer. I
had carried the ring for many years and now, finally, amongst the
powerful assembly of mountains shaped like the Ancients of the

Land, with their heads and shoulders bent in an eternal conversation, my long journey came to its conclusion.

I inhaled the leaf-falling autumn air, cool with a hint of winter soon to come; snow had already brushed the higher ridges, leaving a delicate layer of white lace. In this awaited and tranquil moment, I imagined Aleksi's face and recalled his tremendous admiration for the great Lakota chief Crazy Horse. Through my memories and the story imbedded in the curvature of the ring, the Black Hills and the spirit of Crazy Horse would now know of their great import and healing to this man, a Russian artist five thousand miles away.

It was the bravery and legendary history of Crazy Horse, known for his dedication to his people and for preserving the Lakota way of life that had captured the attention of Aleksi, who then fashioned the story into a spiritual ornament of personal hope. This devotion of Crazy Horse, which so affected Aleksi, is what required I make my journey—really only as an unexpected carrier of Aleksi's message of gratitude that I was honored to deliver.

I slowly turned in a circle to behold the numinous quality of the Black Hills and to offer my respect to the spirit of Crazy Horse and the Lakota people. The wind came up all around me and snowflakes suddenly drifted down like fairies from the silvery skies. The Iron Curtain and Soviet Union were no more, and Aleksi was now free to travel. But I did not imagine that he, an elderly man of simple means, would find his way soon, if ever, to the ancestral grounds of Crazy Horse, and so I left his brass ring here. If he could never touch this ground, at least the work of his hands would.

───✦───

It was December 1989, and the Berlin Wall had just come down weeks before I arrived in Germany. The Velvet Revolution had also flourished in what was then Czechoslovakia, and although these two startling transformations altered the landscape of consciousness throughout Europe and the rest of the world, the dismantling of Communism in the Soviet Union would not occur until several years later.

I longed to experience the homeland of some of my ancestors. Rocky, a dear friend and fine American artist, had a similar wish, and the two of us decided to make our way from Germany to the Soviet Union. Milan, a kind and talented Czechoslovakian painter who professed a rough knowledge of Russian, accompanied us. I went to meet the forests and cities, artists and cultures—but additionally, in the secret place beneath my breathing, in the shape of my unspoken thoughts, I hoped to carry a little of the winds of freedom lifting up with the rising of new, liberating dreams in a transforming Europe—a Europe relieved of outmoded walls and borders. As an American, was it inappropriate for me to dare such a wish for Russia, for people of another, older country that I could only perceive through the lens of my own cultural perceptions? Even so, it seemed to me that the zephyr of freedom unfurls the human spirit in much the same way no matter what land we call home. In that way, I dreamed into the beckoning wind.

There are certain openings in history that seem to amplify our adventure as a species, reminding us of the unsleeping eye of the ages (as the Greeks might say) with a poignancy that is electric in the movement of humanity's gesture toward freedom. Our German friends were, naturally, ecstatic about the "fall of the Wall;" in our first weeks in Germany, we happily listened to countless experiences of East-West reunification from long-lost family members and friends jubilant in their reunions. We were also shown bits and pieces of the shattered Berlin Wall. Marta, an older woman from Munich, explained to me that almost two hundred people had been killed over the years in the "death strip," the space between the concrete wall and the border fence, as they attempted to flee from East Germany. She held a chunk of cold concrete from the destroyed wall in her hand. It in no way eased the grief of terrible losses but seemed to grant her satisfaction that no others would suffer so.

Within the mysterious timing of life's unfolding, not only was I experiencing the demolition of the Berlin Wall, but I had actually lived for two years as a small child in Germany during its construction. In 1961, after the Korean War and before the Vietnam War, my father was called up by the draft as a physician. By participating in the Berry Plan he was able to defer the draft, continue his schooling, and serve two years in Germany to support the Army Medical Corps. My mother, sister, and I accompanied him, settling in a small town outside Munich. Construction of the Berlin Wall began on August 13, 1961. I had an unexpected historical connection with the Wall, and its fall became a part of my personal story.

The air was ambrosial and heads were lifted high; this ebullient mood was reflected, too, in the lighthearted demeanor of Milan, who had equally vibrant accounts of his last months in Prague before the liberation there. Ignited by a peaceful student demonstration against the Communist government harshly met by riot police, Prague had become the center of burgeoning but still primarily peaceful protests. Eventually these well-attended demonstrations lead to the Communist Party of Czechoslovakia loosening their steely grip on political power. In his best English with hand on heart, Milan said, "We did a bloodless revolution because no one wanted Communism anymore; it's over and our leaders watching the Berlin Wall come down stopped the game. Most especially, they were no longer afraid of change and chose not to fire on us, their own people."

Many years before, Milan had courageously escaped to West Germany. While shadows still lay deeply hidden in his eyes, remembering losses and old fears, he stood with his shoulders squared, proud to tell us of the new awakenings in his country. I was honored to listen. Over the ensuing weeks I would learn to recognize the glimmering flashes of newly felt liberation in Milan's eyes whenever we observed changes in borders and customs, or read transformative newspaper articles, or saw the visible signs of hope when broad smiles were worn as victory banners on the faces of people everywhere.

Divisions, concrete walls, barbed wire fences, and violently controlled borders were not a part of my American consciousness at that time, and yet the exhilaration I felt from the liberation of countries and people needed no explanation. This was a time when the vestiges of European totalitarianism, lingering like a ghost wearing an old, beat-up yoke, were rendered into little cracked pieces right along with the demolished chunks of the Berlin Wall.

The Cold War was ending, the Iron Curtain was corroding into flakes of rust, and I felt the butterflies in my stomach with each new story told, reminding me of the sensation I had whenever I read about the American Revolution. The sounds and gesticulations of freedom breaking loose from the suffocating grip of tyranny is a rhythm and a dance, a full-breathing bodily motion universally recognized—and the deep, free tones I heard in everyone's voices that December were tempered in timbre only by the knowledge that years of hard work lay ahead.

In this extraordinary atmosphere when people actually sensed the turning of power in their own hands, my colleagues and I were struggling to get into the not-yet-freed Soviet Union. It took reams of paper, weeks of faxes, and many hours of waiting in the offices of the Soviet Embassy in Munich before my traveling companions and I finally received the necessary documents to enter the country. As artists without much financial wherewithal, we were unable to pay the costly entrance fees and needed several layers of in-country invitations. Through Aleksi, our host in Moscow, we were eventually invited by the Russian Academy of Arts in Moscow to make a presentation there to students; more important, we received an invitation from a prominent political cartoonist. Bundled in clothes we soon learned were not suitable protection against the audacious cold of Russia, we made our way to the Austrian airport.

After a long and complicated flight to Moscow (we had to stop in Poland for some unannounced reason), Milan, Rocky, and I met Aleksi at the Moscow airport and quickly went by taxi to his apartment. The elevator did not work, so we climbed nine flights of stairs, tumbling our luggage upward as best we could.

While water for tea was heating up on our host's tiny stove, we shyly began the delicate process of exploring the terrain of our communication abilities. Beyond this beginning dialogue, we spared no time in quickly unpacking and delivering to our new friend the items we had carried from Germany. Before our departure, we had asked Aleksi what he most wanted from the West and subsequently stuffed our bags with simple medicines, drawing paper, cheese, and laundry soap, all high on his list. There was nothing really to say about these items; they were not given as gifts but rather accepted as supplies by him. No superficial words of thanks were voiced, nor would they have felt appropriate. Aleksi just nodded with a slightly curled smile as we handed him each provision.

That night in Aleksi's kitchen, with exaggerated hand movements, large exclamations during highpoints of stories, and intense facial expressions (these being our intricate somatic language), we spoke in the manner people do when they first meet and have a shortage of vocabulary. One always wonders what is really understood in these moments, but in the end, it seems all can be settled with a good dose of humor. Milan, after great length, was able to convey an old Czechoslovakian farmers' joke about cows, first to us in German (he spoke better German than English), then to Aleksi in broken Russian. Whether it was the late hour or the warmth of new friends, we all laughed until our eyes were moist and we could no longer catch our breath.

Afterward, as my two companions prepared to bed down, Aleksi took out a small bowl and began to make a simple mixture of glue from flour, water, and salt. He dipped little strips of paper scraps into the mixture and began neatly fitting the gummy papers one by one around the kitchen window to insulate it further, filling the gaps between glass and window frame where the below 30-degree wind was fiercely forcing its way in. As a sculptor at home with my hands, I worked with him in silence late into the night, allowing our shared efforts to be our invisible conversation. Sometimes there is no better way to get to know someone than to work side by side. In addition, beyond attempting to be helpful to our kind host, I believe I worked on that window purely out of a sense of survival. Never in my life had I felt such stunning cold as the temperature of that Moscow winter.

There is a vast multitude of layers to perceive and understand whenever meeting a country, its people, and its culture for the first time, and it is a very humbling experience. I could only hope to grasp a few of the complexities of a culture that has taken thousands of years to develop. I tried to be as present as possible with the tactile strata of lifestyles and beautiful nuances particular to the Russian people, the land of Eastern Europe, and to the historical and spiritual landscape built upon an amazing amalgamation of human experience over generations, involving every extreme from brutal hardship to immense love, beneficence, and creativity.

The following morning I awoke at dawn, having dreamt a conversation between two great Russian artists I have long admired: the painter Isaac Levitan and the composer Rimsky-Korsakov. While these two masters were discussing how to render musical phrases into colors, hues, and lines to portray a philosophical feeling and expose the human body to never-before-experienced realms of sensitivity, I was flying straight into one of Levitan's paintings. It was *The Birch Grove*, a favorite of mine. I cherished the lush impression of the Russian forest that this painting summoned in me, with the lovely white birch trees emerging from a verdant field and the brilliant perspective bringing the viewer into an intimacy with the trees as if presently walking among them. In my half-awake state I marveled at the mystery of how Levitan's nature paintings of the Volga River, moon-filled nights, and Russian fields could so wildly provoke philosophical and spiritual feelings quite similar to those produced upon listening to Rimsky-Korsakov's musical masterpiece, *Scheherazade*. The melody often left me breathless with its enchanting violin solos. If an orchestral piece could enable a human being to actually fly unaided by technology, it would be *Scheherazade*. I did not have wings in my dream but rather seemed to effortlessly soar ever further into Levitan's birch forest.

This was a pleasurable experience and one familiar from my childhood as my mother, a fine painter herself, taught me to virtually enter into the world of an art piece. When I was quite young, maybe six years old, I learned from her to peer into a painting, focusing my attention in such a way as to abandon all peripheral views, and thus to cross the threshold into the painting completely. This kind of seeing allows the image to penetrate our accustomed boundaries, inviting a new dimension of reality to come into focus for us. In my dream, I was meeting the ancient Russian birch trees and knew them to be the keepers of the original language of this mysterious land. The origination of language from the shape and sounds of the trees, valleys, birds, insects, rivers, and mountains of a particular place is well known in the ancient European and Celtic histories, just as aboriginal people everywhere know it today. I understood I needed to listen to the very ground under the city streets, to the calls of birds on rooftops, to the trees carrying the wind, and to the clicking and cadence of the Russian tongue to hear the oldest language sounds again.

Then, rather suddenly, I was fully awake and appreciating, as so many others must have before me, how a person can begin to really know a land and a people through its artists. Seeing the paintings and sculptures created by Russian visual and tactile artists, listening to melodies of Russian musicians, and reading the words of the poets and philosophers from this far end of Europe, I could further touch the heart of Russian geography, history, spirituality, society, and everyday life. Alexander Pushkin, Fyodor Dostoevsky, Anna Akhmatova, Pyotr Tchaikovsky, Nikolai Rimsky-Korsakov, Valentin Serov, Isaac Levitan, and many others had their eyes and ears attuned to the muse of this land, creating a river of inspiration that has streamed past any human-made border or prison of thought. This beguiling artistic flow of creativity surely has known oppression but moves around it and through it, and sometimes even washes itself free.

Over the next few days, searching for warm hats and groceries, we learned through ever-improving conversations and our own experiences what daily life was like for Aleksi. Details from reports we had heard—rationing food with special tickets, bread delivered spontaneously out of trucks to lines of people waiting on unmarked street corners, half-empty markets selling single eggs for a small fortune—were not exaggerations. Aleksi's smiles and kindness fed us and kept us warm far beyond what we could find in physical food and comfort. I tried for the most part not to eat much the first days, knowing I would be back in Germany in little over a week and could make up for my nutritional needs then. The major problem with this well-meant strategy was that after several days the severe cold forced an appetite upon me such as I had never known. I held out until the third day, when Aleksi produced from his cupboard a large cube of butter for our freshly cooked potatoes. As it was, Aleksi and I were lunching alone, and before I realized what had happened, in this one sitting I had eaten the entire butter cube all by myself. I ate it as if it were a block of cheese. I felt embarrassed initially, but my body was ravishingly hungry for fats and oils. Aleksi knew and simply glanced at me, then at the empty plate, and laughed. My lips glistening with butter, I shrugged and sat back in my chair, curious about my bodily reactions, but feeling quite content with the smooth warmth of butter and potatoes filling my stomach.

The potato is no small matter in Russia or for the entirety of

Europe and can be likened more to a political upheaval than a humble grocery item. Most often, we speak of a coup as an act having to do with governments and people, but there is something to be said for the fact that a certain food can transform the power of a nation. Arguably, in the case of Russia, there was a vegetable coup; not in the traditional sense of an act being a sudden seizing of power, but certainly in regard to an act of great brilliance and high success that changed life there—all caused by the introduction of the unpretentious potato. This was followed by the arrival of the sunflower with its precious oil.

Anthropologist Jack Weatherford reminds us that for more than four thousand years the indigenous people of the Andes have cultivated the potato, producing an amazing three thousand or so varieties to suit a range of environmental conditions. After the Spanish conquest of the Americas, the potato, along with many other marvelous human and earthly treasures, made its way to Europe. At first, the potato was only accepted and eaten by European monarchs (in part because of politics but also because it was something exotic and unknown, and consequently feared by the general populace), but eventually the folk of the land grasped the value of this underground tuberous gem.

So strong was the potato's impact on the food culture of Russia that Weatherford and other historians remark that the Soviet Union might never have developed into a world power without it.[1]

Prior to the European arrival in the Americas in the 1400s, Russia was dependent upon grain crops, which, due to their high stalks above ground, are far more susceptible to seasonal variations such as rains and cyclic insect infestations. Once the potato, protected beneath ground, was fully adopted around 1840 (having been introduced by Catherine the Great, but not widely cultivated until Czar Nicholas), Russian society and power began to transform because most people were now able to have a hearty, high-caloric, and reliable food source. Eventually, Russia became the world's greatest producer of potatoes.

Sitting in Aleksi's kitchen holding an uncooked potato in my hand, I pondered the power of this generous member of the nightshade family. If a small, innocuous tuber can feed a nation, propelling it to global prominence and causing a paradigm shift in society, what would happen if we focused on a tree, a honey bee, a wind current, or a ray of sun light? All of these hold promise, design secrets, and renewable and sustainable offerings for humanity when we properly listen to and attend to their gifts. Or what if we simply took the time to really appreciate the potato and acknowledged the generations of Indigenous scientists who literally took thousands of years to develop a vast array of potato varieties, including those that so precisely suited these far northern climates? As we race toward ever-greater "modernity" and new technologies of the furthest imagining, a pause now and then to ask what a tuber might offer or what an aboriginal elder might say with her longstanding scientific knowledge, might not only be sensible but essential to a healthier, more sustainable future.

That evening, Aleksi told us about the courageous botanist and geneticist Nikolai Vavilov (1887–1943), who is today recognized around the world as the leading plant geographer of contemporary times. While researching his botanical theories, Vavilov collected seeds from every region of the planet and eventually established the largest seed bank in the world, at that time, in Leningrad. This remarkable collection caught the attention of an international audience, when people around the world learned that many scientists who were starving during the Siege of Leningrad devotedly saved it, including one of Vavilov's assistants, who starved to death surrounded by these edible seeds.

Tragically, under Stalin's regime, Vavilov was imprisoned in 1940 on the charges of advocating "bourgeois pseudoscience." In reality, the arrest was a consequence of a power struggle with one of his former colleagues and a conflict of ideology over scientific experimentation. He died in jail of malnutrition three years later. Fortunately, Vavilov's great efforts live on in his important theories and through the Vavilov Institute of Plant Industry in St. Petersburg, which still houses one of the world's largest collections of plant genes.[2]

⟶

By midweek, Aleksi let us know it was time to attend our various meetings. We very much looked forward to these engagements, as they were an opportunity for us to meet people. Yet, for Aleksi, there was a mixture of burden and anticipation. His muffled voice and slumped shoulders as we left his apartment revealed years of answering to government bureaucrats. He would be required to report most of our activities to the local authorities: where we traveled, who we met with, and if, in fact, we had fulfilled our invitational obligations. "The eyes and ears of control are everywhere," he said, at the same time acknowledging how much better it was now than in the Stalin era. In those days, he said, no one dared carry a personal address book for fear that one misstep with the government, real or fabricated, could result in an entire network of friends and family being imprisoned or worse. Soviet botanist Gregory Levin explained the lingering feeling of the past in this way: "Stalin is no more. But like tyrants before him, his ominous figure casts a long shadow over our century, our country, like the period of McCarthyism in the United States."[3] Even with these heavy felt thoughts and words, in a short time Aleksi brushed off his sadness and anger, having clearly practiced his way through this interior maze of oppression countless times before. Surprising me, he quietly laughed and said, "We artists will always be free; we wander in the story in our heads where no one can find us."

Ygor the political cartoonist and his accomplished wife, Svetlana, invited us to their home on the other end of Moscow for tea and to view his work. As we approached the underground, one of the most artistically beautiful in all of Europe, adorned as it is with remarkable figurative statuary, Aleksi mentioned that we needed to make a stop along the way. It was already late afternoon, and the jagged cold of night was beginning to set in, but we simply nodded in agreement while tucking our heads down against the freezing winds. At this point in our excursion, we had stopped asking questions and just scurried after Aleksi with complete trust, allowing our host to take us where he would.

Some time later, we popped up out of the subway near sunset, wound our way through wet snowy streets, and arrived—finally— at the home of Aleksi's ninety-year-old mother, Rozaliya, who immediately began making us tea. We were deeply touched again by the over-generous offerings of food, all the while wishing there were some way to avoid people pulling out their winter stocks just for us. Luckily, I had now become accustomed to stuffing my big coat pockets with German jams and was able to give several jars to our new host.

Rozaliya had also invited a young friend of hers who spoke excellent English. For the first time during our visit, we were able to speak unencumbered by our poor Russian skills.

The table, spread with cookies, small loaves of bread, and cut-crystal demi-bowls filled with homemade jellies, radiated plenty— but my eye went to the bright, moist orange that had been precisely cut into very thin circles. There was just the one orange, spread neatly like an oriental fan on an antique painted plate displaying a Russian farm scene. The orange was so beautifully presented, each slice a haiku poem to be appreciated in its perfect litheness. I did not eat any of it, feeling the weight of the offering. Then I noticed Rozaliya looking at me sternly and realized there was, in such a situation, a delicate balance between good intentions and offending one's host by not receiving precious sacrificial gifts. With fork held lightly in hand, I slowly reached out and as ceremoniously as possible picked up one of the circular slices. Once on my plate, I sliced the juicy round into bite-sized sections and ate each one with relish, looking up to find the family elder staring at me with distinct approval. Our eyes suddenly caught and we both laughed. She explained how everyone feeds guests the best they can so that they can celebrate life and be fed well in return. Truly, I thought to myself, it is both wise and sweet, this appreciation borne from the not-having of things and then unexpectedly having them in some small way, as delicious as the fresh orange now melting slowly in my astonished mouth. Just as I was thinking how good it is to be alive and taste the fruit of the Earth, Rozaliya turned to me and said she believed that when humans die, we become spirit clouds and can see the whole Earth from the sky, floating above the land, blessing it with our eyes. Instinctively, we all looked out the window to see the big Russian sky filled with gigantic, salmon-colored clouds in the now sun-setting hour.

By nightfall, we finally arrived to see the works of Ygor, the political cartoonist. Gentle Svetlana could not hide the fact that she thought we were insane to come to her country for the first time in winter and poured us one cup of hot tea after another as if it flowed from an endless waterfall. We stayed quite late into the night, having the sort of conversation that is rich in riddles, side comments purposefully intended not to be repeated, and flowery cultural exchanges. This was followed by Ygor showing us his politically and culturally relevant cartoons. One of his drawings has stayed with me, the way certain moments in our lives stand out, crystallized into perfect memories that we return to as anchor points of comprehension: the scene is an expansive Russian wheat field and a farmer is bent, plowing the fields with his knees. There is no farm equipment, machinery, or even animals in sight, only a long-faced man dragging his knees through the soil. Ygor said this summed up his view of how the farmers of Russia had been treated during the Communist era.

The following morning, after an early and enthusiastic visit with students at the Academy of Arts in Moscow, we all took a train to the countryside to visit with Yasha, a farmer friend of Aleksi. Some days earlier Rocky and I had requested to see the northern forest and also to meet a young artist, Julia, who Aleksi informed us was a very talented painter. She was also one of Yasha's two daughters.

The small village was a half-day's train ride northeast from

Moscow. Rocky, Milan, Aleksi, and I huddled together to fend off the cold, crouching on wooden benches on the antique Soviet train boasting not a breath of heat. We brought with us oil paints and fine brushes for Julia and German chocolate bars for her six-year-old sister, Nadiya.

Shivering, we arrived at the house of Yasha and Anna and met some of their extended family while huddling around the kitchen's pot-bellied stove. The house was a converted barn, still under reconstruction, and the children were up in the hayloft playing on their makeshift beds of straw. I noticed all the men in the family brandished mustaches and beards against the cold—and they were now dripping with melting icicles in the heat of the kitchen air.

The six-year-old was a magical girl with a wandering dreamer's eye who instantly took the chocolate bars up into the sleeping loft to eat them and then make folded paper houses out of the shiny foil wrappings. The older girl, Julia, received the art supplies of paints and brushes with tears of excitement, and we quickly offered to help exhibit her work in Germany. We then walked to the nearby birch woods to pay homage to the beauty of the land while recalling folktales of the ancient witch Baba Yaga—still very much alive on the tongues of country people.

The "wild woman" Baba Yaga is known for both her wisdom and her frightening acts and is a prominent figure in many Russian folktales and Slavic myths. She can be kind and helpful and bring good fortune, but she can also be quite ruthless: when people encounter her, they live or die depending on what they say and do. She lives deep in the birch forest in a little hut that can only be found with a feather, magic thread, or special doll showing the path. I somehow felt she might be watching us.

With the essence of the magical birch trees all around us, we returned from the forest and entered the kitchen through a hallway we had not yet seen. There on the wall, hanging in the shadows, was an aged and cracked photograph of a shaman with his large, circular drum. When Yasha turned, he saw me peering at the photograph with wide, questioning eyes.

He glanced at his wife and then made the decision to tell us. This Siberian shaman was the person he went to see once a year to pray for his land and the health of his family, fields, and animals.

Settled into another cup of steaming black tea in front of a newly stocked fire, he told us more as Julia slowly translated his words. "This shaman comes from the great mountain range of the Altai, known as the Golden Mountains. There are other places of the shamans, some originating from Lake Baikal and further north. We do not speak of them publicly, but they have survived these difficult Communist times. They teach of many things, most especially of the living world beyond humans, about respecting the land and the ancestors. They told me the hardships we have in this country strengthen us."

Siberia is an enormous region of steppe, tundra, and forest that comprises no less than one-twelfth of the Earth's total land mass. I learned from reading the work of journalist and historian Anna Reid that before the conquest of this vast expanse by Russia in the late 1500s, there were about thirty culturally distinct peoples living here with a multitude of languages spoken from Mongol to Turkic and others so unique they exist in a linguistic category all their own. In this fiercely cold region, a person's breath crystallizes, forming clusters that fall upon the snow-covered earth, creating what is called "the whispering of the stars."[4] Here in these ancient lands the Indigenous people and shamans have lived much as they did thousands of years ago, but perhaps not for too much longer now, with the world so quickly modernizing in outlying regions.

In hushed tones as if at any moment we might be overheard, Yasha continued. He told us how, under Tsarist Russian rule, the Indigenous people were completely ignored except for attempts made to destroy their very existence, and now under Soviet rule attempts to further degrade or erase them were commonplace. The Indigenous people were seen as an embarrassment to the Soviet Union, a world superpower with advanced technology. Shamans were forbidden to practice, and some were imprisoned or killed because they chose to not stop living their old time ways. Yasha told us that things had improved somewhat in the past years, but there was surely no welcoming atmosphere. Nevertheless, shamans were still practicing in the mountains and steppes, riding their beautiful horses and playing their sacred drums just as in olden times.

In her research about the endurance and conditions of Siberian shamans and Indigenous populations, Reid summarized it this way:

> The tsars tried to replace shamans with priests. The Communists ostracized and imprisoned them, and under Stalin shot them or threw them out of helicopters, saying that if they could fly, now was their chance. If shamanism had survived all this, other aspects of native Siberian culture probably had too.... On a continent that was theirs before Russia existed, native Siberians are not extinct, but excluded.[5]

Not surprisingly, historical references to the native Siberian tribes were being manipulated or eliminated to hide the ferocious battles between Indigenous Siberians and Russians, many struggles falsely being portrayed by government spokespeople as a simple process of "natural assimilation."

More tea was poured. Yasha pulled slowly on his beard, and feeling more at ease with our sincere interest, he spoke to us about the shamans and their philosophy. He explained that the Indigenous people of Siberia live within the understanding of how important it is to have respect and appreciation for the vibrant, living Earth. The world is a sacred, alive place of mountains, animals, rivers, winds, and grasses—and we humans need to live in a good manner with the Holy Mother of the World. The Buryat shamans of the Lake Baikal region express it this way: To live a life of honor is to live with "tegsh," meaning to live in appreciation and balance with all things.

We drank our tea quietly, listening to the crackling fire, our hearts alight with the feeling of "tegsh."

In the spirit of this excursion to the farmers and birch forest, the following day Aleksi decided to show us what he called the most

important artwork of his life. It seemed that our entire journey
thus far was a test for this particular revelation. Before entering his
studio, he explained to us that, although he loved his country with
all his heart, he also longed for a freedom he could only dream of,
often believing that America held this treasure for him. He said he
did not want to leave Russia, but he wanted to *feel* that he could.

At the far end of the dimly lit studio, firmly cradled by a sunken
wooden floor, stood a life-sized canoe fashioned out of recycled
sheet metal and rubber waterproofing. Rising up from the center
of the canoe was a mast fitted with a large, triangular canvas sail.
Although the entire canoe was beautiful to behold, the most remarkable feature was the image of Lakota Chief Crazy Horse boldly
painted on the canvas sail. Four feathers dangled from the top of
the mast, and American Indian symbols were etched into the metal
craft. Aleksi walked in a circle around what he called his Crazy
Horse canoe and with moist eyes relayed to us his deep reverence for
this chief he had read about throughout childhood. He proclaimed
Crazy Horse as his life-long hero and reason for hope. "Through all
my hard times I have always remembered him. He has been like
this mast for me. When confronted by the government and in war,
Crazy Horse never backed down and stayed true always to the ways
of his people. He fought to protect his people's lands and preserve
the old traditions while never losing his personal integrity, even in
the darkest of times." As Aleksi spoke with Milan translating, I quietly thought to myself: it is true. Like the Siberian shamans who did
not relinquish their drums during this time of Communism, Crazy
Horse never surrendered his spirit to the conquering government.

Looking more closely at the canoe, Aleksi explained to us that
the sections of sheet metal were actually panels that could be
folded up into a kit and carried as a backpack—to the shores of
eastern Siberia where he could sail to Alaska. "The borders of the
Soviet Union block me in, but I, in my canoe, can set myself free
to America." Aleksi had well imagined setting sail to his freedom,
and his canoe, borne from inspired imagination, might very well
have been not only seaworthy but also a powerful force beyond

any bodily imprisonment. I recalled the words of filmmaker Luis Buñuel: "Fortunately, somewhere between chance and mystery lies imagination, the only thing that protects our freedom, despite the fact that people keep trying to reduce it or kill it off altogether."[6]

Aleksi's canoe and story conjured up for me the great complexity of the country he was dreaming about—my native home. North American history embraces a wide arc of extremes that are not easy to reconcile, let alone fully comprehend or convey to a person from another country.

Our beginnings are certainly muddled. We Americans raised our precious flag of freedom and independence after a brave war fighting against tyranny, yet we must not forget that we raised this same flag on ground saturated with American Indian blood and the sweat of Africans forced into slavery as well as the death of thousands who never survived the ocean passage from their African homeland. Before the large-scale migration of Europeans in North America, there were between fifteen and twenty-five million Indigenous people living throughout the land, yet with disease and war this population was quickly and violently reduced to fewer than one million people. The history of people in transitions, flights, conquests, displacements, and migrations, no matter the cause, is never a kind subject. In America, this traumatic history has yet to be fully acknowledged, let alone healed.

Later that evening, having returned from Aleksi's studio, we gathered once again in the kitchen to navigate through our emerging thoughts. Aleksi, Rocky, Milan, and I could not avoid the obvious. The devastating history of the Indigenous people of Siberia and North America after invasion was painfully similar, and we recognized the difficult irony that these aboriginal peoples often hold an enormous wealth of knowledge essential to resolving today's ecological, sociological, and spiritual problems. It was in this mood that Aleksi gave me the brass ring he had made. The ring was rather massive, and the geometrical designs on it reminded me of ancient labyrinths symbolizing the inward journey to know ourselves and the greater universe.

A few years later in 1991, the Soviet Union dissolved and the borders of the former USSR opened. While this was cause for tremendous celebration, simultaneously the door of a complex and difficult economic and political maze was also opened. While this was indeed a long-needed yet challenging commencement to the end of totalitarianism, human freedom could not then, and cannot now, be realized with only a change of government. The Black Hills of South Dakota, the Golden Mountains of the Altai, the memory of Crazy Horse, the horse-riding shamans, and the natural voice of our searching hearts all invite many more questions concerning freedom. By listening to these questions—deep within our inner stillness—we can hear sounds of magnificent beauty and refined consciousness that can lift human freedom over contrived borders and walls. As Crazy Horse prophetically stated: "I see a time when all the colors of mankind will gather under the Sacred Tree of Life and the whole Earth will become one circle again."

6 Reconnecting on Other Shores

Part Two: Cloud Blossoms

Whether sculpted or painted, etched or carved, the eyes look directly at observers no matter where they stand. Art lovers as well as critics have commented upon this phenomenon regarding certain figurative artworks throughout the ages—the intriguing way in which the gaze of the portrayed follows the viewer around the room. For instance, the eyes of *La Gioconda*, or Mona Lisa, peering out from her painting at the Louvre, appear to be watching everyone no matter where they are in the full 180 degree arc of the room.

While this mystery of artistic talent has beguiled me on several occasions, what riveted me to one particular spot in the Hong Kong Museum of Art was actually the non-moving, penetrating gaze of a wooden statue of Kuan Yin, the Goddess of Compassion. She was hundreds of years old, greater than life-sized, and her eyes pierced mine from only one singular point of view. Anyone wanting more than a superficial engagement with this masterpiece was required to stand directly in front of it: not to the left or right, not from across the room. No, her eyes did not follow the viewer. Instead, she requested and invited you to experience her full grace and wisdom by engaging your attention, all at once, squarely on—

or not at all. Shunning any side-glances or attempts to hide, you needed to meet her face to face.

As I prepared for my journey to Asia, at the top of my list was a wish to see some of the innumerable statues of Kuan Yin that I had researched. Diverse in size and form, these magnificent images were artistic beacons emanating the light of compassion throughout mainland China and Hong Kong, where I was traveling. This first Kuan Yin statue that I saw in Hong Kong was carved brilliantly. She sat calmly with dignity, her right hand resting on bent knee. The carving was simple, yet hewn with a great deal of passion. So full in expression, especially in the forceful gaze, this Kuan Yin fulfilled the entirety of my longtime wish. I simply stood there, transfixed by her beauty and natural majesty.

None can explain exactly why a certain piece of art, music, or poetry becomes an exquisite incantation to the very spirit of life—how suddenly, without warning, it can deliver us into a full state of ecstatic appreciation. As a sculptor, I could only hope to create works that evoked so much emotion in people and generated this same desire to delve into the soul of the world.

Kuan Yin's full name is often given as Kuan Shih Yin, which means, "Observing the sounds of the world," or "One who hears the cries of the world." She is known in the West as the Goddess of Mercy. While traveling in Asia, I learned that Kuan Yin is the most beloved and widespread of any Goddess of the Chinese, and many Japanese and Koreans equally revere her under similar names. She offers kindness, aid, and compassion to all who seek her.

There are various renditions of Kuan Yin, and one image portrays her with a willow tree branch in one hand and a delicate vase in the other. It is said that, to be truly compassionate, one must be flexible like the willow, which can bend far in the greatest of storms and then bounce back again without breaking. The type of willow wand Kuan Yin carries is from the weeping willow tree, whose long, draping branches and leaves reach not skyward but toward the Earth. Raindrops like tears, both of sorrow and joy, run down the bowed branches to give water to the land. This, too, is an act of compassion. The vase holds the nectar of compassion that she sprinkles upon her worldly children.

I would sense Kuan Yin's benevolence in every footfall of my unfolding journey in China. This merciful Goddess especially came to mind when, on board my flight to Hong Kong, I learned the startling news that my home country's armed forces had begun to invade Iraq. I knew many people were going to die and immediately called upon Kuan Yin in my mind, wishing that her compassion and wisdom could somehow overwhelm the odds and stop the bloodshed to come or at least ease some of the suffering. Throughout my travels in the following weeks, as soon as people felt comfortable with me, they would inevitably ask, "What is this war about? Why is the United States bombing Iraq?"

My friend and colleague Wyolah journeyed with me to Hong Kong and mainland China to assist with my bronze monument projects and to support young Chinese artists in rural areas by funding an art exhibit. As with all my travels, meeting the people and the land as best I can is equally important to me as any business or other opportunity. Without these encounters, the art ventures become meaningless and empty of vision. In light of this, I had the honor of meeting a very special woman in Hong Kong: Xiao-lian, a wealthy and prominent woman of the city.

Her presence was that of grace and majesty. Surely, if regal qualities could be passed on through generations, Xiao-lian certainly possessed them as an ancestral gift. We sat around a luxurious rosewood table at one of the hotels that she and her husband owned. With the elaborate classical décor, interior waterfalls cascading down from ten stories above our courtyard, elegant assortment of dainty dishes, and consummate service by her staff, we could have been at the court of a princess from one of the old dynasties.

To back up a bit: I met Xiao-lian after I had been in Hong Kong and China for a week. As anyone who has traveled there knows, Hong Kong is a city of lights—a glowing, blazing, glittering, flashing metropolis that could light up a moonless night as if it were Las Vegas two times over. We were told that this lively port city, once a colony of the United Kingdom, never sleeps and that you could buy almost anything twenty-four hours a day. We would find this to be true.

However, even before the dazzle of city lights demanded my attention, what aroused every cell of my being was a mysterious, all-pervading fragrance. The spice-filled air of the streets and our hotel, although unfamiliar, quickly became comforting. Our sense of smell exists in the oldest part of the brain and has the power to connect us to the deepest part of our memory. In my case, the scent of the Hong Kong air transported me to fields of summer wildflowers from my childhood.

I soon became fond of reciting restaurant and teahouse menus. They read as verse from poet-scholars of old—a cup of tea might be described as the sacred drink of the ancestors, poured from liquid jade streams, originating high up on the Nine Sisters Mountains. It might go on to tell that every winter, when the blossoming trees sleep, the sisters carry clouds upon their shoulders. These clouds, resembling blossoms, rain upon the mountains and create the jade streams, which in turn water the tea plants. Such poetic words, found on everyday menus, lulled me into the song of the people and that of this ancient and deeply lyrical land.

I then remembered that one of my first attractions to China was through Chinese literature. In college, I learned of a remarkable Tang Dynasty poet, Xue Tao (also known as Sie Thao or Hung Tu). Born around 768, she was among the most famous and skilled poets of her time, and there are many stories of her composing exceptional, precocious poetry well before the age of ten. She also was an inventor and is said to have revolutionized the technique of papermaking, among other accomplishments. Her genius brought her widespread recognition, and Wei Gao, the military governor of Jiannan and Xichuan, became her patron. Because of her position, which did not diminish even after Wei Gao died, she came to know and influence prominent figures of her day. Later in life she became a Taoist priestess, which is reflected in the elegant poetry of her maturity.

Here is a poem of Xue Tao's translated by Mary Kennedy:

It is Told of the Cloud Touching Temple

It is told of the Cloud Touching Temple

that one walks only on moss,

even in the wild wind, no dust is blown.

It is so near to Heaven that the walls of hibiscus

are level with the clouds.

All is waiting for the poet and the moon.

It is told of the Cloud Touching Temple

that flowers crowd the steps,

float on the stream, blow into the sky

across the mirror of the descending Queen...

changing the clouds into gardens for her delight.[1]

Back to the gracious Xiao-lian: I sat across from her, surely the wealthiest woman I had ever met, and an unseen presence whispered the poem in my ear. I wanted to run my fingers, the tools of my craft, down one of her perfect cheeks to see if it was stone-smooth as jade. I was a bit embarrassed to have these thoughts, but it was not the beauty of her skin that intrigued me so much as its extreme inelasticity.

After our initial meeting, I began to see past Xiao-lian's flawless composure. She had a hard strain in her face, and it made me want to offer her a journey to the Cloud Touching Temple. Xiao-lian had the most elegant yet guarded smile I had ever experienced: her curved lips were very small and formed a tiny, perfect bow. She was a tremendously kind woman, but, as she told me, a woman who had no privacy or freedom to be herself—her spirit stowed away in the depths of centuries of feudalism and "proper" upper-class feminine behavior. She told me that, while she dearly loved Hong Kong, women there were commonly kept in check with old-fashioned standards and treated as second-class citizens. Even as a woman of rank and privilege, she had to act in a very specific manner in public to maintain face and respect. This is true of many people in high positions anywhere in the world, but somehow she wanted me to understand her particular experience as a Chinese woman.

Despite Xiao-lian's personal challenges, she was an important contributor to her city, offering assistance to many in need, practicing the ways of Kuan Yin, through her many charitable organizations. It was through this work that she found a way to share her passion for her country and deep love for people in a properly acceptable manner despite societal constraints. I admired her.

It was also one of the few times I felt equal sympathy for someone wealthy—this sad billionaire—as I did for some of the poverty-stricken artists Wyolah and I had visited from the Chinese countryside. It crossed my mind that these "poor" artists were happier than one of the richest, most elite women of Hong Kong.

Xiao-lian explained to me that Hong Kong was a city that demanded performance and that it was most assuredly a man's town. She stated everything in a matter-of-fact tone, but I could feel her unnerving grief as it pulled at me beneath our conversation like an invisible ocean undertow, concealing a wave of words purposefully not spoken.

Her suppression reminded me of several older people I met in Shanghai earlier in the week. They told me about the years of the

Cultural Revolution, which are still too near to them, the scars and wounds still raw even after several decades. Some of the brave and inspiring older women I also met in Hong Kong and mainland China shared pieces of their past. I watched their faces stiffen as they remembered things, terrible things. I saw, just beneath the surface, girls who were woken up in the middle of the night and dragged out of bed to watch their mothers and fathers being beaten and carted off to prison. All the items in their homes that were reflective of education or wealth, no matter how slight, were thrown into a huge bonfire and burned. The girls were stripped down and their so-called "bourgeoisie clothes" also tossed into the flames, while they were left to stand alone in the night and wonder if they would ever see their parents again. As it was, some families were never to see one another again.

I was told that sexuality was greatly suppressed and not spoken of during those difficult years. I learned that women were raped under the guise of being interrogated and as a test of their loyalty to the Communist Party. As men became more frustrated with repressed natural sexual expression, the rapes increased.

⌁

These thoughts drifted in my mind as I visited with Xiao-lian, and I felt in my pocket for the stone I had carried with me all the way from California. Before taking a moment to be too shy, I gently reached across the table to cup her hand in mine. She was startled but not resistant, and I realized that this was breaching some un-spoken custom. I asked her to open her hand palm-upward, which she did, now curious. I quietly said that I had something to give her from the Pacific shores of California.

Then I gently placed a crimson-colored stone in her hand. It was fashioned naturally by water and sand into the shape of an almost perfect heart. There was no mistaking its message. "From the heart of the Earth," I said, "to honor your heart, Xiao-lian."

For some time we sat in silence. She did not look up but simply stared into her hand where the heart-stone rested, as if breathing life into her entire body. Soon, small droplets of tears wandered down Xiao-lian's jade cheeks, wetting the little stone, making it even redder.

I did not move or say a word; this would have been truly impolite, I thought, and an insult to the years of shielding she had built. I wanted her to feel safe in this public space, and my silence, I hoped, assured her of this intent. In the interim, while time had stopped for us, her staff scurried about and had not noticed anything unusual, or so they acted. This is the way it had to be; she could not afford to show even the slightest emotion.

I had carried this stone from the Northern California coast, not knowing where it would go or who would receive it; now I wanted this little heart-stone to do a big task. I wanted this unassuming gift from the sea to comfort Xiao-lian for just a moment. She held the unrefined rock—not a precious, faceted diamond or some ornately carved gem more familiar to her, but instead a wild stone chiseled by the turning of ocean waves—tenderly, turning it over in her smooth hand. This touch of wildness amidst a magnificent but ostentatious cornucopia of manufactured riches cracked the atmosphere, creating an opening to freedom and reality I will not forget.

After some time, Xiao-lian whispered a simple but clearly unrestrained "Thank you"—not to me, but to the grace of the moment—her voice now beautiful and free.

Trails to the heart are like this, even when we approach them late or lost: they are enduring like a seashore bounding the ocean of the soul. The heart-shaped rock from the heart of the wild was a stepping stone to Kuan Yin's compassion. Xiao-lian looked up with a warm, authentic smile; it was no longer hard to imagine her walking in the Cloud Touching Temple, where Kuan Yin offers her compassion to all.

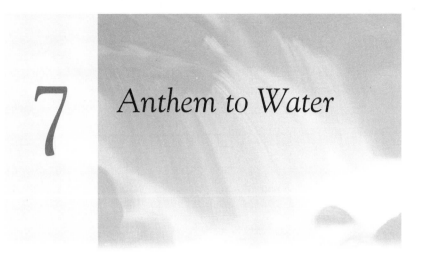

7 Anthem to Water

Part One: The Heart of Liquidity

The way to the heart of humanity is water.
—NORTHERN UTE ELDER, OIL AND WATER CONFERENCE,
SANTA FE, NEW MEXICO, 2006

The sage's transformation of the World arises from
solving the problem of water. If water is united, the
human heart will be corrected. If water is pure and
clean, the heart of the people will readily be unified and
desirous of cleanliness. Even when the citizenry's heart is
changed, their conduct will not be depraved. So the sage's
government does not consist of talking to people and
persuading them, family by family.
The pivot (of work) is water.
—LAO TZU

Intimacy with Nature is a mystery whose enterprise, like moving
water, is to flow past boundaries and to invite connectivity. I do
not know exactly when it happened: perhaps while on an adventure when I was ten years old, discovering an arrowhead along
the banks of Big River and imagining the flint knapper who walked

this water course before me, or maybe during a summer swim as I weightlessly flew underwater, dreaming of curious sea lions who glided upstream with me from their ocean home. It might have been years later as I canoed miles upriver to catch a glimpse of a fledgling osprey or while listening to the invisible Old Ones whose whispered bardic tales are carried on the river's ripples only after dark. Somewhere in these events, my body became a part of the Big River Watershed. The waters' spirit cracked open my heart, bidding me to always remember that this natural beauty is not only a luxury to revere, but also an indispensable key to our collective coherence as a species.

The blue-green flowing course reminds me that we cannot live without water. The simple and profound equation is this: water is life. Yet, the startling reality is that today, more than one billion people worldwide do not have access to safe drinking water, resulting in nearly two million fatalities a year due to waterborne diseases. Most of these deaths are among children.[1] With water scarcity increasing due to human population growth, pollution, and climate change, clearly our relationship to water must change.

First and foremost, we must secure access to clean and safe water as a basic human right for everyone in every country. This will require not only changing our detrimental use of water, but also ensuring that no institutions or corporations impede on this life-giving right to water. Communities around the world are now engaged in critical struggles to protect their local waters, and it is time that we uphold water as a global commons for all.

To support efforts to protect and defend water, we also can look beneath the surface of the stream into the deeper currents of our understanding about it, and in this manner begin healing our relationship with this irreplaceable liquid.

Whenever I live in a place—countryside or city—or visit a region for a length of time, I like to meet the bestowing watershed or reservoir. These local water circulations are the life-givers of the land, nourishing all trees, plants, and animals of a given region. These liquid terrains cradle the water in which I bathe, with which

I clean my home, and that I drink each day and imbibe into my every cell. It struck me some years ago as an artist working on water awareness projects that this element is always generously giving to us. This led to the question: What was I doing to appreciate and protect the water? In this vein, it became essential that I come to know more about these magnanimous waterways and, most especially, to thank and safeguard them. What would it be like to visit a friend who had labored all day to create a marvelous meal for me, the guest, which I then ate without pause to give thanks? Or to be nourished by my mother as a child and never acknowledge that my very survival depended upon her ceaseless giving?

Big River in Northern California is part of the Mendocino watershed where I spent much of my young life, and as an adult still do, learning from the river's riddles and moods. This gentle, sauntering body of water, whose sloping banks are adorned with willow, fir, and redwood trees, emerges just south of town to join the Pacific Ocean. I do not take in this beauty lightly; the redwood trees and the entire river's integrity have almost been lost on numerous occasions due to efforts to log even the last hoary stands. My body still flinches in reaction to these thoughts. Taking in this beauty fully involves awareness of the river's story, her health, her wonders, and her battle—like that of many rivers around the world—to survive.

One afternoon while dangling my feet over the edge of the bank at the mouth of the river, I observed that there is a precise moment when low tide at this estuary reverses in a grand planetary gesture that is yet so subtle only water birds and river creatures seem to really know it. Captivated by this thought, I tried to see exactly when this tidal change occurred. All the waters that have been mysteriously pulled back to sea begin to steadily return, bringing life to a myriad of empty canals that branch off the main course of the stream. Like earthworms suddenly caught above ground after a rain, the canals lay shriveled and cracked in the hot sun. The incoming tidal waters purl against the high grasses, bending the shape of the land and reviving these parched "invertebrate" canals.

Like many, I have always been enamored with water. This precious element seems the ultimate teacher of movement and shaping, both physically and spiritually. Everything has been touched by the primordial hands of liquidity. Water has sculpted the very landscape of our world. White-foamed waves fan across the beach, creating quilted patterns in the sand. Snowmelt rivers shape mountain, gorge, canyon, and alluvial plain. Deltas form when a surging river encounters the calm of an ocean bay or when a halcyon lake spills out onto the land. Craggy shorelines are chiseled by waves. Ancient ice fields send glaciers down mountains that cut valleys and polish granite into giant stone bowls fit for a feast of the Mother of all Mountains. These contours and lines have defined our common ancestry, for we, too, are shaped by water. As we look with our salty, ocean-filled eyes upon these fluid-cut forms, so, too, is our consciousness molded. We often dream of water when we are endeavoring to transform ourselves.

Not only is this fluid element able to carve and define form, it can also be shaped into any. Water openly embraces the volume of all things that enter it, yielding to every surface and shape, enveloping a thing completely or, if in motion, gliding around it. As I walk Big River, I watch tumbling streams effortlessly flow around several large boulders and then just as easily accept a tossed stone. I think how I would like to emulate this powerful characteristic whenever I meet obstacles in my path, and how, reflecting on Lao Tzu's words on citizenry, I wish governments would make use of this natural yielding way of the waters, this ability to tolerate and even embrace others unlike itself.

Delving further into this stream of consciousness, I think the unique properties of water have a lot to teach us about living in balance with the Earth, each other, and our very own nature. After all, at an average of 70 percent liquid, we are primarily unmoored water strolling about this planet.

When water enters any crevice, container, or living entity it will round each corner, bending into every imaginable form. In this sense, water gives with enormous benevolence, offering itself equally to eager creek beds, wildly raging rivers, shy rivulets, thundering rain clouds, snow-draped mountain peaks, epic seas, peculiar lakes, and fairy-sized dewdrops. As if this were not enough, water willingly rises to unbelievable heights in trees and reaches boldly into vast, hidden aquifers. Then, with complete abandon, water enters and vivifies the bodies of all living beings, from bumblebees to giraffes, human beings to jaguars. Water streams through us all so that we can live. Although we might not always remember it, water is a friend from whom we have no secrets, for the hands of liquidity know us intimately, having touched every part of us.

Viewing the entirety of our Mother Planet's hydrologic cycle, we learn that humans are as much a part of the cosmic movement of Earth's lifeblood as are the plants, animals, and oceans. Water is moving through all of our bodies in one giant circulation. When Indigenous people teach us that the sacred waters, plants, and animals are our relatives, this is not metaphor or myth, but a spiritual awareness and respect for scientific occurrences. We, and I mean the big *We* of all growing, moving, living beings of the Earth, are literally sharing the Earth's water, and these are the same waters that existed millions of years ago.

As the most ubiquitous element of our physical embodiment and the very life-force of our home in this galaxy, perhaps there is a message bubbling up from its depths that deserves our full attention at least for a moment. Given our make-up of 70 percent water, we are, in fact, more like each other than not. No matter our ancestry, ethnicity, religion, nationality, or DNA, we are most essentially water, and water has no known prejudice, just an affinity for us all.

Hegel observed, "Water is the element of selfless contrast, it passively exists for others.... It is its fate to be something not yet specialized ... and therefore it soon came to be called 'the mother of all that is special.'"[2]

There is a fountain of knowledge that wells up from this mother-of-all-that-is-special, this water of life. Are we asking? Are we listening? I wanted to understand (or rather to be reminded) how water could simultaneously be so very pliant and yet so cohesive. I sat under a redwood tree that cast a silvery-green shadow on the river and summarily retrieved my antique university biology textbook from the bottom of my daypack.

I read that one of the most remarkable qualities of liquid water is how it binds together and is cohesive in an unencumbered, sovereign sort of way. This fluid togetherness, as many of us learned in school, is called hydrogen bonding. A water molecule, H_2O, consists of two hydrogen atoms and one oxygen atom. However, the hydrogen bond in a water molecule rapidly and consistently flickers on and off. The speed is astonishing: scientists observe that every ten billionth of a second the bonds hold, then release, their connection.[3] Water not only bonds within a single molecule but also bonds and shares electrons with other water molecules due to attractive polarities. These intermolecular bonds are also engaged in a flickering dance, holding and releasing, connecting and letting go, to create a seemingly paradoxical event that is supple and yielding while simultaneously maintaining wholeness and integrity. This property also creates what is called surface tension.

A tranquil pool along the river catches my attention. In the shallows, a white feather is gliding like a gossamer sailboat, poised for a voyage with dragonflies and bees as its sailing crew. Curling upward, the feather is held up by the water; it is floating. Pliancy and cohesion together: we would do well to model our thoughts and behavior after these liquid attributes.

I would like to float international conflicts on the back of the river, to sail people's broken hopes on the water's belly, and then to send downstream, by the thousands, new dreams that glide and bend around the world's current obstacles. Surface tension is coherency of the water teaching us of the possibility of cultural and intercultural cohesion and the power of our collective dreams to hold aloft our ideals. To absorb this possibility, our hearts need to be open and flexible like water. As Lao Tzu said, if water is united, the human heart will be corrected. It is wise to be governed by water. Those seeking to live well in their communities, and within the larger community of the Earth, will tell you that adherence to the deeper teachings and ways of the watershed are essential.

Floods, tsunamis, tidal waves, undertows, torrents, avalanches, storms, and riptides are also exhilarating faces of water's governance. Water is life-giver and death-deliverer, and we should respect water and study its natural laws. This is particularly true now as we face the consequences of climate change. The ways of water are increasingly reflecting our human actions through a multitude of extremes: from long-term droughts and unseasonable floods to massive glacier melts and rising sea-levels.

The guiding ways of water can be found everywhere. There is an Indigenous saying that the moon is the heart of the forest. When I first heard these words, I was enchanted by the poetic imagery. Only later, after some contemplation, did I realize the moon is, in fact, directly affecting the movement of water in all the trees and plants of the forest, gravitationally, pumping and pulsing as a heart does. Biologists have studied how water moves and expands in trees and how, in addition to suction and ionic bonding, this movement might be linked to the cycles of the moon and the corresponding forces of lunar gravitational pull.[4] Farmers throughout the ages have worked in concert with these forces, claiming them to foster healthier, stronger plants and better crop yields. While plants and trees devoutly look to the cycles of the moon for their rhythm in rise and fall, so, too, do the oceanic tides pay this same homage. Can we humans, as personal vessels of water, disbelieve that we, too, are deeply influenced by these same lunar-water cycles? What is ebb and flow in our bodies?

Certainly every woman who reflects upon the sky's silvery disc and her own monthly lunar cycle knows that she is intimately part of this relationship between the moon and her internal tides, and accordingly, the bigger circle of life.

When water falls from the sky or is thrust from ocean spray it naturally forms the shape of a sphere. What better symbol of wholeness than a complete round? During the early morning, we can see spherical drops delicately balanced on grass blades and up-turned leaves welcoming the day as gemlike eyes blinking brightly into the rising sun.

When water is pulled by Earth's gravity, as with a river drawn to the sea, it reconciles beautifully its spherical inclination by cre-ating spiral motion and curving shapes. Looking along the shores of Big River, I see this reconciliation in the meandering arc and bends of the water's pathway. The curves tell the tale of how water likes to travel in a spiral walk. Liquid whorls are a marriage of water spheres in motion with Earthly gravity.

Staying true to the river's full story, I am pressed to ask myself: What is our relationship to this artful spiral marriage? Only mod-ern humans have attempted to defile this natural flow of water, straightening the spirals into rigid pipes, suppressing mighty river gyrations behind huge walled dams, and subjugating waterways to linear cement canals. My heart hurts just thinking about these unnatural confinements.

Dams and diversions of river water have multiplied tremen-dously over the last half-century as the demand for water globally has more than tripled. Water for agricultural use and hydroelec-tric power top the charts. Since 1950, the number of major dams worldwide has grown from 5,000 to 45,000.[5] Many rivers have been drained dry because water is lost through evaporation in dammed reservoirs and then diverted and siphoned off all along the length of a river, drastically decreasing or stopping the flow altogether.

In her book *Last Oasis*, Sandra Postel of the Global Water Policy Project tells us, "The Nile in Egypt, the Ganges in South Asia, the Amu Dar'ya and Syr Dar'ya in Central Asia, the Yellow River in China, and the Colorado River in North America are among the major rivers that are so dammed, diverted or overtapped that little or no fresh water reaches its final destination for significant stretches of time."[6]

Each drop is so small, so almost unannounced, it is hard to imagine that the little rivulets made of droplets borne from snowmelt in the Rocky Mountains are the source of the headwaters of the mighty Colorado River. Some Indian people of the region call this river the great Ice Serpent. Twisting and spinning on her descent of more than 12,000 feet, the Colorado winds through deserts, mesas, and the Grand Canyon. Along this journey, the river turns red with vibrantly colored crimson silt. With this ruby-hued heart flow, the Ice Serpent glides on through the canyons to meet with her love, the Sea of Cortez. Yet today, even when the Colorado reaches with all her power toward this familiar welcoming sea, it may or may not be hers to embrace. She is an embattled ancient dragon with torn skin and pierced scales, drained, dammed, and diverted. Still she powers on with all possible strength to trickle home to her natural destination, the sea. As a Californian, I am painfully aware of my state's participation in the hijacking and heartbreak of the Colorado River. I ask: What happens to the well-being and very spirit of the water when we stop this primordial, sacred flow?

While I was in the Southwest interviewing Indigenous elders for the documentary film *Our Living Waters*, Loya of the Northern Ute remarked, "People have many heart problems in America today because we are damming too many of the rivers. Beavers can dam rivers without damaging the flow because their dams are small and they know how to help the waterways with their work. But now with all our big dams, we are stopping the natural movement that was meant to be. This stops the flow of Mother Earth's lifeblood, her heart circulation."

At first, I wrestled with her words because of Western medical perspectives on the cause of increased heart disease. However, as I meditated further upon Loya's insight, it came to me that no matter how we wish to describe the reasons for heart disease in our time, there is clearly a deep wound in people's hearts because of the tragedy of subjugating all that is wild. We know, consciously or subconsciously, that each day we are losing more of the natural symphony of water and the wild heart of the land, and that is simply not good for our hearts. Loya went on to say that because her people have been displaced from their original lands, generations' worth of wise water management from these long-maintained regions is also being lost. Her people suffer from what she called "historical trauma." She told me about her deep longing to go home to her ancestral land, to rightfully dwell there again where her ancestors' bones are buried. With these words, our shared emotional waters spoke from our eyes. The Colorado River strives toward home; Loya, too, wants to go home.

⌐

The sun is now directly overhead, marking splashes of gold on the glistening skin of Big River. Loya's words are still echoing in my mind, and I wonder if rivers, too, are experiencing this "historical trauma" as they are displaced, diverted, straightened, and made static. I come upon a bottle that has been tossed along the riverside trail. There is water trapped in it. Stagnant water reflects the absent rhythm of death because water must move to live; it is its nature to be in vibrant motion. I cannot help but think that damming rivers is a great offense to the wild rights belonging to water. We speak, as we certainly must, about the universal human right to water, but I wish to add that we need to address water having its own rights. I believe an inherent benefit of respecting the clean, free-flowing right of water to remain as undisturbed as possible will be the rediscovery of our own ecological and spiritual equipoise with this sacred element.

Water as mover and shaper also shapes the history of our civilization, forming where we live and influencing how we fashion our daily lives. It is to this present and future shaping that I now look, not to wallow in laments but to be informed and conscious.

Recalling the European nature philosophers of the 1800s, Theodor Schwenk states in his extraordinary 1965 book on water and air flow forms, *Sensitive Chaos*, "Humanity has not only lost touch with the spiritual nature of water, but it is now in danger of losing its very physical substance…. It is being realized that the living circulations of water cannot be destroyed without dire consequences and that water is *more* than a mere flow energy or a useful means of transport."[7]

As we have become an ever-expanding industrial civilization, water is used without restraint as a mechanism in almost every aspect of manufacturing and as a waste container for every form of contaminant imaginable. Today, due to chemical poisoning of waterways and waterborne diseases, millions of people die annually. A 2010 United Nations Environment Program study reports that at least 1.8 million of these fatalities are children under five years old—that is one child every twenty seconds.[8] Maude Barlow, the national chair of The Council of Canadians and the director of the Blue Planet Project, warns us, "The destruction of aquatic ecosystem health, and the increasing water scarcity, are in my opinion the most pressing environmental problems facing humankind."[9]

Although in water-wealthy countries problems of scarcity are often hidden, most of the world is currently thirsting for pure, clean water to drink. While we here in North America can still for the most part turn on any faucet or spigot and expect clean water to pour out, people in many countries, most often the women, must walk for miles each day to collect water for their immediate needs. A woman's other daily tasks only begin after an arduous journey of fetching water—a trek that can take six hours or more in some regions in Africa and India—and carrying containers that can weigh up to fifty pounds when full. Sadly, the water so hard-won is often polluted, slowly or quickly sickening the household. It is no wonder people in these regions are shocked to learn that in North America we even flush our toilets with clean water.

Even though 70 percent of our Earth's surface is water, the main portion of it, 97 percent, is salt water. Much of the remaining 3 percent that is fresh is held in snow and glaciers, leaving about 1 percent available. Unabated pollution is reducing the purity of this invaluable 1 percent. Further, the impact of climate change is increasing hot spots around the planet, while watershed run-off is being reduced from shrinking glaciers and fewer wet snow packs. As we look toward mitigating increasing water crises, we no longer can do so in isolation—scientifically or politically— from the climate crisis.

At the same time, our human populations are growing rapidly, and scientists predict that by the fast-approaching year 2020 thirty-five nations will experience severe water shortages.[10] Already, a third of the Earth's population is struggling from inadequate freshwater supplies.[11] It is important to remember that there is the same amount of water on our planet now as there was a thousand years ago and thousands of years before that, but the number of people does not remotely resemble that of a thousand years ago. We need to listen to what the water is telling us and develop a new consciousness about this life-giving element. Good water practices are at the core of a viable Earth etiquette.

Mikhail Gorbachev, former president of the Soviet Union and current president of Green Cross International, wrote in the foreword to Water, The Drop of Life:

> Water, like religion and ideology, has the power to move millions of people. Since the very birth of human civilization, people have moved to settle close to it. People move when there is too little of it. People move when there is too much of it. People journey down it. People write, sing and dance about it. People fight over it. And all people,

everywhere and every day, need it.... Let us acknowledge that access to clean water is a universal human right, and in so doing accept that we have the corresponding universal responsibility to ensure that the forecast of a world where, in 25 years' time two out of every three persons face water stress is proven wrong.

Without water security, social, economic and national stability are imperiled. This is magnified where water is shared across borders—and becomes crucial where water stress exists in regions of religious, territorial or ethnic tension. Thus we are faced with a mighty challenge.... Just as we are moved by water, we must now move in order to save it.[12]

The importance of working together as a world community is one of the messages that water seems to be telling us. Water molecules do not exist individually on their own, and it is their very nature to be in continuous relationship with one another. It is within this dynamic of bonding with other water molecules that water exists in all its extraordinary forms.

With fresh water shortages affecting the entire planet, the potential for cross-border conflicts inevitably arise. Can we be wise Earth Citizens, and, like the example of water, realize the need to collectively address these water challenges? At this poignant moment, can the Global Community come together with a new understanding of water as a sacred commons that belongs to our living Earth, to all species, and to future generations?

As I have learned from colleagues working in the field of water stewardship, water is best cared for by the inhabitants of each local water basin. As with many land-based issues, local communities often know what is best for the particular complexities of their region. The watershed itself also has a natural integrity that needs to be respected, and so it is prudent that these communities en-

compass the entirety of a water basin and not be divided and estranged by arbitrary political borders. As Theodore Roosevelt once
advised, "Each river system, from its headwaters in the forest to its
mouth on the coast is a single unit and should be treated as such."[13]

Water is reflecting back to us that we have an opportunity
to respond now in a timely and creative manner with healthy
community relations to successfully navigate cross-border water
conflicts and to help people who are suffering from an immediate
lack of water resources.

Whether a civilization has been built around a complex irrigation system sourced from rivers or next to springs and wells or
from desert cisterns, water brings people together. In this sense,
it is truly the universal solvent, dissolving separations and creating unison. Water asks us to look at our interdependency with
the land, our entire bioregion, and our neighbors—and then to
look at our sense of security and our lifestyle. Water asks us to
remember we can die without it and then to remember others can,
too. As a universal solvent, water encourages us to dis-solve and
re-solve disharmonies with our neighbors and the natural world
in which we live and from which we receive our water, our life.

There is a myriad of innovative water resource solutions, and
the one I wish to mention here is particularly appealing in its
elegant simplicity and energy efficiency, emulating the laws of nature. Often I think of drinking water coming up from the ground,
but people have been harvesting rainwater and mists from the sky
for thousands of years.

In the small Chilean coastal village of Chungungo, water shortages had become an increasing problem. In looking for solutions,
villagers observed that the leaves of the town's plentiful Eucalyptus tree were collecting coastal moisture and, with the help of
Canadian engineers, designed a plan to follow nature's example.

In the mountains above the village, huge mesh nets, acting
as Eucalyptus leaves, catch the coastal fog. The droplets are fun-
neled into pipes that carry the sky water into tanks for Chungungo. The people there call the process "harvesting the clouds."

Similar fog-collecting projects have also been developed in other countries such as Mexico, Croatia, Namibia, Oman, and Nepal.

Our ancients also knew this way with mist. The Roman author Pliny the Elder recorded that people living near the Holy Fountain Tree in the Canary Islands collected most of their water from fog-gathering tree leaves.

Additionally, in both urban and rural areas, rainwater catchment is a growing source of water conservation and collection. Rainwater that is collected from the roofs of houses and buildings can make an important contribution to drinking water, and in communities around the world, rainwater collecting technologies and classes are on the rise.

Concerning the resolution of transboundary issues, new technologies will certainly be instrumental. Dr. Jerome Delli Priscoli, speaking at the eighth Stockholm World Water Symposium, explained that through satellite technologies, countries sharing watersheds have the ability to accurately view the water use in an entire region, leading to more openness and clarity in negotiations, as there is no longer the possibility of secreting data.[14]

Walking further upstream, I focus my sights on the bottom of Big River, observing stones and moss beneath the surface, and realize I am peering through transparency. While the river has her enchanting mysteries, there are no unwholesome secrets here. The water speaks of openness and the beauty of translucence. I imagine our world leaders sitting by the river to see the dignity and power of transparency, and then to act accordingly.

In his keynote address, Dr. Priscoli went on to state the need to look deeper into what water is offering to us as a society:

"The symbolic content of water as cleansing, healing, rebirth and reconciliation can provide a powerful tool for cooperation and symbolic acts of reconciliations so necessary to conflict resolution in other areas of society.... Rekindling the sense of sacred water ... is one way to facilitate the escalation of debate on water cooperation to higher levels and thus impact the capacity to reach cooperation and to manage conflict."[15]

The understanding that water is sacred and the very essence of life is universal to Indigenous cultures. This is also true for people who live close to the land, as any farmer will tell you. Because of this respect, many societies have acknowledged water as a shared commons. In recent years, however, this perspective has radically changed. In our consumer market-driven world, water is increasingly becoming a commodity for sale. When water becomes merely a product, it then also becomes accessible only to those who can afford it and is no longer available to all of the world's inhabitants. Citizens in communities worldwide are taking a stand to protect their local water basins from commoditization and are learning how best to care for and defend this irreplaceable source of life. It is both prudent and a source of pride to know the water landscape and water protectors of our home regions.

One thing is for certain: over these next pivotal years, as a great teacher, water will fill, envelop, and reflect the dreams and relationships we choose to imagine and create. In addition to innovative technologies and more inclusive and protective water basin management, renewing our appreciation of the spiritual nature of water will be a key component in steering a healthier course than the direction we have taken so far.

As we can see, water is also a mirror. It is the oldest reflective surface known to humans, and it is in this mysterious liquid glass that we first had the opportunity to see ourselves. Water is not only a cosmic mirror reflecting all of creation back to itself in images of lakeside trees, animals that come for a drink, mountains that cradle the waters, and the ever-changing water-bearing sky. It is also a mirror for the inward-looking eyes of the human soul. In this sense, the water mirror is personal and many-faceted, and the more courageous and curious we are, the more we will see. We can gaze at the reflection of our society in water, behold our actions, and ask: what are we building in beauty, and what are we destroying?

In these waters, we can see our individual and cultural dreams reflected back to us. We have the opportunity to search for new dreams surfacing on the mirror and ask how we can regain our awareness of the spiritual nature of water, and in so doing, heal our relationship with it. I am reminded of the mirror of Galadriel in J.R.R. Tolkien's *The Lord of the Rings*. This magical mirror "shows things that were, and things that are, and things that yet may be."[16] In another, more historic instance, Hellenic seekers traveled far distances to the Temple of Delphi to seek council by peering into the bowl of divination waters.

This most ancient water mirror also reminds us that at one time people everywhere openly honored this divine liquid. In civilizations worldwide, water was known to be holy, each droplet a miracle of life. People pilgrimaged frequently to sacred wells, divine springs, mystical lakes, and healing baths. A river was a holy place, a magic water-serpent that our ancients sang to for their very lives.

The word *mirror* and the word *mari*, which is one of the oldest names for the ocean, have similar linguistic roots. People celebrated the mirroring seas with various names in different lands: Maria, Marina, Marian, Miriam, and Myorrha.

Mari, the Mother Sea or Mother Ocean, was most frequently depicted wearing a blue robe representing the ocean and a necklace of pearls representing the white foamy waves.

Many modern words such as *marine* and *maritime* still express these ancient Mother Sea names; in the German language, meer means the sea and in Old Norse it was *merr*. The Russian *more*, the Welsh *mor*, Old Saxon *meri*, and Spanish *mar* are all words for the sea or ocean.

Place names throughout the Middle East, Europe, and Africa also honor the sea in this way: Mar-Mari, Mara, Marian, and Pal-Myra, to mention a few. It seems everywhere we look, humanity has held a deep reverence for this great body of water since the beginning of time.

Almost every civilization believed that life originated in the sea and often referred to the ocean as the sacred Womb Waters, or Mother Waters. In the many languages that attribute gender to nouns, the ocean is most often feminine. In the old Sumerian language, the word *mar* meant both womb and sea.

Several wonderful creation stories of the indigenous people of the Americas relate how animals, often a turtle or muskrat, sometimes a raven, are sent to the bottom of the ocean to collect mud from which the Earth Mother is then molded.

One compelling Japanese creation story describes a giant mystical carp that vigorously awakens from a long sleep in the ocean. Its wild thrashing creates a tsunami from which the Japanese Islands are born.

In classical Greek mythology, the Titan Goddess Tethys and God Okeanos are the deities of water. Their liquid stream girds the entire world, and it is from this vast body of circulating water that all things could be formed.

An aboriginal tribe in northern Australia tells the beautiful story of All-Mother who arrives from the ocean shaped as a rainbow serpent with her children inside of her. These children are the original ancestors of the land.

With a spiritual relationship to water universally understood, there were sacred water sites in every part of the world. This was true for the early Celts throughout Europe for whom holy water sites were central to many ceremonies. Later, with the spread of Christianity, many of these older spiritual traditions came under attack, and their holy sites were destroyed.

Yet, an important truth remained: even with widespread devastation and loss of many lives, the love and worship of water did not die. The old practices were not annihilated, and people continued to pilgrimage to their venerated springs and wells. Because of this resistance, the church began to convert pagan sacred sites to Christian places of worship by building nearby or directly on top of them. Eventually, after many years, the old Earth-honoring ways and Christian traditions began to merge. Although how this initially came about is a tale of terrible bloodshed and grief, it is also a living testament to the ability of water to bring about an unusual reconciliation between diverse worldviews that we might not expect.

Today, at many ancient wells and springs both in Europe and in the Americas, Christian saints are celebrated with festivals and ceremonies that were once old-time holy days. Some of the rituals creatively blend the old with the new by carrying on a variant of the old cultures with lovely traditions like Well Dressing, in which wells are beautifully adorned with leaves, flowers, fruits, grasses, stones, and feathers.[17]

Water has held an ongoing place of sanctity both symbolically and physically in our modern world, although not always apparent in a larger cultural or secular context. Islamic, Buddhist, Christian, Jewish, and Hindu traditions all impart the story of four sacred rivers of life that originate in Paradise and flow to the four directions of the world. In many recountings, these rivers symbolize nourishment, enlightenment, spiritual strength, and passage to death.

Ceremonial washing and cleansing have been a part of many religious rituals, throughout the ages and carried on today. Immersion in water often symbolizes death and rebirth and the washing away of the past to welcome regeneration. "By means of water, we give life to everything" (Qur'an, 21:30). "Be praised, my Lord, through Sister Water; she is very useful, and humble, and precious, and pure," said Francis of Assisi, in *Canticle of the Sun*.

Millions of people revere the Ganges River as one of the most holy symbols of life today, and many seekers make pilgrimages from all over the world to purify themselves in these waters. Both Jews and Christians have rituals of water purification that are central to their beliefs. The word baptism originates from the Greek word *baptizo*, which means "to immerse."

Today, around the world, people practice a multitude of life-honoring water ceremonies continued since long ago: Mongolians high in the Altai Mountains, Taoists in China, aboriginal people in Australia, First Nations People in the Americas—and many other Indigenous people. Aboriginal elders from diverse lands tell us these water ceremonies are, in fact, keeping the world alive.

In Japan, the water ritual of the tea ceremony is practiced daily.

This ceremony embraces four principles that are qualities of living with inward balance and with the Earth in balance. These principles—Purity, Respect, Tranquility, and Harmony—also reflect water's profound influence on humanity.

The ancient Buryat people living on the shores of Lake Baikal in Siberia call it "the sacred water." This immense body of water, containing some 22 percent of the world's fresh water, is the oldest and deepest lake in the world. This magnificent water temple, glistening between necklaces of snow-topped mountains, is widely venerated throughout Russia as a sacred site that needs to be safeguarded. In every region of the world, in every wondrous waterway, we can and need to regenerate a sacred understanding of water, and in so doing protect it.

I am thinking I need to remember these stories when I am bathing, cleaning, drinking, and washing at my home, bringing these respectful water-thoughts close to my skin. Water cleanses, heals, purifies, vivifies, and sanctifies. Each of these fluid words runs off my tongue like ripples into the river.

Sunset is now near and the coastal mists have rolled in, blanketing the Big River estuary. As I move from the up-river sun to the cool, silvery fog at the river's mouth, I imagine, as in the old time Arthurian tales, that I am walking through the magical mists of Avalon. Before stepping through, I take one last look into the river mirror.

The river tugs at me, and I want to simply and unshly say, I love water. It is a love that I find is universal amongst all people. When a person falls in love, the whole world seems to shift dimension, mysteriously and unaccountably. Where there was no time and other scarcities existed, suddenly there is an immeasurable quantity of time and necessities abundantly met. Where there was conflict and grief, love finds the subtle crevice to enter and bring well-being and plenty. The dynamic of this amorous encounter can suddenly change for us the very formation of the landscape.

I am asking: what would happen if we renewed our wellspring of love for the deeply spiritual nature of water?

Streaming, running, trickling, cascading, bubbling, surging, rushing, meandering, sparkling, splashing—from snow-capped mountains to white-capped sea, there are multitudes of bodies of moving water, our Earth's lifeblood flowing through tens of thousands of veins. This yet-untamed liquid landscape moves through our hearts to the heart of the great ocean, and so I am hopeful because the heart is the most trusted place of power—it has the courage to be vulnerable, humble, and unafraid. The heart knows the way to be strong, loyal, and unflinching. In this way, we can make our stand by water.

D.H. Lawrence writes:

> Water is H_2O,
>
> hydrogen two parts,
>
> oxygen one,
>
> but there is also a third thing,
>
> that makes it water
>
> and nobody knows what that is.[18]

I would not claim to know this third thing; the sacred mysteries are divine riddles meant to be kept by the Earth Muses. I would simply suggest here the possibility that ingredient is water love, the heart of liquidity.

8 *Anthem to Water*

Part Two: Vision Creek

Say, you are in the country; in some high land of lakes. Take
almost any path you please, and ten to one it carries you
down in a dale and leaves you there by a pool in the stream.
There is magic in it. Let the most absent-minded of men be
plunged in his deepest reveries–stand that man on his legs,
set his feet a-going, and he will infallibly lead you to water,
if water there be in all that region . Yes, as every one knows,
meditation and water are wedded forever.
–HERMAN MELVILLE, *MOBY-DICK*

When you throw a rock into the water, it will speed on the
fastest course to the bottom of the water. This is how it is
when Siddhartha has a goal, a resolution. Siddhartha does
nothing, he waits, he thinks, he fasts, but he passes through
the things of the world like a rock through water, without
doing anything, without stirring; he is drawn, he lets himself
fall. His goal attracts him, because he doesn't let anything
enter his soul which might oppose the goal…. Everyone can
perform magic, everyone can reach his goals, if he is able to
think, if he is able to wait, if he is able to fast.
–HERMANN HESSE , *SIDDHARTHA*

Tony and I are walking along the Marin headlands just north of San Francisco, discussing water justice campaigns and water awareness projects. He looks at me with crystalline eyes that remind me of shimmering glacial ice. But they're not reflecting any cold; his blue emanates from a depth of soul as venerable and vulnerable as the glaciers. He suddenly asks me when I first became interested in water. I know that he is not looking for a one-dimensional response. That's one of the cherished elements of having good allies: the questions we ask each other require us to ask more of ourselves. It's a deeper dialogue, not a practiced answer. I am thinking that such pressing queries are, potentially, part of our evolutionary unfolding as a species, for they have the possibility of creating never-before-articulated ideas. I am quiet for a long while as our pace slows, letting the resonance of the ocean waves permeate the space between our thoughts. As a coastal dweller all my life, there is no time I can remember being without the influence of the aquatic realm, yet I am listening to my colleague's deeper question and wondering if it is one that can be answered adequately. I suggest we sit down for a while so that I can tell him a true story about the meaning of water in my own life.

⤙——

This is not a tale of wisdom, but one that gave me wisdom in the experience, in the unfolding of what happened. And, even given the pure folly and dangerous innocence of the effort, I still would not have wished it any other way.

It was not the only time, but it was the very first time, that I fasted from both food and water. It was not so much the fasting that might be brought into question, but rather that I had decided to approach the venture alone, in the wilderness. I had backcountry skills both physically and psychologically, having been taught by wilderness instructors as well as working as an assistant guide for others on numerous occasions, but certainly never under these conditions and without a companion for safety.

I was nineteen at the time, and, like many that age, I was seeking a broader philosophical foundation for life than that which my culture or university courses offered. There are significant queries that either we call to us (and are then haunted by) or we stumble upon because of circumstances; both were true for me. These questions were not just mine, of course, but inquiries that have always intrigued humans.

At the time, I was drawn to a diverse array of spiritual texts, and I realized that fasting was a common thread in many spiritual practices. In Asian, Middle Eastern, Nordic, American Indian, and other traditions, fasting was described as a profound mystical experience. Through fasting, perceptions and perspectives were altered and the spiritual senses were deepened. Specifically, I understood that, as our bodies thirst and hunger, the portal to the deeper universe, in all its wonder and divinity, could open to meet these longings.

I was reading *Siddhartha* by Hermann Hesse, and it was this book in particular that finally set me on my way. Two prominent messages in the story penetrated my youthful consciousness and took up position there, beckoning me to explore further:

1) Siddhartha believed that he could attain enlightenment on his own through self-discovery and inner reflection. A significant step in this path of attainment was the practice of physical abstinence. I was quite taken with this idea of self-reliance along with self-discipline and simplicity. A child of privilege in wealthy America, I, too, would learn to do without.

2) I gleaned from his story that there was something quintessential about water, specifically rivers, that brought about spiritual development. I would be like Siddhartha and go to the river. My place of fasting would be what I later came to call Vision Creek in the Northern California backcountry. There, when it was time to end my fast, I would be able to drink from wild flowing waters. (This was when we could

still drink directly from these northern streams because they were not yet so polluted.)

I didn't know what enlightenment meant or even if I wanted to be enlightened, but I did want to become a fully alive and awake person, and I wanted to reach for something greater in my life. Humanity's negative impact on the planet had also begun to enter my awareness, and this, too, lured me to search for answers.

Innately, I understood that the *not* having of something, by choice, could produce a spiritual thirst and hunger in me, and I wanted to know what that was. However, when I set out with my backpack into the forest in which my special creek flowed, what I didn't fully realize or seriously address was that I might be having a very real encounter with death. Certainly, I was nervous about how I would endure physically, but my thoughts revolved around remaining disciplined in my decision not to eat food or drink water—rather than actual bodily processes.

I would fast for three days, I determined. Exercising a little caution, however, even with my sprightly enthusiasm, I decided I would have my last drink the morning of the first day, then go through the next two full days without a morsel or a sip, ending my fast at dawn on the fourth day.

—◦—

The sound of flowing water is a song, an ensemble, and every brook and rill, river and lake, ocean cove and inlet sea has its own unique melody. Derived from spring snowmelt and winding through a myriad of hidden rivulets, Vision Creek snaked its way down through the mountains, nestled between fir, oak, madrone, and pine-clad forests. It was not a large creek when it emerged, but certainly one with a deliciously cold stream and a most mellifluous ripple. It was this sweet-voiced melody that pulled me to the spot.

The ravine where the creek flowed was quite steep, but just forty feet above it was a small meadowed shelf. I had walked through the area once before and knew it to be a place where human-made time seemed to cease, and the land could speak freely in the language of birdcall, chanting leaves, clacking stones, murmuring breezes, thrumming grasses, and all the Earth's natural poetry.

I traveled with very little: my sleeping roll but no tent, a bag of nuts and dried fruit so that I might have the energy to hike the eight miles back, my pocketknife, and no flashlight but matches and a lighter in case of emergency. Water being the element central to my meditations, I decided to have no campfires. The stars at night would be my light.

Already a full day's hike into the mountains, I arose the next day at first light to make my way to Vision Creek. Arriving at the meadow by early morning, I settled my belongings into a leafy bed where I would stay. Then, unhurried, I wandered down the ravine to the creek, where I drank and cooled my body in the wetness for the last time (I had decided to not even touch water during this fast). The day was quite still; cicadas were chirping their high-pitched songs to the world, and I allowed my thoughts to go downstream, sending each one along a ripple. Later that afternoon I watched two newts mating in a tranquil eddy in the shade. Holding hands underwater, they spun in a circle dance, and I thought to myself—what a wonderful way to initiate lovemaking.

Evening appeared in colored banners across the sky, and I walked, moving slower than usual, to my sleeping place. I watched the night sky gradually break into stars, feeling the meadow a place of calm, a place where it seemed all things, no matter how grand or minute, were held in balance. But I was not quite yet in this rhythm; I was looking for something to happen and questioning why I had come. My thirst had begun.

By the next morning I could detect changes in my body, and I felt quite slow and vulnerable to the world. The beauty of the land was overwhelming and I wanted to give this place a gift for allowing me as a visitor. I walked to an oak tree by the meadow's edge and, after asking permission from the trees, collected some fallen branches and sat down to work, carving two wooden dolls for Vision Creek. One of the dolls was a girl and the other a boy. Curly green and white mosses became their hair and layered leaves their clothing, all sewn together with thin grasses.

There are moments of stillness that can open our consciousness to the rhythm of the ages: when we inhale the summer air and feel sunlight in every breath, when we watch a cloud moving silently across the vaulted sky and recognize the expanse of our mind, when we rest beside our sweetheart after lovemaking and feel eternity in our serenity, when we gaze upon the full moon over the sea and dream with our ancestors. In such stillness our memory awakens—an ageless, planetary memory that has always been there, just beneath our thoughts.

All day while I carved, I listened to the ballad of Vision Creek as the stream recited to me her history, of times long ago before humans walked beside her banks, and then of times when people first drank from her, fished her waters, came to her for healing, bathing, and prayer. Then I envisioned, with the creek's suggestion, the coyote, bear, jay, puma, deer, squirrel, raven, and all the animals that came to drink from her and still do. Drinking was very much on my mind, and I focused on my dolls.

As the day neared sunset, I remembered a wild rose bush not too far up the path. The bush in this season was dressed in red rosehips, and I thought of rosehip necklaces as the perfect adornments for my dolls.

The little rosebush was further up the trail than I had recalled, and by the time I returned it was almost completely dark. I was suddenly very tired and weak, and I lay in my sleeping bag looking up into the night, aware of just how profoundly thirsty I had become. If I lay very still, I thought to myself, the strong thirst will pass. Some hours later my insides started to feel like shriveled parts and my tongue a thick leathery thing that stuck to the roof of my withered mouth. I wanted to sleep my thirst away, but I became acutely acquainted with the sound of Vision Creek splashing and chortling in a most alluring manner with clean, cool water, just a little ways away.

It had been two days so far, and I very much wished to maintain my fast another day as planned, but the enchanting song of flowing water was speaking to me of relief, which I now deeply craved. As I touched my parched mouth, my lips having split earlier in the day, the provocation of the tumbling water became intolerably haunting—no longer a gentle melody but an arrhythmic taunt throbbing in my head.

Without moon, the night was jet black. Yet even so, before I could stop myself, I was crawling toward the water on hands and knees, feeling my way to the ravine. Driven by thirst, my body seemed to have a mind of its own, and I crept to where the bank dropped down to the creek. It seemed quite steep, and I clutched foliage on low-growing brush to steady myself. I sensed manzanita bushes, young oaks, and some poor ferns I knew I was mangling in my desperation to get at the water. The angle of the slope was much sharper than I had remembered, and I suddenly started to slip. The ledge that I had been inching down dropped off abruptly, and I grabbed for the upside of the hill, pressing my face into the brush and dirt the better to hang on, trying to keep on gravity's good side.

Having just caught my downward slide, and with my heart pounding in my ears, I stopped and tried to evaluate the situation. I realized the sound of the creek was echoing off the banks, fostering an illusion of proximity, and, in the utter darkness, I had chosen a route too high up. My efforts had only further increased my thirst, and I was completely exhausted. The most intelligent thing to do seemed to be to return to my camp and let this difficult moment pass. Just then, a light breeze lifted across the ravine toward me, redolent with the fragrance of the mountain stream. I did not know the smell of water could be so sweet and, although I did not want to get hurt, I now absolutely had to have water.

Focusing to recall the lay of the slope, I reached out into the darkness on all fours, moving cautiously but with determination toward the crooning ripples. In only a few moments, I was once more nearing a steep angle on the hillside. I quickly tried to catch myself as I started to slip, but it was too late—I was dangerously skidding downhill again. Snagging brush, I grasped at the rough branches with all my strength to break my fall, adrenaline pumping furiously. A manzanita bush graciously grabbed back.

My muscles were trembling as I crawled very slowly back up the slope. Thoughts of breaking my leg or worse were dashing and crashing through my mind, and I could smell the distinct metallic scent of blood. Feeling the ground out ahead, I crawled to a small, flat shelf just big enough for me to lie down. I caught my breath and quickly made an inspection of my condition, running my fingers along the cuts on my arms and legs. I was relieved to find that nothing was too serious or broken. Suddenly, I was startled by my own mad laughter: somehow I'd found it funny that, by bleeding, I was leaking precious liquids. It was also a nervous laugh because I was embarrassed for taking such a risk in the dark. I heard a calm but firm voice inside that warned, "Stop. If you break a leg out here on this mountain, alone, you could die, and for what? How holy would that be?" The water song still haunted me, and I tried to remember what I was doing out there.

It might seem unbelievable or at least unbelievably naive, but I had not anticipated one of the most obvious consequences of a complete fast from both food and water. Beyond the more desirable effects of altering mind and spirit for new insight, which I had longingly awaited, I realized that I was probably in the first stages of dying. I was not afraid, but I became vividly aware—beyond my extreme physical discomfort—that I was driven fiercely by my immense desire to live.

"Water is life," I quietly said aloud to the forest, "and I want to live. I want to give to and experience life's beauty, mystery, and power." These words meant something very new to me, and as I followed this trail of understanding, my terrific urgency began to quell. I was still extremely thirsty, but the willpower I had exerted in order to get to the water, the violence of my desire, and my uncontrolled determination now yielded to other sensations and forces.

Water is sacred. Water is healing. I am born from water. I will die without water. Water quenches my thirst, and the entire Earth needs water to live. Drink deep, drink long, and drink joyously from this ever-flowing wellspring of life.

This is what I felt. This is what came to me.

The sound of the creek was once again a soothing symphony of silvery splashes and tinkling stones. Too exhausted to climb further, up or down, I nestled onto the shelf of flat earth, covering myself in the forest loam created by innumerable transforming leaves. This living ground gave me the moisture it held and I dug my bare feet into the soft soil, feeling the comforting dampness.

I could not yet sleep. In my mind's eye, I began to see a crystalline water molecule, and I became fascinated with the mystical magnetism of water, the source of which I understood to be its inherent asymmetry.

Within the composition of H_2O, the oxygen atom has a stronger affinity for electrons than do the two hydrogen atoms, and electrons are more closely linked to oxygen's nucleus than to the nuclei of the two hydrogen. The hydrogen gives a slightly more positive charge because of this unevenness. This asymmetry is what gives water its unique ability to be structured and unstructured, to be integral to itself while open to shaping and being shaped by the world in an ever-moving, limitless conversation. Composed primarily of water, humanity is one drop, one jewel, in this liquid conversation.

The Japanese painter, writer, and museum curator Okakura Kakuzo (1862–1913) explains the nature of this asymmetry by way of the Japanese tearoom. Similar to the design of a traditional Japanese garden, with its arrangement of rocks set irregularly, so, too, is the tearoom a place of dynamic aesthetic asymmetry.

Kakuzo, in his elegant 1906 publication *The Book of Tea*, writes: "The tea room is an Abode of the Unsymmetrical inasmuch as it is consecrated to the worship of the Imperfect, purposefully leaving something unfinished for the play of the imagination to complete.… The art of the extreme Orient has purposefully avoided the symmetrical as expressing not only completion, but also repetition. Uniformity of design was considered as fatal to the freshness of imagination."[1]

Author Andy Couturier, from whom I learned about Kakuzo, concludes, "Empty space is a place to think, neither same nor opposite."[2]

I was imagining my thoughts being sculpted by this asymmetry and by water's "empty space," where my mind had room to wander. People make pilgrimages to water in order to reflect and contemplate, to immerse themselves in an exchange with life, to have a conversation with water's open arena of asymmetry. When people meditate with water, all things can be re-imagined in the dynamics of water's peculiar unevenness, in the liberated space of such fluctuating liquidity.

Sleep now came in fleeting pieces. Even the cool night air could not keep me any longer from my dreams, while the night-long water hymns, sounding up from the creek, eroded all that was left of me.

I awoke at dawn, dreaming of a frantically dancing creature. Long, knotted hair spun from its monstrous head, and, although startled, I stepped closer. The writhing braids jumped through the air on their own as if alive. Reaching out, I took hold of one wild strand and discovered it was a snarled twine of oil, tree sap, blood, and water. The creature spun around to look at me and said, "Loose the braids to free the heart of the world. Untangle the oil from the water, sap, and blood."

While at the time I felt this dream was something important to remember, I had only a glimmer of comprehending its meaning. It is one that has continued to unfold as the years pass.

——

At this critical ecological and societal turning point in human and planetary history, it seems much of the metamorphosis has to do with liquids.

The Amazon rainforests and large areas of the Boreal Forest and the Athabasca River of Canada are being destroyed due to oil exploitation. Indigenous communities in these regions suffer from disease and threat to their survival due to relentless pollution and land loss from these extractions. The blood and treasure that have been spilled, especially in the Middle East and Africa, over oil and other resources such as natural gas and water, demonstrates how surely our entanglement with our planet's liquids is at the center of this strife and unfortunate legacy. Our destiny at this pivotal moment involves wise choices as we struggle to sever these liquid strands and set them free, to finally cut through this epoch's Gordian Knot.

I did not understand the all-pervasiveness of global conflicts that last day of my fast at Vision Creek. This education came later over time, but I did know undeniably that the way humans had been living needed to be re-imagined and reshaped and that this reshaping needed to emulate the design of nature in elegant, sophisticated balance with all living things. I understood, in a deep sense, the words of John Muir: "When we try to pick out anything by itself, we find it hitched to everything else in the Universe."[3] I also knew I was very, very thirsty.

To move after I awakened that dawn, my third one there, required what seemed to be more energy than I could muster. Even my clothes had begun to feel too heavy to bear. The nature of water is to move, to flow, and I now realized I could hardly move without it. I became content, after some effort, just to watch my thoughts and listen to what the forest and creekside offered me without my having to move. Butterflies and dragonflies painted the day in colossal streaming bands of colors. Mosquitoes were in great abundance with their high-pitched whine and quick sting, but I no longer desired to swat them away. Let them drink, I thought. I imagined just letting go and dying there, becoming food and drink for the forest creatures—and I did not find it an objectionable idea. There is a sense of peace that tempts a person to let go even further in this state of mind.

I looked forward to my first sip of water this miraculously granted next morning with both excitement and anxiety because I wondered if these remarkable sensations would leave once I drank. I feared that with one swallow, this new consciousness would be lost forever.

My thoughts dissolved into the stream, and my mind wandered as it followed a madrone leaf gliding on the surface; it became a little boat carried on the current. Where will it go? I pondered. How many towns and cities will it pass by on its way to the ocean? Vision Creek kept singing to me of integrating the whole story, from mountain stream to cities of millions, and all that came with it. How could I bring this song of forest and meadow, valley and river, home to where most of my human family lived in cities often deprived of even one wild sound?

Beyond these musings, most of what transpired during that final numinous day are things not to be spoken of unless in the presence of another of like mind and heart, or are meant to be given back only to the oak and pine, hills and brook, and to the many creatures of those wild spots. There are circumstances and times for oral traditions and the power of sound and song to govern: so here, let me move on to say what happened the morning when I first drank.

How does one approach the very essence of that which gives them life?

The early morning sun sent shanks of light through the tree branches, transforming Vision Creek into a stream of shining liquid gold. The tinkling sounds were a symphony, a poem of shimmering life. I waited. My thoughts rested for a while on people who do not have immediate access to adequate or clean water: in war-torn countries; in refugee camps; in places where women walk most of their day in quest of enough water for their families, burdened and enslaved by the need for water. I thought of poverty-strained countries and low-income communities near industrial centers where pollution has poisoned the waterways, sickening and killing the children and the elders. I thought of people who die without water while crossing borders in deserts. Yet, I needed only to take a few steps to reach this stream of clean, refreshing, life-giving fluid. This was a privilege that I wanted to respect. Only a few paces away, the beautiful creek was surging and sparkling, and I could almost hear children's laughter and the sounds of play in the stream.

Bending to approach the water, I felt very shy and overwhelmed with appreciation. Tears formed in my eyes, and I was amazed that my body could even produce them in this state of dehydration. The drops traced paths down my dusty face, and I watched several tears fall unexpectedly into the creek. Our waters touched and blended.

Tears are our way to bring water from its wellspring inside us— trickling down our cheeks onto the earth, into the river, watering the land—when our hearts are so full the water must flow through our eyes.

I slowly slipped my hands into the creek, feeling that my skin was only a thin veneer between the water and me. Washing my hands clean in the bright, cold stream was entirely euphoric, and I took my time. I cupped them together, realizing that our hands are our first and best chalice. And then, reciting a hundred passionate *thank yous*, I lifted the water to my lips and inhaled its heady, sweet aroma. As reverently as possible, I took a little sip—and was wholly electrified.

I could actually feel the water entering and flowing through my veins, awakening every sense, re-hydrating my withered existence. As I drank more, every cell seemed to tingle and spark back to life. I also remember thinking it wise to drink slowly after a fast, and for some moments, I did hold back. Then, the intensity of my thirst became a wild thing on its own course. I laid belly-down on the soft bank with my head dipping in and out of Vision Creek, drinking and laughing and feeling quite ecstatically and miraculously alive.

As the water flowed into my body I became aware that I was imbibing the River Jordan, the great Ganges, deepest Lake Baikal, the Nile and Amazon Rivers. I was drinking the Great Lakes, the Yangtze of China, and all the waters that have flowed through my ancestors' veins, through the fluid-pumping hearts of all the people of this land and other continents, through all the transpiring trees, all the plants, insects, fish, and mammals from all time, since the beginning of this unusual and marvelous watery blue sphere we call home.

Reason alone cannot know what water is, because the heart and spirit that guide it follow rivers of consciousness delicately strung upon a million moons that have circled the Earth, pulling the waters to and fro, within and without, for countless cycles. We cannot live without water; that much we know for sure, and we are all connected in the great life-stream.

After some minutes, I was amazed to feel how quickly my thirst was quenched. I promised myself to remember always the Great Wanting. I looked into Vision Creek and felt the water looking back at me. "I will never forget you," I whispered to the stream of life.

Then, I jumped in. All the long morning, as cold as the creek was, I was entirely an aquatic creature. Laying in the sun to warm, offering gratitude to every stone, flower, bee, and leaf, I began to think about my mother feeding me milk from her breast and how milk is our very first liquid when we are born. I suddenly had an immense urge to see my mother and recognized that it was time to meet with people again. Family and friends were calling, and I drank from Vision Creek one last time, knowing that this was how I would gather the strength to walk home.

I set the two little wood, leaf, and berry dolls near a gentle pool and bowed a fond goodbye to the singing creek whose waters I now had become.

I must tell the whole story, because later, there was a different song—one of unnatural silence.

Several years later, on a break from my university studies, I hiked in to Vision Creek to pay homage and to listen to the stream's water songs, only to discover that the beautiful creek was no longer running.

Total silence. There was nothing but a bit of moisture in the ravine. No moving water. No more flute music. No more lyrical splashes. No more secret poems. No more swirling hymns. No more mirrored pools. Simply, no more flowing water. Fish would no longer swim here; the creek was dead and dry. There was a lump in my throat the size of the ocean, and I later learned that a poorly executed timber operation some miles upstream had silted the entire creek out of existence.

Upon seeing the unexpected and unwatery grave of my lovely creek, an eerie sound issued unprompted from deep within my body like that of storm waves ferociously slamming cliffs.

I recalled the words of Suquamish Chief Seattle when his tribe was forced to transfer their lands to the federal government in 1855: "The shining water that moves in the streams and rivers is not just water but the blood of our ancestors. If we sell you our land, you must remember that it is sacred…"[4]

I lay down in the meadow, and the entire mountain seemed to grieve with me. I pledged in that moment to give my voice to the creek, to the waters.

There are times—and we are seeing many more of them—when we need to make a stand for protecting our Earth and to voice her stories and needs. Even if we are not understood at first or are thwarted in our efforts, it is one of the most important things we can do as individuals of courage and compassion.

There are a hundred thousand ways to do this, and each person can find his or her own way that stirs personal passion, from water justice campaigns to watershed restoration projects, from education to the arts. Each voice is a rivulet adding to the river of necessary life-sustaining power and momentum capable of changing the course of our human relationship to water. Every drop counts. Every contribution to the combined flow of change for the better is valuable.

The little creek continues even now, in its stillness, to sculpt my character and influence my thoughts and actions. The ever-changing melody strung on Vision Creek's liquid turbulence, cascading through forest and meadow, splashing upon stones—this ancient anthem streams through my veins still. I will not forget. You have given life to me, and so it is that I came to the water, so it is that I must sing water's praises still.

9 Hypatia's Pearls: Democracy Ancient and Modern

In the twilight, colorful illuminations sparkle and glance across the Aegean Sea—bright, undulating gemstones reflecting the Grecian full moon in a path of sapphires, emeralds, rubies, and diamonds. I am huddled near the shore with my two companions: Lydia, a fine painter especially adept in the use of color, and Litsa, a leading Greek archeologist. We use the last of the day's light to touch the land fully again with our eyes. We are in northern Greece, in Thessaly. It is June.

The object of our immediate attention is a small flower, a marguerite, growing in a low meadow at our feet. This flower adorns many ancient fresco borders throughout the islands of Greece. No more than an inch in diameter, the delicate white daisy is named after a pearl. The French name "Marguerite" is derived from the Greek "margaritos," both meaning "pearl." In Germany, this same flower is known as the Meadow Pearl.

Pearls, both those of the sea and of the meadow, were worn by women portrayed in the Grecian and Minoan temples of antiquity, especially those found on the island of Crete. Elegant marguerite hairpins fashioned of gold were found in Cretan palaces, and folklore indicates that it is possible "marguerite" actually refers to the island of Crete. The root word "mar" means ocean or sea, and befittingly, the island of Crete was known in ancient times as the Pearl of the Sea.

While Litsa, Lydia, and I admire a carpet of little white flowers we recall a recent journey we took to Crete, where we met an elderly woman, Oresteia, who shared with us stories of her frightful childhood, when Hitler's army came to her island. The German soldiers killed many Cretan resistance fighters and tortured women in her village. The Germans made plans to come after the young girls for their use and pleasure, but the Cretans cleverly and bravely took the targeted women and girls to a high mountain cave to hide them. Later, resistance fighters caught the Germans in a firefight at a narrow pass. The girls, including Oresteia, were thus spared, but her village was burned to the ground by the retreating German soldiers. That year, many people perished from starvation and cold since food and fuel supplies were destroyed, but still the town prevailed, she told us.

This emboldened sense of resilience captured my heart. A spirited vivaciousness still lives not only on Crete but also in the Greeks I met throughout my excursion. My companions explained to me the Greek pride they have always felt, as do their fellow citizens. During World War II, when many European countries were collapsing under Hitler's armies, the Greek resistance continued, lasting longer there than anywhere else. Greece repelled the Fascist Italians in 1940, marking the first Allied victory in the war, and only then did Hitler send in troops to secure his southern flank. In Crete, however, there was such ferocity of combat by Cretan civilians and Allied Forces that many historians argue the struggle caused the fatal delay of the German invasion into the Soviet Union. The Germans, forced to postpone an autumn attack, met their famous defeat outside Moscow in the bitter Russian winter of 1941.

This Greek sense of independence and autonomy is longstanding. Greek national history includes surviving Turkish Ottoman rule from the fifteenth century until Greece's declaration of independence in 1821. During this time of widespread Turkish occupation, Greek Christians created secret schools where children were taught to speak the forbidden Greek language and learned their denied history.

As my colleagues spoke about Greek history, their eyes seemed as bright and sparkling as the gemlike ripples of the moonlit Aegean. We sat in a field speckled with marguerites while dusk turned to night. The full moon rose higher in the hilly eastern sky, and I suddenly lost my breath as I realized that this white sphere is, in fact, the pearl of the heavens. Throughout these Mediterranean lands and into Egypt, the marguerite flower is known as a representation of the full moon, and the flower is commonly called the Moon Daisy. Gazing at the luminescent white beauty, we wondered on this night just how many other women might be looking toward our shared moon. We imagined women gathered together under the full moon throughout the ages, beyond nationality and time, into the greater mysteries of life and the universe.

I had come to Greece primarily to explore installation sites for my sculptures and to speak at a Culture, Art, and Environment seminar that I had been invited to convene.

Beyond these professional pursuits, the allure of touring Greece, for me as for many, held the promise of a timeless encounter with some of the oldest of our philosophers, artists, scholars, and poets who speak through the epochs with eloquence and seamless relevance to us today. Throughout the country, grand architecture and monumental yet humanistic art reflect a continuum of sophisticated design, while Greek philosophic, scientific, and cultural accomplishments still provide enduring and utterly pertinent wisdom.

"Hellas," as the Greeks call their homeland, is a beacon of historical light that has shined the world over. Each time the greeting "hello" is exchanged, I am reminded of the depth of influence Greek culture and language has had here in America. The word "helles" means light, and the ancient Greeks called themselves the Hellenes, meaning the people of light. Their Goddess was Helen, who was the Goddess of Light, and her male counterpart, Helios, was the God of Light. When we in America greet one another on a daily basis, we are exchanging, through an ancient Greek tradition, the acknowledgment that we dwell in a world of light.

The following day, after our evening beneath the "pearl moon," my colleagues and I visited Athens, lured by the city's prodigious mythology and history. Litsa reminded me that the city is one of the oldest metropolises in the world: Athens dates back more than three millennia and has long been considered the cradle of Western civilization. The city-state of Athens was known throughout the ancient world for its dedication to the pursuit of knowledge and philosophical attainment as well as for the awe-inspiring beauty of the city's architecture and artistry, which embody these marvelous humanistic quests. What artist of our current era has not dreamed of spending countless days gazing upon the superlative craft and artistry of early Greece?

Athens is also the celebrated birthplace of democracy and its ideals. "The noblest motive," wrote Virgil, "is the public good."[1] The ancient Greeks considered it essential that citizens of the polis participate to actively create this public good, if there was to be one. To Athenians, politics meant that each voting citizen needed to directly and frequently engage the larger issues of the community and be well educated about all public matters, a sentiment of continued and vast global importance today.

Navigating on foot through the congested streets of modern-day Athens, conversing about governance and antiquities, my friends and I made our way to our destination and immediately fell speechless. The Parthenon could do this to anyone, I imagine.

I had never before experienced historical architecture in the same way one might behold a magnificent old-growth forest. The Parthenon's remaining marble pillars, rising up from the Acropolis far above us, generated this sort of lofty awe. The great white stone "trunks" stood tall and majestic atop the plain of Attica. The ancient temple of Athena, built in the fifth century BCE and surrounded on three sides by steep, luminous limestone outcroppings, is the essential symbol of ancient Greece itself and the ideal of Athenian democracy. The columns of the Parthenon, although eroded and cracked from exposure, still radiated their ancient dignity and wisdom unabated.

We three climbed slowly to the summit in the tawny afternoon light. The words of Walt Whitman came to mind as I was finally able to run my curious fingers along the legendary marble ridges:

> We have frequently printed the word Democracy. Yet I cannot too often repeat that it is a word the real gist of which still sleeps, quite unawaken'd, notwithstanding the resonance and the many angry tempests out of which its syllables have come, from pen or tongue. It is a great word, whose history, I suppose, remains unwritten, because that history has yet to be enacted. It is, in some sort, younger brother of another great and often-used word, Nature, whose history also waits unwritten.[2]

The ancient Greek word *demokratia* means, literally, "people power." However, as is usually the case, the political sphere is never tidy in its evolution, and so we must critically question the actual power that is granted to people in governments claiming to be democratic: Who were/are the people so empowered to act democratically? The Athenian democracy of the fifth and sixth centuries strictly gave only male citizens the privilege of democratic government. Women, men not of Athenian descent, and slaves (who were the majority of the population) were completely excluded from any political representation or voice. Since then, the definition and enactment of democratic governance has been an ideal in constant transformation, formation, and reformation.

In this sense, democracy should be more likened to a verb than a noun. In America, as in other democratic countries, we are in the process of democratizing. As Whitman reminds us, there is still a deeper democracy yet to be awakened, and I would venture that, once more eyes open from slumber, this last century's progress will be only the beginning of democracy's morning exercises. In 2008, for the very first time in United States history, both a woman and an African-American took center stage in the presidential elections. With the historical election of President Barack Obama, the ideal of equality and opportunity for all, so central to our democratic constitution, took another critical step forward into reality.

To understand the evolution of American democracy and to assess its further motion forward, it might be helpful to look into some of its often-overlooked origins. In the structural DNA or in the origins of any endeavor, we often find helpful and restorative instructions. One component I would like to explore briefly here is that of American Indian influence.

The first American settlers from Europe were amazed at the personal freedom and equality possessed by the American Indians. In their written reports about the native populations, settlers often commented on the equal liberty and social standing of each person, especially noting that it was not based on property ownership. The example of people living in a primarily peaceful and prosperous society, governed by regional councils without the rule of monarchy or feudalism, and, furthermore, not even dictated by rank conferred by landedness, exerted a profound influence upon the colonists. Twentieth-century historian Charles C. Mann recounts the words of eighteenth-century colonial administrator Cadwallader Colden. Commenting about the Haudenosaunee people (meaning The People Building a Long House), he observed that they had "such absolute Notions of Liberty, that they allow of no Kind of Superiority of one over another, and banish all Servitude from their Territories."[3]

These observations of personal freedom, equality, and new forms of governance soon were communicated to Britain and then throughout Europe, where scholars and philosophers became enthralled with questions concerning changes to the reigning monarchies and longstanding aristocracies. Voltaire and Rousseau were two of the great minds of this time we call the Age of Enlightenment, and they generously drew upon American Indian worldviews in formulating their arguments and expositions.

The experience of freedom also awakened European-Americans, stirring memories of Athens and Sparta, which had powerfully experimented with forms of representative democracy. In addition to these early proto-European models, the founders of American democracy studied and evaluated different systems of Indian councils with whom they had direct contact. In particular, the Council of Haudenosaunee, or, as it was later named, The Iroquois Confederacy, was well known to and in various degrees attended by George Washington, Thomas Jefferson, Charles Thompson, Thomas Paine, and Ben Franklin, the last of whom wrote:

> It would be a very strange Thing, if Six Nations of ignorant Savages should be capable of forming a Scheme for such an Union, and be able to execute it in such a Manner, as that it has subsisted Ages, and appears indissoluble; and yet that a like Union should be impracticable for ten or a Dozen English Colonies, to whom it is more necessary, and must be more advantageous; and who cannot be supposed to want an equal Understanding of their Interests.[4]

The Iroquois Confederacy was a group of five, then later six, American Indian nations that unified to create what was the major political entity in the Northeast at the time of colonization. The nations included the Cayugas, Mohawks, Oneidas, Onondagas, Senecas, and, later, the Tuscaroras, who migrated into Iroquois country in the early eighteenth century. In great part, this united confederacy was formed in reaction to the European threat. And, it was quite a contrast to European models of governance. Instead of a strictly hierarchical top-down rule, it offered governance by councils of elected officials. The political leaders of the Iroquois Confederacy, called *sachems*, did not gain their positions or rank by heredity, as was common in Europe, but rather by election. Leadership based on merit demonstrated an entirely new understanding of both individual citizens and society. Additionally, the *sachems* could be removed from office if necessary. Contrary to the European tradition in which a monarch ruled until death, even when unpopular or unfit to lead, the Iroquois Confederacy included a tradition of "impeachment" for leaders who did not fulfill their duties.

Today, American scholars from different disciplines argue about the level of Indian influence in the design of American democracy, debating how much direct influence, if any, there was. Perhaps the most important thing to acknowledge, in any case, is the undeniable impact upon European-Americans by American Indian culture as colonists experienced, for the first time, the benefits of the individual freedom and personal respect due each person that the Iroquois lived by and demonstrated. The Iroquois Confederacy provided a highly tuned and ingenious model of dialogue and deliberation, and one that included female leadership and decisions based on the future of the next seven generations.

From a broad view, there are many combined streams that form the river we call American democracy, a blending of ancient Greek and Roman efforts, French political theory, the spirit of a new-minded group of settlers, and the sophisticated American Indian law of councils and confederacies. Studying and acknowledging this unique historical blend might shed new insight upon and add strength to the further "enactment" of the story of democracy called for by Walt Whitman in *Democratic Vistas*.

In his 1871 treatise, Whitman prophetically claims that not only democracy's story but nature's history "also waits unwritten."[5] That Whitman so closely associates democracy with nature seems particularly appropriate for our times. How can we truly embrace democracy without simultaneously acknowledging nature? It is clear, given current societal and environmental crises that threaten all life on Earth as we know it, that we need an integrated system of governance informed by the self-balancing model and example of Nature. It is inherent within most if not all Indigenous world views that in order to live in a sustainable society the human laws of the people need to remain in balance with the natural laws of the Earth. During the time of the land-based Celts on the British Isles, a person cutting down a tree was required by law to plant the seed for a new tree in its place. For traditional people everywhere, there is no such thing as having a society separate from the Earth upon which it lives. The community's well-being is completely integrated with care for its land—from sustained harvests to sustainable living.

Respecting nature's laws is obviously not only essential to designing ecologically sustainable lifestyles and governance but also to fair and just representation of all sentient beings. One of the most important laws of nature is the equilibrium of female and male; all life depends upon this remarkable natural dynamic. To reflect this natural law of the biosphere that is Earth, many Indigenous councils took great care in balancing male and female leadership. It was understood that a truly representative government and leadership based upon choices and agreements between *all* humans required the governing body to have adequate balance of power between men and women.

Iroquois society was (and is) matrilineal and a society in which women have always been deeply respected. In their confederacy, women elected the leaders and had the power to impeach them. The East Coast Powhatan-Renape Iroquois are descendents of a confederation that at one time unified more than thirty Indigenous nations. The leader of this confederation from approximately 1657 until 1715 was Queen Anne of Pamunkey Village, who played a prominent role in early Virginian history.

Awashonks, who led her people in the seventeenth century, was a woman chieftain of the Sakonnet, a tribe of the Mid-Atlantic region.

Nanyehi, or Nancy Ward, as the English called her, was the head of the Cherokee Women's Council and a member of the Council of Chiefs. In 1755, she became Ghigau, meaning Beloved Woman, after her bravery in battle and later demonstration of extraordinary diplomacy skills. Nanyehi was a lead speaker at treaty negotiations after Europeans invaded Cherokee lands. She was an advocate of peaceful relations, saying, "Let your women hear our words."[6] Unfortunately, women colonists had no voice in politics; yet, Nanyehi's appeal to the European settler women makes us wonder what would have happened if they did. These are just a few examples of American Indian women leaders.

Although the founders of American democracy were influenced by the American Indian confederations, unfortunately they overlooked that essential component of gender equity in governance. Even after many courageous and sustained struggles, it was not until 1920 that women in the United States finally gained the right to vote. Still, there continues to be a large gap in balanced societal leadership in American politics, and we have yet to elect a woman president. With nature's model in mind, where is the dynamic equipoise of male and female fully practiced in our leadership?

———

Litsa, Lydia, and I looked out over the city of Athens from the Acropolis, as if gazing out at the ocean from the prow of a ship. We sailed the vessel of our imaginations to an earlier time, when the Parthenon was first built and dedicated to the Goddess Athena, who gives this great city her name.

The Athena of antiquity, of pre-classical times, actually had a multitude of names, identities, and myths, as did many deities of old. In his book *The White Goddess*, poet and historian Robert Graves cites scholar E.M. Parr's view that Athene was an inversion of Anatha, also known as Neith of Libya. Parr also states that "An" is Sumerian for "Heaven."[7] With this in mind, I suggest that Athena is connected to many ancient "Ana" Goddesses, which are Creatress Mothers. Some of her earliest names and close associations were with Anath, Athirat, and Ashtoreth. In her earlier origins, she was known as the Canaanite Mother of All. In the understanding of her as an ancient Great Mother Goddess, her name was Asherah among the Phoenicians and the Hebrews, and from Ugarit, the language of the ancient Canaanites of what is now Syria, her name was Athirat. This last name resonates even more with the idea of Athena because it was these early Syrians who phonetically codified language enough to make it teachable to all, thereby removing the power and mystery of the written word from the exclusive class of scribes and those they served. Two millennia later, this democratizing knowledge came to Greece, and the Greeks added written vowels to the consonants that made up written language, making it even easier for the commoner to grasp and use.

The worship of Asherah goes back to Sumer and beyond, where she was called Ashratum. In Egypt, Ashtoreth was known as Asit (much like the Egyptians' Au Set or Female Principle energy).

Over the centuries, beautifully sculpted figurines of Asherah have been discovered by the thousands in present-day Israel and Palestine. These figures have been numerous and ubiquitous, found in open valleys, near rivers, under trees, on mountains, and atop stone altars.

One of this Goddess' titles in both Phoenicia (modern-day Lebanon) and parts of North Africa was Tanith; she was known as a guide and protector of sea travelers. In this form, she was shown often accompanied by dolphins or fish. The symbol of Tanith or Tanit was a full-skirted woman in a pyramidal shape standing with upraised arms and a crescent or full moon overhead. Another ancient symbol of Tanith was the well-known sign of healers, still recognized today—the caduceus, which depicts two serpents twined around a tree or rod known as an Asherah pole.

This tree and pole are significant because one of the most important aspects and meanings of Asherah is that of the Sacred Tree of Life. Often, the Goddess Asherah was honored as a holy tree and worshipped as the Great Mother in special groves.

The portrayal of this Goddess as Ath-enna, An-at, or Athirat can also be associated with the early Egyptian Goddess Ma-at, Maat, or Mast, also equated with the measuring mast of the ancient ships of the sea-going people. The Asherah pole can be viewed as the center pole, mast, or tree of the ships of the ancient Greeks and Hebrews.

Asherah was known to Hebrews of both the north and south, in Jerusalem, Samaria, and Bethel. She was represented by her sacred tree or pole in the First Temple in Jerusalem for well over two centuries before the temple was destroyed by the Babylonians in 586 BCE when they sacked the entire city. This same divine figure was also known as Anath or Atteena in North Africa, later to become the more familiar Athena of classical Greece, who was imbued over time with further meanings and symbols associated with wisdom, war, weaving, and council. Throughout Greece today, we see statues of this classical Athena adorned in battle gear or with her familiar owl, who represents wisdom.

Voyaging further in my musings upon history, I ponder how delicate is the sapling tree of democracy and freedom. Can the little tree rise as a center pole or great mast on board the Ship of the World upon the tumultuous rising seas of our day and those to come? As my friends and I continued our conversation, Lydia offered the startling news to me that it was only in 1829, with the liberation of the Greeks from the Ottoman Turks, that democracy began to flower again in Greece, absent as it had been since 338 BCE. Yes, that is more than two thousand years! Even as it is noted as the birthplace of democracy, Greece has had a fragmented history with its own governmental invention. The original Athenian polis, beginning with the democratic reforms of Solon in 594 BCE, was a democracy that lasted only 250 years. After its demise—attributed to the Greek defeat in battle with Sparta in 431 BCE, which Athens provoked, and then complete summation when Athens was defeated by Philp of Macedonia in 338 BCE—it took millennia for Greece to return to this original form of governance. Edward Gibbon, the eighteenth-century British historian, wrote of this: "In the end more than they wanted freedom, they wanted security. When the Athenians finally wanted not to give to society but for society to give to them, when the freedom they wished for was freedom from responsibility, then Athens ceased to be free."[8]

As the twenty-first century sets its course, here in America it seems especially prudent to study the lessons of democratic history.

The day after our excursion to the Acropolis, Lydia and I met with the Honorable Margaret Papandreou to explore the idea of installing one of my statues in Athens. Mrs. Papandreou is the American-born former First Lady of Greece, now widowed but still working in the public sphere as a strong advocate of peace and women's rights. Her late husband, President Andreas Papandreou, was involved in politics as a reformer in the early 1960s. He served as a leading Member of Parliament in the Centre Union, a political party founded by his father, George Papandreou. In 1967, a military junta overthrew the democratic government, and Andreas Papandreou was jailed as Greek generals installed a military regime. He and Margaret were exiled until 1974, when democracy was restored to the country due to civil protests, a failed Greek military invasion of Cypress, and consequent withdrawal of support by Western powers of the Greek regime, all of which contributed to its collapse. Many former leaders returned to the country soon thereafter, and an election was held. Citizens not only voted for a democracy but for a republic, finally ending the old monarchy. When Papandreou returned, he established the new political party PASOK (social-democratic Panhellenic Socialist Movement) and, in 1981, was elected Prime Minister.

Soon after her return to the country, Margaret Papandreou founded the Women's Union of Greece, an organization to fight for changes in women's legal status within the family and the labor force. She also has been very successful at connecting Greek women activists to the global women's movement. In thinking about our upcoming meeting, I could not help but notice the derivation of her name—from Marguerite, the moon-ocean daisy of Greek lore—another remarkable pearl discovered on my journey.

En route to her home, we drove past a life-sized bronze statue of President Truman, commemorating the end of World War II and

American support of Greece. As we whizzed by the bronze figure, Lydia nonchalantly commented, "Oh, he's back again." Catching the perplexed look on my face, she informed me that every so often, but on a rather regular basis, groups claiming to be Marxists or Anarchists bomb the Truman statue to bits. Then, somehow, the figure dutifully is made whole again. Lydia further explained that Truman has friends and enemies alike in Greece. Some say that Truman is Greece's greatest benefactor because after the war, when Greece had its own power struggle, he armed Greece with airplanes, cannons, and even mules imported from Missouri, to help with the fight against the Communists. On the other hand, Marxists or Anarchists in Athens see Truman as the Father of the Cold War and have anti-American sentiments toward what he symbolizes. They associate his economic and military aid, even though not directly related, as later supporting an oppressive totalitarian regime in Greece (widely criticized for its human rights record) that had overthrown the center right government in 1967. Nearly forty years later, President Bill Clinton issued an apology for the United States' past support of the military junta.

The bombing of Truman's statue came to mind again some years later as I set to recording my journey to Hellas. Coincidentally, Lydia called to inform me that the American Embassy had just been bombed. Since the beginning of the Iraq war in 2003, the distaste in Greece for American international politics, not surprisingly, had grown considerably. During the same visit of which I write, we met at the embassy to discuss my public art project with the American ambassador Nicholas Burns. The Marxists, Lydia told me, had just blown up part of the very same third-floor room in which we had met, as well as the adjacent public bathroom. Apparently, the bombers were not trying to kill anyone, Lydia clarified; they were actually aiming their rocket at the embassy shield (a large disc on the outside of the building displaying the embassy's coat of arms) but missed. Instead, the munitions went off inside the ambassador's reception room. Fortunately, the ambassador, his staff, and the public escaped harm that day.

As a concerned American artist, I wondered what I could do to help mend this terrible tear in international relations. The words of Kofi Annan, then Secretary General of the United Nations, came to mind: "Artists have a special role to play in the global struggle for peace. At their best, artists speak not only to people; they speak for them. Art is a weapon against ignorance and hatred and an agent of public awareness. Art opens new doors for learning, understanding and peace among peoples and nations."[9] These are words I have hanging above my design table in my art studio.

We drove north from Athens through a landscape of silvery stone mountains on our way to the Culture, Art, and Environment event where I had been asked to speak. Creatures shaped of rugged rock appeared as the Grecian Gods and Goddesses that have never forsaken this land of theirs. Passing by ancient olive groves and vineyards with the azure-blue Mediterranean gracing the horizon, I suddenly knew the story that I wanted to share at the upcoming seminar.

I had researched Hypatia, a remarkable Greek teacher who studied in Athens and taught in Alexandria during the late 300s and early 400s CE. As the head of the Platonist school at Alexandria, Hypatia dedicated her life to promoting traditional Greek rational thought. It greatly dismayed me that, like so many remarkable women, all mention of Hypatia had been omitted from most history text books. Because religious zealots destroyed so much information about the past, the primary source of our current knowledge about Hypatia comes from the remaining letters of one of her students, Synesius of Cyrene, who later became the Bishop of Ptolemais. As one of the most renowned mathematicians of her time, she edited *The Conics of Apollonius*, which provided the fundamental ideas for hyperbolas, parabolas, and ellipses. As a leading astronomer, Hypatia wrote *The Astronomical*

Canon, likened by later scholars to Ptolemy's *Handy Tables.* She also designed such tools for scientific research and measurement as the astrolabe and hydroscope.

Clearly, her discoveries and teachings belong next to the great works of the familiar Greek stars: Socrates, Plato, and Aristotle. I thought to myself, if one of the necessary balancing forces in nature is woman's equality with man, the brave and brilliant Hypatia was certainly an example to be remembered and included in our histories. Yet, it is not only because of gender or as an academic anomaly for the times that she is significant. Hypatia's life also marks a peak historical moment when scientific inquiry, so central to a true democracy, was to be silenced and cast into a dungeon for some centuries. Hypatia's story seemed a poignant example for discussion at the seminar, as leaders and opinion-makers in our current century struggle in truth-telling, from honest environmental and economic analysis to the import of women's pivotal role as societal change-makers.

With a desire to inspire the seminar participants, I told the story as follows, based on my historical research.[10]

The Valley of Thessaly, 420 CE

The new acquaintances, Clio and Philomena, slowly walked along the precipice to an outcropping of stones where they could safely sit and look out over the valley spread below them.

"As I promised, Philomena," began Clio, after a thoughtful silence spent gazing into the distant hills, "I will tell you of the scholar with whom I had the great honor to study in Alexandria, a teacher by the name Hypatia. I traveled to study with this learned woman some years ago." As soon as Clio had spoken Hypatia's name, her eyes brimmed with tears and she quickly turned her face to hide them from Philomena's questioning gaze.

In a low voice, resuming her composure, Clio began her story:

"As a mountain woman from Olympus, and proud of this I will add, you must understand how amazing it was for me to see the grand city of Alexandria. My first days before meeting the great philosopher, I walked the town. My eyes burned at night because I hardly blinked the entire day long, not wishing to miss any of the unfamiliar beauty, although the city was already in decline from the height of its splendor a century before, and some monuments and great buildings were already in ruins."

Remembering her excitement about the city helped quell the pain. "Shimmering white marble temples and fine sculptures adorned the town. Beyond the flowering trees that embraced the city roads like jeweled necklaces, you could see the great port where ships from far lands were anchored.

"Glowing day and night as brilliant as a star shining on Earth, the famed Lighthouse of Alexandria marked the port harbor. At the top of the lighthouse, a magnificent curved mirror reflected sunlight during the day while a continuously burning fire provided light during the night. Sailors claim they can see the light from great distances that go beyond logical sense. The design of the lighthouse is only one of many marvels that I experienced in the old city, but, perhaps more importantly, it was the culture of the city that impressed me the most.

"I was able to see the vestiges of a great city that at one time was at peace with its widely diverse population and mixture of nationalities, trades, and beliefs. Yes, the city was still rich with culture and full of travelers from abroad; on every street, I heard languages from places I cannot name. It was in this city that Hypatia taught students from all over the world. She was so loved as a central figure in Alexandria that a letter sent from anywhere addressed informally "To the Philosopher" would be delivered to her as a matter of course. To understand the importance of her life, you need first to know of the tumultuous time in Alexandria and the decay of the Great Library that has now almost completely vanished.

"The location of this greatest of libraries was, not by mere happenstance, built in Alexandria, at the crossroads of many great lands. The library was part of the ancient temple and museum located in Bruchion, near the palaces and royal gardens. This temple-school held a wealth of information and wisdom: ship building, geography, mathematics, international diplomacy, law, hygiene, agriculture, medicine, business records, chemistry, metallurgy, art, music, textiles, war strategies, and practically every other matter of concern to educated citizens as well as civic leaders.

"The atmosphere of the great library welcomed visitors and scholars alike with lecture and dining halls and beautiful courtyard gardens. Everyone who studied or taught there could see the famous inscription, 'The place of the cure of the soul' carved into the wall of the main hall, which contained the vast collections of irreplaceable scrolls.

"Sadly, the Great Library of Alexandria has been repeatedly damaged over the years by fire and war, and now only the tiniest fraction of the knowledge therein has been saved. Some say that, as before, the Library will have another renewal after these terrible times in the city, but I do not know.

"The most recent unrest at the Library was at one of its temples and was instigated by Pope Theophilus, who ordered the destruction of the Temple of Serapis. You see a great conflict had been stirred between a faction of the newly ruling Christians, earlier Christian groups, and the older Pagan establishment, a conflict that continues today.

"Theophilus knew, like others of the expanding regime, that as long as Pagan temples or records of the old knowledge and sciences existed, people would not truly embrace the new religion. Theophilus gained permission from Rome to destroy the Serapeum, in order to better exile the Pagans from their place of gathering. Some have reported that the destructive fire at the temple was also meant to burn the adjacent library, thereby eliminating precious knowledge and carefully documented histories that might contradict the Pope's view of things. The vast structure of the temple was burned to the ground, and the huge flames could be seen and felt throughout the streets of Alexandria.

"Hypatia was in the city and witnessed this assault, and when she spoke of it to me, her grief was clear to see. The spirit of the citizens of Alexandria was greatly injured by this terrible atrocity; it was a grave wound, Hypatia said.

"Because Hypatia experienced these attacks on the temples of learning firsthand, I honored her courage all the more for continuing to teach in public when clearly the new city atmosphere was anything but welcoming or tolerant. As the leaders of the new ruling religious order slowly strangled the free flow of knowledge not to their liking, it became more difficult than ever to openly teach the earth sciences, mathematics, and the old mysteries, but Hypatia never faltered in her commitment to pass on all that she knew to her pupils.

"Not only were the new religionists destroying Pagan temples, but they were working to destroy ancient knowledge by rewriting the histories, translating and transcribing them to fit their preferred worldview.

"I found these attacks very confusing because many of my Christian friends here in Thessaly and from Alexandria hold violence in great disdain and instead follow more closely the words of peace and kindness from their religious founder, a gentle carpenter from Galilee across the sea.

"But please, there is so much to say about the erudite and deeply courageous Hypatia, and I wish to speak of her further now as a way of keeping her memory alive. She was a remarkable philosopher and diplomat who taught of the scientific mystery and beauty of the Earth and all the Cosmos. Prior to the new religionists' arrival in the city, she was admired and respected by the ruling elite of Alexandria and dearly beloved by her disciples. Because she was dedicated to educational freedom, Hypatia rejected any involvement in religious or other such rivalries, and she remained open-minded toward all spiritual beliefs, including Judaism and Christianity. In fact, many of her friends were Christians. It was only after the arrival of the new patriarch, Bishop Cyril, who came to rule over Alexandria, that Hypatia suddenly became feared and hated by a small but dangerous group of Alexandrians.

"Throughout many lands, important politicians called upon the famous philosopher to request her advice on matters of philosophy and state, and she held powerful cultural and political positions throughout the city of Alexandria. Many of Hypatia's most loyal students were men who later rose to prominence politically and socially, and, of course, this made her dangerous in the eyes of Cyril, because he considered her teachings heretical.

"She was, as I said, a prominent teacher of mathematics and astronomy, as well as of earth sciences and ancient mysteries; thus, her lectures and discourses attracted the most dedicated scholars. However, upon his arrival in the city, Bishop Cyril immediately forbade young Christians from attending her lectures because he did not want them experiencing her powerful presence or enthusiasm for natural science and ancient earth philosophy. Hypatia's love of earth knowledge and all the classical Greek sciences was completely unacceptable to the new religious factions in Alexandria. I say factions because there were other Christian groups in the city that respected the original tenets of tolerance in the teachings of Jesus. Clearly, a chaotic power struggle with religious implications was underway in Hypatia's Alexandria.

"But let me tell you yet more about this venerated teacher. Hypatia was well tutored from youth, bestowing upon her an un-rivaled and unrestricted education that her learned father, Theon, himself a mathematician, scholar, teacher, and writer, made possible. As she grew into young adulthood, her friends and teachers were some of the greatest scientists and thinkers of Alexandria, all of whom challenged her to question and explore her world. Hypatia excelled in philosophy and mathematics, and eventually she made her own mathematical discoveries and developed scientific instruments such as astrolabes with which to study the stars. The young woman also immersed herself in poetry and the arts, developing rhetorical skills in speech and personal presentation.

"Particularly inspiring to me was not just her lecture subjects, but how she taught them. Hypatia spoke most eloquently of the beauty of nature and the cosmos. She could describe the cycles of the moon with such gracious poetics as to elicit reverie as well as scientific enthusiasm. We often studied outside in her garden, overlooking the great port, and sometimes at night in order to observe the stars and other heavenly bodies. Astronomy was one of her most beloved sciences because, she said, it brought valuable measure to the human mind. Moreover, no other scholar could claim as much dedication to truth, to the value of observation, as she.

"Hypatia taught that in order to best gain inner wisdom and to understand the very beauty of knowledge, we must ourselves be beautiful. She had forceful words for students who did not want to internalize this basic truth: to care for the self and to know the beauty of one's self was of the highest good.

"Hypatia shared with us her devotion to the Goddess of Wisdom, also known by her ancient name, Sophia. She explained to us that a philo-sopher is a lover of Sophia, *philo* meaning love, Sophia meaning wisdom.

"She asked us how we could invite ourselves and humanity to be inspired and excited with the love of wisdom and knowledge. Knowledge is not a single spark but rather a continuing fire that all—together and individually—must keep alive if they wish to learn and grow their entire lives. She asked us to contemplate the reward of experiencing the presence of Sophia in our own lives, how much happier we are when motivated with direction and growth and curiosity, tending to the bright fire of our mind. Should this flame be dimmed, she warned, the heart would also dim and humans would fill this void with domination and violence.

"Hypatia taught us to question our world and allow the mysteries of life to move us to higher levels of thought. True self-inspiration demands continuous energy, and to keep the fire of our minds burning bright, we need to contemplate deeply and study life fully each day. This depth is achieved through self-observation and by developing knowledge about and appreciation for all of creation. When we know ourselves, we then can see the world in a clearer and more honest light, less encumbered by our attitudes or outside forces.

"For many years, people dedicated to the old traditions and earth sciences had been subtly persecuted throughout the city, but things grew steadily worse under the rule of Cyril. Unquestionably, Hypatia would garner no respect from this new ruler, no matter what she did or did not do.

"Cyril intensified religious schisms and demanded the eradication of all spiritual disciplines that did not uphold his own orthodox beliefs. He deported longstanding citizens and leaders out of the city and eliminated many others. As religious tensions exploded in the city, political tolerance for freedom and acceptance of diverse beliefs greatly diminished.

"Hypatia declared, along with the more courageous leaders of Alexandria, that the bishops and other religious leaders should not hold power in areas intended for imperial and city administration. She fought to keep a separation between expanding church control and normal municipal affairs, seeing that the two forces, once bonded together, would inevitably cost people their precious individual freedoms.

"The new patriarch also realized that Hypatia enjoyed a wide influence not only with the leaders of Alexandria; her disciples included many prominent dignitaries who ranged as far as Syria and Constantinople. Adding to the distress of Cyril was Hypatia's friendship with and influence among Roman functionaries and church leaders. Hypatia supported Orestes, the new imperial prefect of Alexandria, who strongly opposed Cyril's rule. This alliance further diminished the philosopher's position with the patriarch.

"Beyond her political ascendancy, Hypatia's teachings of earth science and rational philosophy posed substantial danger to Cyril's success as a bishop and to his agenda to gain personal power by appropriating full governance in Alexandria through ecclesiastical means. Furthermore, because of her tolerant views, she declaimed the rule of a single male godhead and male dominance in general.

"The fact that this great teacher was female also immediately threatened not only Cyril's authority, but also the natural rule of all men over all women, the latter population deemed virtuous or valuable only when submissive. Thus, the patriarch decided that he must ruin Hypatia and send the wisdom of the ancients into extinction with her.

"To stir the fear and anger of the city's most dangerous extremists, Cyril and his followers conspired together and began to circulate slanderous rumors attacking Hypatia's reputation.

"They told the citizens of Alexandria that this learned scholar was secretly a demonic sorceress who was using evil spells to control the good people of their fair city. The propagandists terrified the populace, saying that Hypatia was a fiendish entity, a witch skilled in the dark mantic arts. As a woman she was particularly vulnerable to claims of witchcraft. This vicious propaganda spread at a time when the city was in great turmoil anyway, as political and religious groups now openly fought in the streets. Cyril ensured that the blame for this unrest was laid at the feet of Hypatia and the high officials she supported.

"In time, the menacing assertions denigrating Hypatia bore the patriarch's desired outcome. A mob fired up by a circle of religious fanatics decided to murder the great philosopher and rid the city at last of this trouble-making woman.

"Early in the spring of my last year in Alexandria, Hypatia was returning home after a lecture in the city when she was torn from her chariot by a group of hate-filled men and hauled to the Church of Caesarion. They stripped her naked and then killed her by scraping flesh from her bones with broken bits of pottery. The mob brought her destroyed body to Kinaron, where it was thrown into a burning pyre."

Clio bit her lip to quell her tears. "Hypatia was brutally silenced by their treacherous deed," she whispered.

Philomena and Clio sat quietly, peering over the valley below, neither wishing to speak for some moments. Finally, Clio finished her tale:

"Tragically, Cyril and the instigators of the slander and those who actually murdered Hypatia were never punished for their heinous crime. With Hypatia's presence gone from the city, the open pursuit of knowledge with tolerance for differing world views—once a source of pride and identity for Alexandrians—has greatly suffered."

—✦—

That afternoon, Philomena and Clio walked toward the higher mountains to cast off the after effects of this grievous tale. The rocky trail twisted and climbed in an unexpected direction, exposing steep folds in the high mountains. To Philomena's wonderment and surprise, cradled in one of the uppermost mountain bowls was a hidden lake sculpted and formed by ice sheet and snow. Clio stood at the lakeshore. "Have you noticed the shape of this lake as you approached it from the trail?"

Philomena shook her head, indicating she had not. "Come stand here with me. You see the long rays that reach out from the center in all directions?" she explained as she drew her finger in the air, following the edge of the lake in a distinct pattern.

"The lake is in the shape of a star, and it is called the Lake of the Star Mirror. Like the stars overhead, the lake speaks to us of destiny. When we look into this shimmering mirror, the lake speaks to us of our life." Philomena now could see the star shape of the lake, as clear as the face on the moon, which, once revealed, is never forgotten.

Every evening, throughout the summer and autumn, Clio meditated with the magnificent lake, and at night, she watched the stars make their sky journey across the great mirror in reflection.

She could tell the changing seasons and the coming of greater and lesser natural events by peering into the blue sapphire waters. As her eyes rested upon the liquid mirror, she would dream. During the warm summer nights, when the magical water bowl held the prophetic constellating gems of the heavens, she would swim with the stars and open her mind to all of creation.

Clio explained: "The lake-mirror sees all and reflects our inner nature, our inner self. "Who are you?" asks the lake. We gaze upon the shining surface and see ourselves, who we are and who we can become. Our fears, pains, joys, ignorance, strengths, and weaknesses are all revealed by the lake, reflecting back to us our very essence."

That night after their walk up the mountain, Philomena sat by the lake as Clio spoke quietly, allowing the sounds of the lapping water to be heard though her words: "Every person has a star that belongs to and can guide each of them to their own destiny. This destiny is created by human choice. These choices become our life direction. Look above you and behold the fires in the sky; look about you and see the stars reflected in the waters; contemplate with the lake.

"The madness of our time swirls about us, violating innocence and stealing all reason. It is a madness and fear borne from ignorance and a great emptiness of heart. A madness like this feeds upon itself and begins to appear normal and so becomes all the more dangerous. Remember this, long and hard though the battle for reason and freedom may be: There is justice in time as long as we keep questioning and acting upon our better hopes and aspirations. Our lives, our actions, can effect a greater cycle. We can begin by asking ourselves: what does reason tell us? But we must also ask with our hearts; we can seek truth-telling of and with the heart.

"I think truth-telling is something we can give not only to ourselves, but also to the world. Giving our heartfelt truth is the question for us all in every age. Hypatia's courage and intelligence lives on through the giving of this story. What she gave her people lives on through the generations. There will always be daunting human sufferings, but how we face our challenges, and what we learn from and give of them, is our choice." With these words, Clio affixed a band of sea pearls on Philomena's head so that the lustrous white beads cascaded like glowing stars down her midnight-black hair.

⤙⤚

Several days after the ecology and culture seminar, we stopped at a small bookstore in nearby Volos. Litsa noticed a photograph of an ancient fresco representing three Cretan women wearing long strands of pearls elegantly wrapped in their hair. I couldn't help wondering who these pearl-clad women might be. And, with all this attention recently cast upon these precious beads, I began thinking about their actual origin. Pearls are formed in a most unexpected place and in a most surprising way. They gradually "grow," hidden inside the shells of certain mollusks; given the rather rough and rugged look and feel of these shelled creatures, one would hardly suspect the smooth round treasure held within.

The process begins as a response to an irritant, such as a parasite or just a grain of sand inside the shell. The mollusk surrounds the foreign entity with layers of crystalline calcium carbonate, which are held together by an organic hornlike compound called conchiolin. These layers are called the nacre, or, more commonly, mother-of-pearl.

Now, there is a thought I want never to forget. Nature reveals to us that luscious beauty and innovative design can be born, not only from some form of attraction or harmony, but also from an irritant.

As for the other pearls—those shaped by human consciousness and the pull of human evolution that we call pearls of wisdom— they, too, are often formed in unexpected places and in surprising ways. Provocative questions and hard-won decisions, grating injustices that stimulate the courage to imagine a different world and the bold actions they inspire—these are the irritants or seeds that generate such pearls of sagacity.

The pearl of modern democracy in America, even with its imperfections, began its formation with rebellion in response to the irritation of onerous rule from abroad. This resulted in independence from Old World tyranny, surely guided by American Indian examples of freedom and liberty.

The hard-won and magnificent pearl of a racially just government in South Africa was the direct result of Nelson Mandela's release from jail and rise to presidency. This pearl formation started with the irritant of the complete unacceptability of racial inequality, a modern stance sustained by enlightened governments worldwide.

The pearl of Martin Luther King Jr.'s dream of racial equality in the land of democracy and the pearl of courage worn by Rosa Parks when she refused to sit in the back of the bus were the outgrowth of defiance of the status quo. The pearl of women's suffrage in the 1920s was propelled further when women were first imprisoned for protesting for their rights, an act of civil disobedience such as those deemed necessary for democracy to truly thrive as described by writer-philosopher Henry David Thoreau in 1849. Only in exercising our right to follow our individual and collective conscience are these pearls possible; they are born of a necessary response to discomfort, not bountifully granted by higher-ups at their pleasure.

The pearl of Mohandas Gandhi's non-violent resistance movement, Satyagraha, was formed in response to British colonial rule (specifically, the irritant of unfair taxation). It led India to independence and inspired freedom movements around the world.

Rachel Carson's controversial against-the-grain book, *Silent Spring*, written in 1960, initiated the ecology movement we have today, and so was the turning point in worldwide environmental awareness. Carson herself had to endure personal censure, friction, and ill health to get her message out; it cost her dearly. The ecology movement is a pearl of great price and should be respected as such.

The colossal irritation of global climate change and its chaotic effects, the "inconvenient truth" named by American Vice President Al Gore, has the potential to propel an unprecedented global movement toward a new age of, we must hope, planet-saving sustainability—a pearl that might be described as the world itself, a world we can treasure and keep safe as the ultimate biologic jewel. We shall see.

Most of these ideas, revolutions, awakenings, and transformations at first seemed out of place, foreign to their home, perhaps frightening. Only later, with time and education—like the most brilliant iridescent sea pearls that come from the most densely overlapping of layers—did they become the beautiful and essential gems we now know them to be. All this to say, it is often agitation for a more beautiful and just world that gives rise to our collective pearls of wisdom and provides a vital force for a thriving democracy.

As I look upon the pearlescent full moon over the ancient Aegean Sea, I see that she shines with ageless luster through deep, long nights over an Earth that knows no borders when it comes to moonlight and wisdom.

10 Around the Fire: From Global Warming to a Renewed Hearth

In the time of distant knowledge when the flame made wise men think, metaphors were a form of thinking.
—GASTON BACHELARD

In the introduction to his book *The Psychoanalysis of Fire*, Gaston Bachelard writes, "If all that changes slowly may be explained by life, all that changes quickly is explained by fire."[1] Although modern human beings have been around for perhaps two hundred thousand years, it has been just within the past two hundred years—a mere eye-blink in our planet's long history—that we humans have consumed the enormous amounts that we have of ancient sunlight stored for millions of years in oil, coal, and natural gas. Moreover, in less than one hundred years, this energy consumption has injuriously affected the climate and all life on our planet. We know our Earth has been through massive climate changes in previous millennia and related massive species extinctions, but this new trial by fire caused by today's industrial world has ignited deep stirrings and global inquiry concerning our societal choices and the very existence of our species.

And so I have come to sit with the fire.

Using a well-worn knife given to me by a close friend, I begin to accumulate wood shavings with which to start a small campfire. There is an art to laying the little chips and positioning the kindling in such a manner that air is properly welcomed into the piled twigs and sticks, giving sufficient oxygen to the nascent flames. Once this is done, I arrange the larger pieces of wood, unhurried, folding them inward to create a conical flower. To do this task in such a deliberate way is, for me, a kind of honoring of the fire.

Once it is lit, I ponder the incandescence, warmth, sizzle, and sparks along with the sheer mystery of the mercurial flames. Immediately, two moods are conjured: one of poetic contemplation and quiet reverie as the flames lap the air; the other of another sort entirely, for fire has many dispositions—it is the spirit and spark of energetic inquiry. The blaze grows quickly and, rising up with its golden spires, a question flares, pressing in and up, heated and relentless. How did we get from the warming, transformative hearth fire of the home, the fire   celebrated around the world in every folk and spiritual tradition, to fire-powered weapons of mass destruction and the looming catastrophe of the toxic chemical fire of global warming? As a species, we are courting calamity, facing the end of civilization as we know it, and, lest we dive like hypnotized moths into the extinguishing flame, I think it best to slow down and take some time with these thoughts—here, by the ancient fire, the same fire that burns in the hearth and the heart.

I am not seeking an irrefutable, all-encompassing answer; rather, I am simply sitting with the glowing flames, and so with the very source of the elemental power in question.

The campfire burns bright in an open meadow within a circle of centuries-old Douglas Firs whose large trunks this night have become the stage and screen for a cast of ever-changing shadows and contoured shapes. As the fire undulates in a gentle breeze, shadows trace their metaphoric forms on the tree trunks where firelight and darkness meet: mysterious birds in flight, delicate arcs of butterflies, nimble jumping children, dazzling lightning bolts, and horses galloping across dark fields.

I am in a forested area of Northern California called Nadelos, a Sinkyone word that denotes a special ceremony around the fire when the community gathers together to recount traditional stories. Tonight, I try my best to offer the story I know, even with its missing parts and unknown outcomes.

In every land, for thousands of years, humans have gathered around a fire to tell their stories, especially after the sun goes down. In the night, when the business of the day has quieted, time moves beyond appointed hours and becomes less linear and more spherical. In the beautiful darkness, when time expands in all directions at once, allowing countless centuries to be captured in a seamless instant of recognition, we sit with the whirling flames and flickering embers as they open doors in our imaginations.

These campfire gatherings are special times when our words can be offered to the animals, mountains, rivers, and stars. Trees may bend in the wind to hear of our human journey and add their influence. I watch the flames weave golden tapestries into the sky while, just underneath the sound of the fluttering blaze, I hear the crackle of the burning sap narrate another kind of story.

Since the beginning of human time, we have assembled around the fire not only to tell our tales, but also to dialogue, deliberate, and dream. This night, in my imagination, I invite several distinguished leaders and elders to be seated with me in order to learn from their council across the glowing blaze. I am listening to their warnings about our rapidly warming planet. Perhaps you, dear reader, can imagine sitting by this same fire with me, and together we can see into these matters of the Great Crisis and Transformation of our time.

Scientists are telling us that climate destabilization due to carbon dioxide emissions and other heat-trapping gases is occurring faster than originally estimated, and we are running out of time to change course. Human use of fossil fuels, as we drive our cars, heat our homes and offices, and power our industries, is the main source of excess greenhouse gases in the atmosphere. Additionally, current industrial agricultural practices contribute significantly to global greenhouse gas emissions.[2] These are some of the most important contributing factors to our current predicament and the ones that spring to my mind while sitting with the flame.

Many prominent thinkers are so alarmed by our self-inflicted blindness and approaching yet still-avertable calamity that they spend much of their time and resources trying to reach us so that we might see our true state and act to change it. When Dr. Rajendra Pachauri, along with former Vice President Al Gore, accepted the 2007 Nobel Peace Prize on behalf of the Intergovernmental Panel on Climate Change (IPCC), he said, "If there's no action before 2012, that's too late. What we do in the next two to three years will determine our future. This is the defining moment."[3]

At a 2007 Google conference, Dr. Jane Goodall warned, "We have reached a point in time that if we don't act now ... it will be too late. Global warming is real."[4]

Today, there are approximately 387 parts per million (ppm) of carbon dioxide in the atmosphere, which is 37 ppm above the level climate experts such as Dr. James Hansen, director of the NASA Goddard Institute for Space Studies, have deemed environmentally sustainable.[5] Heat-trapping gases in the atmosphere are causing unprecedented warming, and climate scientists state that a rise of just 2 degrees Celsius would put hundreds of millions of people in danger of flooding, severely reduce the availability of fresh water, and dramatically increase droughts, causing catastrophic and widespread food shortages, among other ill effects.

The Director of the Environmental Justice and Climate Change Initiative, Nia Robinson, correctly brings to our attention the following consequence of such a deleterious change: "People of color, Indigenous Peoples, and low-income communities are the first to experience negative climate change impacts like heat death and illness, respiratory illness, infectious disease, and economic and cultural displacement. Climate policy must protect our most vulnerable communities."[6]

The Lapita Navigators, an Indigenous people living on several remote atolls in the tropical Pacific, are already losing their homes and crop fields to rising sea levels. Their entire culture and livelihood is at stake as the islands they live on are flooding further each year. The terrible irony is that the islanders—like many Indigenous populations around the world—have not been carbon polluters, yet they are the ones suffering the immediate consequences. Activist and filmmaker Steve Goodall's documentary, *Some Place with a Mountain*, tells the ongoing story of the Lapita Navigators and shows how their story is a wakeup call to the world.

However, even for those who think climate change is a scientific hoax, everyone can see that with peak oil upon us the age of fossil fuels is coming to an end. Any country not wanting to be left behind should immediately look to the clean-energy future to keep pace economically and technologically, if not to save the very planetary biosphere itself and so their nation.

Moreover, as this book goes to print, the worst environmental disaster in U.S. history is unfolding. On April 20, 2010, British Petroleum's Deepwater Horizon drilling rig exploded from trapped oceanic methane in the Gulf of Mexico, killing eleven workers and resulting in an unabated oil spew gushing into the ocean from miles down. It is estimated that an astonishing 60,000 barrels or more of crude oil are rushing into the Gulf every day.

Like many, I can't stop thinking about the blood-like red oil surging out from the wound at the bottom of the sea. This tragic moment demonstrates the worst of our fossil fuel addiction and seeming inability to respect natural laws. The spill is also bringing to light the danger of trying to extract every last drop of oil by encroaching upon ever more hazardous and sensitive locations.

We have no idea how long it will take to restore the destroyed ecosystem of the Gulf Coast or even if it is possible in any sort of timeframe that makes sense to us. How can we even measure the loss of unique wildlife in this region and the loss of thousands of livelihoods, not to mention an entire way of life, a self-sustaining culture that has been built along the coast by fishing families for generations? And, we can remember that these kinds of extractions have caused other devastation the world over from the Persian Gulf to the North Sea, from the Amazon to Canada. Many people are wondering if this will be a turning point in our use of fossil fuels. We shall see, and, in the unfolding, let our tears of grief and care lend to the washing and healing of the darkened and sullied shores, tend the dead and dying innocents—the innumerable creatures who have inhabited this sea and wetland for millennia before we were even here. This tragedy is one of many mounting reasons why we need to transition to a clean energy economy.

And so I have come to sit with the fire.

I am watching the borderland where the light cast by the fire ends and the darkness of the forest begins. This is where my thoughts wander as I take in the words of my fellow citizens and venerated speakers about the state of our world. Our modern society seems to be living in the borderland. I recall how many of the old fairytales speak of a wanderer lost in a wild forest at night, alone and hungry, perhaps near death, when suddenly he or she sees a light, a modest hearth fire or a lit lantern, glowing from a little hut through the brambles and the thicket. Hope is restored as the wanderer musters enough strength to make it to safety.

Yet, our present tale is different. Here in the borderland, where we are just now, nothing is certain about how and when we will make our way forward to the comforting hearth that we can only imagine.

In the preface to environmentalist David Orr's book *Down to the Wire*, he warns us that we are now entering the period that Harvard biologist Edward O. Wilson calls "the bottleneck."[7] Wilson describes it this way: "We have entered the Century of the Environment, in which the immediate future is usefully conceived as a bottleneck: science and technology, combined with foresight and moral courage, must see us through it and out."[8]

Orr goes on to say: "Some may quibble about the timing, but it is clear that we are heading toward a global disaster that has the potential to destroy civilization. But the conversation about changes in governance, economics, social norms and daily life that must be made to avoid the worst of what lies ahead is only beginning. In short, the level of public awareness and policy discussion does not yet match the gravity of the situation."[9]

Looking into the glowing blaze before me, I recall that over the last year, while reading various environmental articles, more often than not I have seen the term "sustainable communities" coupled with the word "resilient." This has jarred my attention. Sustainable is one term, meaning "able to be maintained at a certain rate," or "conserving an ecological balance by avoiding depletion of natural resources." The word "resilient," on the other hand, is defined as "able to recoil or spring back into shape after bending, stretching, or being compressed." The dramatic increase in the literature of the use of resilience as applied to sustainability seems to be preparing us to understand and internalize the truth of our planetary predicament. Overall, I like the meaning of resilience; it has a built-in strength to it and can mean "able to withstand or recover quickly from difficult conditions." I am registering that it indicates we have already taken a difficult turn for the worse. The real question seems to be just how far the impacts of climate change have already bent, stretched, or compressed our communities and bioregions out of shape—and whether or not our eyes, ears, hearts and minds are open to recognizing it.

We can get an earnest dose of reality by remembering that global warming is not an abstract threat for many of the world's rural people, like those living in Bolivia. The World Bank reports that Bolivia's Chacaltaya Glacier has lost 80 percent of its surface area since 1982.[10] In the Andean highlands of South America, water scarcity due to an alarming rate of glacier melt is a serious problem right now. Environmentalist Bill Mckibben's startling

2010 book title, *Eaarth: Making a Life on a Tough New Planet*, seems to succinctly sum up our global situation.

Thought leaders like Dr. Joanna Macy, a general systems theorist and proponent of Deep Ecology, can help guide us through this time by reminding us that we need to "recognize that denial itself is the greatest danger we face. We have the technology to make sweeping and effective changes. But not much can be done until we're ready to acknowledge the situation we're in, to let it sink in…. That profound inner movement of acknowledgement brings a great release of intelligence and creativity."[11]

The flames are forming shapes as the breeze shifts and a wing of fire suddenly shoots up from one of the burning logs, then turns just as quickly into a spiraling nautilus. I am mesmerized by the fire-dance and changing shapes, marveling at how the flames sculpt and influence my thoughts into new imaginings. It is here, by the fire, that I can acknowledge fully our historical crossroads as a species, and it is here, by the flames, that I find an abundance of intelligence and creativity.

Another speaker appears at my evening gathering: Nobel Prize winner Al Gore. He begins the final chapter of his 2009 book, *Our Choice*, with these words:

> Not too many years from now, a new generation will look back at us in this hour of choosing and ask one of two questions. Either they will ask, 'What were you thinking? Didn't you see the entire North Polar ice cap melting before your eyes? Didn't you hear the warnings from the scientists? Were you distracted? Did you not care?'
>
> Or they will ask instead, 'How did you find the moral courage to rise up and solve a crisis so many said was impossible to solve?'
>
> We must choose which of these questions we want to answer, and we must give our answer now—not in words but in actions.[12]

Across the fire, I imagine the grandchildren of our generation looking at us with these questions in their eyes.

Yes, it is a time of action, and much of it is needed by everyone—sooner rather than later. Experts from many fields report that we already have the technology needed to solve the climate crisis—from solar, wind, and geothermal power to smart grids, local organic agriculture, and efficient mass transit systems. As an example, environmentalist Lester Brown tells us that, in just the three states of Kansas, North Dakota, and Texas alone, there is enough wind energy that can be harnessed to meet our national energy needs.[13] China is also endowed with plenty of wind energy—enough to double that country's current electrical generating capacity.[14]

The Internet connects people and conveys information in ways that have revolutionized our capacity to collaborate and act in unison as a global citizenry. We can distribute renewable energy on Internet-like grids. Yet, global climate experts and leaders stress that the greatest obstacles we have in making the changes we need (within the timeframe scientists have indicated is essential) are not physical, but rather stem from our lack of collective will and the inability of our governments to act for this greater good. This is not a technology challenge but one of maturity, morality, and motivation.

The stillness of the forest around me and the low snapping of the fire invite further contemplation. There is no doubt that new technologies and those already in existence need immediate implementation, and that bold political actions are necessary to alter our current destructive course. However, we also need to create the inner conditions for this scale of transformation. It seems apparent that uncovering and then changing the beliefs and ways of thinking that got us into this crisis in the first place are actions that are equally central to the solution. The crisis began with worldviews, philosophies, and beliefs now very much out of step with current reality; it only makes sense that renewed understanding and a transformation of values will be essential for significant, rapid, and enduring change—such that allows the biosphere to survive and recover from human predation.

Global warming highlights a time of multiple rankling crises: water shortages, soil depletion, food sovereignty struggles, corporate deregulation and consequent unbridled profiteering, economic collapse, extreme poverty, disregard for Indigenous peoples' rights, population displacement, deforestation, and species extinction are all indications of long-festering societal misadventures, misbehaviors, and misunderstandings with ourselves, others, and the natural world. Yet, in this uncertain passage, there is a remarkable and precious opportunity to re-evaluate societal narratives, daily lifestyles, and cultural values as we, alone and together, look into who we are and re-imagine our relationship to our home planet and one another.

Closing my eyes, I feel the warmth of the blaze on my face and imagine Haudenosaunee Chief Oren Lyons stepping into the firelight. His deep-toned voice reaches across the glowing embers: "It seems to me that we are living in a time of prophecy, a time of definitions and decisions. We are the generation with the responsibilities and the option to choose The Path of Life for the future of our children, or the life and path which defies the Laws of Regeneration."[15]

What does it mean to choose "The Path of Life?" The warning of imminent biological doom from scientists makes it clear that we need to choose and act quickly, as well as wisely. To draw upon our full potential as a conscious and conscientious species seems imperative at this critical juncture, and that will require not only external information but also knowledge from our innermost being. Taking time for inward reflection is not only intelligent but also gives us the necessary vision to move forward. To paraphrase a Japanese proverb: Vision without action is a daydream; action without vision is a nightmare. This kind of visioning or inward contemplation begins with quietude so that we can listen to a deeper, more mature voice inside and to the natural laws and rhythms of the Earth. When we allow ourselves to be intimate with nature, we can remember that we are inseparable from the community of the rivers, forests, and animals around us. We can remember that all people, all species, share one sky. This intimacy with our living planet is one of the most crucial components in generating deep care for the Earth and each other, and it may be the very inspiration that fuels the "collective will" that climate leaders are telling us is necessary to make the change to new lifestyles, new values, new justice, new legislation, and a new, post-carbon, economy.

The natural world offers us enduring lessons in design, sustainability, balance, and ecological health while also echoing back to us our sacred place in the greater community of the Earth. With insight gained in the stillness of the mountain, desert, or forest, as well as in a city park or home garden, we can be more certain that our actions will address long-term and enduring goals, a larger vision, bound also to bring us deeper satisfaction, and not just immediate superficial fixes.

When we sit with the quiet of nature we are reminded of time, that it can take hundreds of years to grow a mature tree, thousands to make a mountain, but only a day or a year to destroy them for short-term gain. It is here in nature that we can best learn the practice of foresight, of actually seeing ahead, and adopting the long-term goal of care for "the seventh generation," an elegant concept of sustainability long held by the Iroquois Nation in their Great Laws. We need laws that will not harm future generations. What would happen if meetings held by world leaders and decision makers were to take place over a slowed-down, two-week period in a wild forest or mountain wilderness—instead of within the insulated urban chambers of the most frenetic cities? Or, for a contrasting perspective, what if the meetings were held atop one of the devastated plateaus in Appalachia created by disappeared mountaintops, the tragic result of one of the most destructive methods of coal mining, which uses dynamite to remove entire mountain peaks? While these kinds of meetings surely are not going to happen in any foreseeable future, I bring forth the question because, all too often, in political frameworks the sensate inclusion of the natural world is not even remotely considered or invited, even though it is the very fate of the Earth we are discussing, not to mention the life that persists and wishes to thrive everywhere.

Many people have had the experience of walking along the lakeshore, hiking in the woods, or working in the garden when suddenly the answer to a nattering problem becomes clear. Likewise, many a scientist, thinker, and poet have journeyed to the forest, glen, or seaside for clarity and inspiration. Through such contemplation in the midst of nature, we can call upon different ways of knowing and thinking, inviting creativity to bring us new societal innovations, as well as personal insights. When immersed in the natural world it becomes more apparent that global solutions need to address both people and ecosystem, recognizing that they are inseparable. And, while world leaders and captains of industry hold on to the notion that we can postpone serious reductions in fossil fuels, nature is clearly demonstrating to us through massive ice melts that Earth's natural laws cannot be ignored or manipulated. In short, there seems to be no substitute for the measure and perspective we receive when we directly experience ourselves as part of our living planet in the great sea of the universe.

In times of reflection, we can experience the breathtaking, not to be underestimated, beauty of our Earth. This vital force of beauty can stir our deepest longings to live nobly and to be mindful that we are part and particle of this numinous experience called life. And, while connecting with nature will not suddenly straighten out the human world's misadventures, being rooted to the Earth as we make the decisions that will affect all our futures seems only prudent, both ecologically and personally.

Reflecting in a deep manner also means looking at our attitudes, beliefs, and values in nonjudgmental quietude and then learning from what we find. It means attending to inner wounds that need healing so we can best care for ourselves and be mindful not to externalize our wounds onto the world. With any imbalance or illness, healing can only be achieved when the source of the disease is discovered and skillfully remedied. When our societal wounds are acknowledged, only then can the healing salve be applied. In this current time, one of the greatest healing salves needed is that of humanity's renewal of our sacred and loving relationship to our Earth and to all of life. The late renowned scientist and writer Stephen Jay Gould asserts, "We cannot win this battle to save the species and environments without forging an emotional bond between ourselves and nature as well—for we will not fight to save what we do not love."[16] Discovering our intimate relationship with our Earth is an essential part of discovering the nature of who we are and how we connect to the larger story of existence. Without an emotional connection, we will not be motivated to care. Without knowledge of how we—personally, ecologically, culturally, and historically—are connected to nature and the larger cosmos, we will not easily find our way forward. A culture deprived of its origins and place in nature ultimately will not be sustainable.

In essence, we need *inner* climate change in order not just to survive but to creatively thrive in this uncertain passage—this untutored moment in human evolution. Our resilient Earth, we are soothingly told, will doubtless survive; the question is, how well will humans? What decisions are we now making that will affect the well-being of the next generations and the habitability of the Earth? Moreover, beyond our own human survival, what are the implications of so much planetary death, due to our choices, of animals and plants that have until now stood the test of time?

And so I have come to sit with the fire.

I am burning eucalyptus that I brought with me so as not to use wood from the fir forest and risk further disturbing the ecology of this delicate region. The embers flutter in molten orange and reddish-yellow hues as the forces of convection move through the burning limbs that were once alive. These "tree bones" are, in fact, made up of stored sunlight, and I find myself thinking that nothing, nothing at all, occurs upon this Earth that is not somehow powered by the sun. Every event here is directly or indirectly a "solar event."

In the beginning time in the life of our Earth, a remarkable event took place: the energy from the sun was assimilated into the body of a single-celled proto-bacterium. This is a process we call photosynthesis, and it is so complex that how the single-celled organism or its chloroplast splits water (which is only one part of the process) into its atomic components is still not completely understood.

Scientists say this event took place at least 3.8 billion years ago and, effectively, all of life from then on directly or indirectly depended upon photosynthesis for food. Imagine that photosynthesis is fundamental to almost everything we know about life, and yet, beyond our brief contact with the idea in high school, most of us never think about or hear of it again.

Earlier in the day, when I collected the wood and split kindling for the fire, I used the "fire" in my body to accomplish the task. My breakfast of cereal, strawberries, and pears, which depended directly on sunlight to exist, provided the metabolic energy. Every time we eat, move about, warm our homes, drive our cars, build a house, make materials to build a house or a city, grow a garden, or e-mail a friend, we depend on energy provided—one way or another—by the sun.

In the awareness that sunlight is the energy powering the life force on our planet, it is no wonder that, throughout the eons, people worldwide have celebrated the generosity and essential nature of this great golden sphere. People all over the world have rituals to greet and thank the sun and ask for its blessings.

One of the rarest events on the Jewish calendar is a ceremony called the Blessing of the Sun, which occurs only once every twenty-eight years. Known as the *Birkat Hachamah* in Hebrew, the blessing is recited in honor of the sun when the solar cycle is complete and the sun returns to the same position in the sky in which it is believed to have been at the time when the world was created.

The summer solstice ceremonies of the Hopi include pilgrimages to special altars and elaborate dances in appreciation of the sacred Sun and all of life.

Beiwe is the arctic Sun Goddess of the Saami people of Finland, Sweden, and Norway, and she is honored at seasonal ceremonies. Beiwe journeys through the sky to ensure that new plants grow, and she is the protector of the reindeer who feed upon the greenery.

The ancient Inca held an annual Festival of the Sun called the Inti Raymi, which marked the winter solstice. One aspect of the ceremony was the tethering of the sun to the Earth, and in Machu Picchu there still stands a stone column for that purpose, to this day known locally as the Intihuatana, or "hitching post of the Sun." The ritual of tying the sun to the Earth during the winter was to ensure it did not escape during the longest nights of the year.

One of the best-known midsummer rituals in many parts of Europe is the lighting of bonfires and leaping over them. There are many layers of meaning to these ceremonial fires. Some have to do with guaranteeing prosperity and avoiding misfortune, and others celebrate the fire and the sun as sexual energy or in association with fertility since the sun energy is the source of all life on Earth. In these ceremonies, young people jump over the fire and the onlookers predict whether they will marry soon.

At daybreak on New Year's Day at the Futamigaura seaside near Ise, Japan, thousands of people gather to await the rising sun, Amaterasu, the Sun Goddess. Near to shore are two rocks in the sea called the Wedded Rocks. Named Izanami (female) and Izanagi (male), they represent the original couple in Japanese traditional history. In The Land of the Rising Sun, people pay homage to this glowing sphere as it rises in the soft colors of dawn over the Wedded Rocks and pray for a year of good health and prosperity.

The Hindu God of fire is Agni, and he is born again each day, just like the sun.

Beyond countless sacred sun ceremonies and rituals, grand monuments from pyramids to stone circles have been built worldwide to revere the sun. Clearly, our ancient ancestors had no misunderstandings about the life-sustaining power of the great fire in our sky.

The sun contains about 99 percent of all the mass in our solar system, and is so large that it could hold more than 1.3 million Earths within its sphere. "Gigantic" doesn't even begin to allow my imagination to grasp this kind of scale! The surface temperature of the sun is approximately a mere six thousand degrees Celsius, but, at its core, the sun is an amazing fifteen million degrees Celsius! It is here, in the interior, that the intense combination of temperature and pressure causes nuclear reactions to take place. The energy generated from these reactions takes a whopping one million years to reach the sun's surface. What does this mean? Well, for one, an extraordinary four million tons of pure energy is released every second in this process. The sun is actively "metabolizing" itself by the millions of tons per second and giving this transformed energy to the universe—to us. We on Earth are the fortunate recipients of this colossal gift, without which life on this planet could not exist. The sun is offering a one-way gift, for, in time, it will burn up its own fuel source and will die—go out, like my campfire. Scientists tell us that the sun is about 4.5 billion years old and will "live" in its current form for about another five billion years before eventually becoming a non-life-sustaining "white dwarf."

I stir the little sun-fire in front of me and another thought comes to mind: One of the things that led up to this perilous moment of human history is a lack of ordinary, but very powerful, appreciation. When did we stop remembering the sun's gift to us each day? When did we forget where our food and water comes

AROUND THE FIRE   239

from? We speak of food, but do we remember the chickens, fish, tomatoes, rice, wheat, peas, beans, greens, etc., that make up our daily diets as well as all the unseen people involved in providing for our sustenance? It is this very absence of appreciation that requires our reflection now. Lacking awareness and appreciation, we have substituted strange and unsustainable means of satisfying our hungry-for-meaning souls. (One powerful way to support a change in our awareness is by growing a vegetable garden—even a small rooftop garden can cultivate a surprising cornucopia of appreciation and meaning.)

While many of our spiritual traditions do encourage gratitude, many times it is difficult to translate this into daily action. Often the appreciation is left behind after the mealtime grace is said, the Thanksgiving dinner is over, or when we leave our houses of prayer. For some of us, even these simple gestures and rituals are no longer practiced. One need not be religious, however, to make a small gesture of appreciation for that which is given every day.

In the absence of understanding and recognizing the gifts given by the sun and by life itself on a daily basis, people of today often feel empty, abandoned, without support. In an attempt to fill the hollow, we have overfed ourselves with material goods and tasty but lifeless commercial foodstuffs. We have used the often-unacknowledged gift of the energy of solar fire to make and consume more stuff than we know what to do with, much of which simply ends up in garbage dumps and will last as non-biodegradable pollution for millennia. If people around the world lived like most of us in the United States, it would take at least three additional Planet Earths to meet the need!

In her powerful short film and book, *The Story of Stuff*, activist and researcher Annie Leonard quotes retailing analyst Victor Lebow's "solution" to ramping up the U.S. economy after World War II: "Our enormously productive economy ... demands that we make consumption our way of life, that we convert the buying and use of goods into rituals, that we seek our spiritual satisfaction, our ego satisfaction, in consumption … we need things consumed, burned up, replaced and discarded at an ever-accelerating rate."[17]

We have followed this course to its tragic "success," and it has made people feel emptier than ever. Leonard goes on to tell us that "in the U.S. we have more stuff than ever before, but polls show that our national happiness is actually declining."[18] It is well past time to honor and measure new indicators of wealth and well-being other than consumption and economic growth.

And so I have come to sit with the fire.

The flames have consumed several large branches so far. All that is left of them are ashes—ashes that offer valuable nutrients back to the forest soil. I want to learn the ways of consumption not from misguided modern mercantile-based beliefs, but from Sun and Fire.

The thought of fire induces divergent feelings and experiences. Fire can be warming and romantic; it can light the way. Uncontrolled fire can be scorching and destructive; it can kill the unwary.

I remember a hike in the Sierra Nevada Mountains one early spring in which I was caught in an unexpected rainstorm. I struggled to light a fire in order to keep warm in the unrelenting downpour; the smallest spark was glorious to see, and I fought to keep the tiniest flame alive. Ironically, the following summer I fought with all my strength alongside my neighbors to put out a forest fire that threatened our land.

We are drawn to fire but also learn at an early age (if we are lucky) to not get too close lest we get burned, like an unsuspecting moth. We know that fire warms us and cooks our food but also that uncontrolled fire consumes and incinerates all without discernment. We know that the flame, once in the hands of humans, can be a great tool or a destructive weapon.

We have used fire in its myriad forms to build many wonders of civilization. In contrast, we have used fire, in the form of toxic chemistry and the weapons of war, to wreak havoc upon our world. The Industrial Revolution and the age of machines quickly oriented modern civilization to depend upon the extraction from the Earth of coal, oil, and natural gas, all fuels originating from the sun's energy and transformed from plant material into stored fire. The fossil-fueled Industrial Revolution struck as quickly and suddenly as lightning relative to the entire time humans have strolled about the Earth, and now we must ask: Can we use the creative fire of inspiration and the urgent fire of passion to imagine and construct a world without fossil fuels just as quickly?

The essence and presence of fire is about transformation, a phenomenon that has captivated us since ancient times. Our multivalent, sacred, and yet somehow peculiar relationship with fire is universal. When we turn to the many fire-origin stories and myths from cultures around the world, we find that often they impart a warning of sorts. Many of the old stories tell us outright that fire is not freely given—it must be stolen. In his book *Myths of the Origin of Fire*, social anthropologist James Frazer relates how fire-bringers are often legendary cultural figures—animal or human—that steal the original flame and then offer it to the people.

There are numerous American Indian stories in which Coyote cleverly snatches the fire, but the thief can also be a turtle, raven, frog, or fox who slyly makes off with the flame. In a Navajo myth, after Coyote is able to trick the guardians of Fire Mountain by lighting a bundle of sticks tied to his tail, he runs down the mountain to give the fire to the people.

The Andaman Islanders in the Bay of Bengal tell a myth about how the kingfisher stole fire from a magical creature called a Bilik. When the kingfisher is caught in the act of purloining the flame to deliver to his people, the Bilik throws a firebrand, hitting the kingfisher on the back of his neck: bright red feathers on the bird's neck still mark the spot today.

Some Indigenous people from Victoria, Australia believe a fire-tail wren or finch brought the original fire to the people. The small red-tailed bird stole it from the sky or, as is sometimes told, from the crows.

In South Africa, the native San tell us that Ostrich held an ember under its wing until a praying mantis stole it and gave it to the people.

Indigenous people living along the Amazon River basin in Brazil convey a story about a boy rescued by a Jaguar. The boy learns how the Jaguar cooks food over the fire and then steals a hot coal for his people so that they, too, can cook their food.

In various cultures, there are myths about the stolen fire being given to the wood. Then, an animal like Coyote teaches humans how to retrieve the fire from the wood by rubbing two sticks together. These kinds of stories may seem strange or old fashioned to our modern ears, but they are quite enlightening and insightful if we stop to consider how profound it is that trees were, in fact, given fire to hold by the Big Fire, the sun, not to mention how much skill it requires to rub two sticks together to make fire and the alchemical magic of the first spark and flame. Then, when the fire flares, another remarkable thing happens: the once-brown, earth-colored wood burns with a bright orange and golden flame, mirroring the colors of the sun, its source, its origin.

And then there is the well-known Western myth of Prometheus, the Greek hero who steals fire from the Gods for human use and creativity. Zeus had decided to withhold fire from humankind, but Prometheus (Greek for forethought), in his fondness for humans, stole it and delivered it to mortal kind hidden inside a fennel stalk. The myth goes on to relay that Prometheus, chained to a rock, is eternally punished for his deed by an eagle that eats his liver each day, only to have it regenerate each night.

Elders, storytellers, mythologists, psychologists, artists, and philosophers, among others, have weighed in on why the fire is stolen rather than given. There are many interpretations, and, as in any good tale that has survived through the ages, we can each look into the story as a mirror and an allegory and reflect upon our own thoughts and conclusions.

The stolen-fire stories suggest that our ancestors long ago wished for us to be mindful and respectful of this sacred element. That the flame is not freely given can warn us that the technology of fire is a double-edged sword: the fire allows us many comforts while also giving us the power to harm ourselves, others, and the natural world in which we live. Fire gives us the power to change the world for good and for ill; the way we wield it has a tremendous impact on the natural environment. The old stories indicate an unusual relationship—the fire has to be stolen because the guardians of the flame are not sure that humans should have it or can control it. On the other hand, if we are to have it, we need to understand that fire is a hard-won prize and we need to make an adequate exchange for its use; otherwise, it *is* a theft. Apparently, we have not yet made the proper offering in return nor learned how to use it responsibly.

I am not suggesting that we should not have fire. We are all the better for fire's gifts, and it is likely that our very humanity and evolution as a species depends upon the secret of fire; I just find it greatly instructive that so many of our ancestors around the world placed an unmistakable warning on this sophisticated elemental energy.

The myth of Prometheus was recorded 2,700 years ago and yet continues to appeal to us today. At its core, it conveys key dilemmas of our age as much as those of the past with its layers of reflection on our ambivalence about our own human progress or lack thereof. German environmental sociologists Andreas Klinke and Ortwin Renn examined the Prometheus story in one of their risk management studies. They reasoned that the myth has survived the ages because, during times of technological change, humans struggle for reconciliation, and the Prometheus story speaks directly to these uncertainties. Klinke and Renn remark that the myth is actually the history of our Western culture.[19] This theme can be further recognized in the full title of Mary Wollstonecraft Shelley's enduring eighteenth-century novel, *Frankenstein; or, The Modern Prometheus*. One aspect of Shelley's novel addresses the question of humanity's ability to handle the new technology of the time with any wisdom. The contemporary social psychologist Hans-Christian Roglin also looks deeply into the dilemma, writing: "Modern people love the products of technology, but suppress the process by which these amenities of life are produced."[20]

Some of the old fire stories maintain that the control of fire is what distinguishes humans from animals. The early deities apparently gave animals many gifts, but to the humans alone was fire given.

In this vein, I learned a harsh but illuminating piece of history from Heinz Insu Fenkl's essay, "Fire and The Fire Bringer," which demonstrates how seriously we regard our relationship with the flame.[21] When the British began violently colonizing Tasmania in 1803, the settlers claimed that the Tasmanians were so ignorant and primitive, and their skills so rudimentary, that they no longer knew how to make fire. They had so deteriorated as a race that they could only obtain fire if ignited from wild nature, as from lightning striking a tree. The Tasmanian native people also did not wear clothes, even in the severest winters, other than fur capes mostly donned for spiritual and cultural purposes. In the colonizers' prejudiced and uneducated "logic," they rationalized the awful hunting and genocide of the Tasmanians by declaring them no better than "savage" animals due to their nakedness and inability to make fire, qualities that marked them as less than human and, therefore, fair game.

There was, of course, a vital piece missing to this story. The Tasmanians did, in fact, know how to make fire. Exploration journals from the eighteenth century document that the Tasmanians used wood drills to make fire. The British cultural lens and bigotry at the time could not perceive that a highly sophisticated indigenous reverence, not a lack of technological skill, was at work: in respect to their sacred Dreamtime Law, the Tasmanians actually *chose* not to make fire much of the time. Their spiritual way of life so honored this gift of nature and nature's timing of the gift that they did not normally forcibly wrest fire from Nature until She granted it.

Among the Tasmanians, as with other Indigenous peoples that I have encountered or read about, there was, and still is, a profound understanding of the gifts given to us by the natural world and a time-honored respectful effort to stay in balance with them.

Fire is an expensive, beneficent, and dangerous gift, and it requires an enormous amount of reciprocity and discipline to use it in a sustainable and balanced way. Many Indigenous people tell us that the self-destructiveness of our top-heavy culture is a direct consequence of our general disregard for proper "payment" for the things we have taken from the Earth, from Great Nature—our ultimate mother. Simple agreements and natural understandings, such as not cutting down more trees than are replanted, harvesting wild plants with care to leave enough for next year's growth, putting nutrients back into the soil after the harvest, and making sure that all our actions care for—or at least will not harm—the next generations, are all part of giving to and caring for the places in which we live, the places that sustain us. Yet, there is more to such reciprocity; it includes an awareness and appreciation for the gifts themselves, which can be expressed through stories, songs, and poetry of praise, as well as ceremony and spiritual practices of gratitude. These are actions that, at the least, promote and pass on the respect for nature and the Earth's bounty befitting to a civilized people.

And so I have come to sit with the fire.

On an impulse, I pull out my knife again, turning the handle just so, and the flames reflect off the shiny blade. In the deep of the night, the mirrored surface reflecting the fire becomes a piece of flame in my hand. It is a steel-blade fire, returning the knife back to its point of origin, back into the depths of molten metal that once churned and flowed in the crust of the Earth. The blade has a dynamic history: unless it called a meteorite its parent, the metal originated in some star's supernova. It was once a piece of a star hurled out from fiery depths long, long ago with the matter that coalesced to form our entire solar system.

The iron was alloyed with other metals and carbon, heated again in a blistering fire, and then forged to form the knife I now hold. The friend who gave it to me had initially received it from an Iraq War veteran. He said the knife had never hurt anyone. While it was carried for protection on the soldier's tour of duty, the blade had never drawn blood, even there in battle-torn Iraq, where too many civilians and soldiers were killed or wounded, and where, beneath the desert the oil that fuels both war and technological civilization as we know it is coveted and sought. Holding the knife, I think about how our civilization extracts metals and fossil fuels from the Earth through mining and drilling, and how our weapons and wars are tied to these massive extractions and deadly dependencies.

Fossil fuel extraction sites often resemble war zones: the horrible malformation of vast landscapes due to strip mining and open pit mines, the flattening of entire ranges due to mountaintop removal, the destruction of ancient rainforests, and the poisoning of thousands of miles of watersheds from extraction processes. People and wildlife in these regions suffer severe consequences, ranging from illness to extinction.

The U'wa, an Indigenous people living in the Andean cloudforests of Colombia, have had no misunderstanding about the perils of extraction. In their tradition, petroleum is the blood of Mother Earth and they maintain that it should never be taken out of the ground. They call oil "ruiria" and explain that this is the source of all plant and animal life as well as the human spirit. If it is taken from the Earth, the planet will no longer live and the people will die, they tell us. When Occidental Petroleum came to drill the oil from their lands in the 90s, the U'wa protested, stating that they preferred collective suicide than to watch the destruction of their community and lands. It would be a worthier death than at the hands of the exploiters, they said. The community had also already witnessed the ruinous results of oil extractions in nearby territories. Their fierce stand, in addition to support from international groups moved by the U'wa's powerful dedication and message to the world, generated successful results. In 2002, Occidental Petroleum withdrew from U'wa territory. In part, the company claimed this was due to digging a dry well in an early phase of the project and resultant economic issues, but the ardent protests surely weighed heavily on their decision.

"Leave it in the ground" is an explicit message delivered by Indigenous people, a growing body of scientists, environmentalists, activists, and Mother Nature herself. Perhaps this massive adjustment can best be heeded when we retrieve from our memory a time when we all understood our Earth to be living and sacred, and that our Mother Planet was not to be defiled.

Turning the angle of the knife anew, I can faintly see my reflection in the mirror of the steel blade. I remember my friend's contorted grief thinking about the war as he handed me the knife, asking if I would please use this weapon as a tool in my sculpture work. He asked that this knife, a weapon that had been to war, be turned into a tool of beauty-making.

And so I have come to sit with the fire.

I later learned that the date of my retreat here at Nadelos coincided with the National Clean Energy Summit 2.0, hosted by U.S. Senator Harry Reid in Nevada in August 2009. There, he announced in his keynote address that it is time for a "clean energy revolution."[22]

Reid compared the importance of the Summit, and its date, to the American Revolution, stating in his opening comments:

It was on August 10, 1776 the word reached London that the Americans had drafted the Declaration of Independence. The

Revolution that followed set our nation and the world—but especially our nation, on a long journey towards prosperity and global leadership.

Today, August 10, here in Las Vegas we're firing the first shots of a new revolution to regain that prosperity and restore that leadership—a clean energy revolution that will create millions of jobs across America ... "[23]

My work in recent years has led me to address climate change solutions with leaders in the United States and abroad. One of the essential components of any long-term solution that is clear to many of us is that new "green jobs" will not only reduce carbon emissions that lead to global warming but also provide good long-term employment: a win-win strategy, advocated by such organizations as the BlueGreen Alliance and Green For All.

Worldwide organizations like the Climate Prosperity Alliance propose that investing in a global infrastructure of renewable or sustainable energy sources such as solar, wind, and geothermal power will lower carbon emissions as well as create a clean-energy economy to replace traditional oil-dependent industrial practices. Europe is aiming to construct a multinational energy grid (a distribution network) in the next ten years, which is essential to the use of renewable energy sources and the storage of energy. China is also well underway with its own programs to develop renewable energy sources, taking some of the lead positions worldwide in manufacturing wind turbines and solar panels. The Brazilian government has agreed to reduce carbon emissions by nearly 40 percent by 2020, which includes a commitment to reduce deforestation by 80 percent by 2020. Yet, the world remains far from greenhouse gas reductions that effectively aim toward the necessary 350 ppm, and therefore, we must ask daily: Are these measures enough, and are we implementing them soon enough to avoid global calamity?

All nations must take steps to decrease global temperatures, which means settling contentious political and economic differences. As an example, "developed" countries must be prepared to take responsibility for their extremely high percentage of carbon emissions that have continued unabated and even increased over many years. It is only fair and just that funds from developed countries be given to developing countries to help with adaptation measures to the damage caused already by high polluters, and foster the ability of these countries to move directly to carbon-free energy sources. The potential solutions to climate crisis and global economic issues are conjoined parts of an international negotiation that has the future of all nations and peoples hanging in the balance. As they are interdependent issues, effective action on these global problems is more difficult and yet still urgent, and a high-level decision can become either an obstruction or the gateway to solutions that can secure our own and our children's future and that of the biosphere as a whole.

The need for coordinated government policies and action plans to address the climate crisis was recognized at the highest level of discussion: the Committee of Parties (COP) body of the United Nations met in Copenhagen in the winter of 2009 to address the climate crisis. However, as was anticipated by many climate leaders around the world, the conference concluded with only the most minimal of accords: a nonbinding agreement that, even so, did not meet the necessary reductions in carbon emissions.

Yet, scientists like Dr. James Hansen point out that this nominal agreement could actually be an opportunity. He writes in a December 2009 news article: "The centerpiece of the old approach was a 'cap-and-trade' scheme, festooned with offsets and bribes—bribes that purportedly, but hardly, reduced carbon emissions."[24] With only an interim accord coming out of Copenhagen, he and others see a chance for better solutions.

Specifically, Hansen supports a fee-and-dividend (or cap-and-dividend) approach because it seems to be the most beneficial way to achieve the goal of carbon emission reductions by placing a predictable and real price on carbon. At the moment, we are challenged with the difficulty that fossil fuels are still, on the face of it, the least expensive source of energy. Hansen writes: "... in the end, energy efficiency and carbon-free energy can be made less expensive than fossil fuels, if fossil fuels' cost to society is included."[25] A fee-and-dividend approach takes into account real costs that have been ignored, such as the health of people and ecosystems and the existence of future generations.

Furthermore, there is widespread agreement that cap-and-trade policies would likely achieve insignificant carbon reductions, and in the long run would create a worse problem because it would lock in today's dangerous levels of emissions for many years to come. Fee-and-dividend is gaining support from many experts and concerned agencies, including the Congressional Budget Office, 350.org, the Environmental Protection Agency, Al Gore, the Sierra Club, many in the business community (including Exxon Mobile), and even the creators of cap-and-trade as a concept.[26]

There is no question that we have come to the point where we can no longer separate energy, economy, and ecology concerns. To these, we must add national security and wars, as they, too, are intertwined inseparably with our basic needs and outlays when we take into account our current dependence on exogenous fossil fuels. The bright spot in this mirthless entanglement is that, as we begin to undo each of these snarls, we will see the old, unsustainable systems unravel. Al Gore puts it this way:

> The security crisis, the economic crisis, and the climate crisis—seem unsolvable in isolation. Yet when we look closely, we can see the common thread running through them ... our dangerous over reliance on carbon-based fuels.... If we grab hold of that thread and pull it hard, all of these complex problems begin to unravel, and we will find that we are holding the answer to all of them in our hand: we need an historic commitment to put people to work building the infrastructure and technology base for a massive and speedy shift away from coal, oil and gas to renewable forms of energy.[27]

In the end, the transformation has the potential to bring about the very societal changes necessary for truly thriving economies, ecological sustainability, and resilient communities *if we make the right choices soon enough.*

To influence, hasten, and improve decisions by world leaders after the failure of the Copenhagen summit, Bolivian President Evo Morales called for "The World People's Conference on Climate Change and the Rights of Mother Earth" held just outside the city of Cochabamba in April 2010. The conference highlighted, among many urgent matters, the great import of civil society mobilizing to press international governments to act ambitiously and equitably.

All of these efforts will play an important role as the international community convenes during these next crucial years for further climate summits through the United Nations and, perhaps more importantly, at local and regional levels.

In a conversation with economist David Korten at the Praxis Peace Institute Economics Conference in 2009, I asked how he imagined the transition might happen from our current economic system concerning climate change to any of a variety of new alternative economies being discussed. I had to sit back and laugh when he looked me in the eye and said, "I think the changes will be rigorous and necessary, but the transition is not and cannot be managed." Not managed! That took my breath away, and I realized once again that, besides what no one alive today can imagine might transpire due to the scale of our worldwide environmental crisis, so much is and will be self-organized at a community and local level. Many people and organizations are already well aware that their own local leadership and organic evolution is central to navigating the years ahead. When Elinor Ostrom, Nobel Laureate in Economic Sciences, was interviewed by *Der Spiegel* magazine about climate change solutions, she strongly encouraged the idea of local strategies:

> I propose a so-called polycentric approach to tackling climate change. We need all levels of human society to work

on this to be effective in the long run. Cities, villages, communities and networks of people have been neglected as players.... We need to get away from the idea that there is only one solution on the global scale. There are many, many levels in between. So we need to take action on smaller levels.[28]

As I prepared for a presentation at this same Praxis Peace Institute economics conference, I came across a powerful definition of wealth from the Inuit: Wealth is a deep understanding of the natural world. I was so moved by the idea that I devoted my entire workshop to imagining what it could mean to live in a community, a culture that holds to this definition of wealth. I asked participants: During this time of environmental crisis, what would it mean for your town or city to base its growth and wellness on understanding the natural world?

My exploration of the idea also led me to economist Herman Daly's important clarification that the economy is a subsystem of the biosphere, and so we cannot isolate the economy from the larger system of the environment.[29] Although these statements seem obvious, we have not been operating our modern economy with any regard to them. No doubt this must and will change, one way or another, in short order.

And so I have come to sit with the fire.

The wind suddenly stirs, causing a flurry of sparks to crackle and spiral upward into the night sky. My gaze traces their ascending trail, and I delight in the way the fiery particles all at once merge visually into the stars overhead. The swirling sparks are rising toward hundreds of billions of distant fires in the sky. These colossal fires are so very far away that they appear as exquisite glinting, fiery gemstones arched in the dome of the sky.

Some years ago, I took a small group of inner-city Bay Area youth camping for several days in the Death Valley desert of eastern

California. Later, the most talked-about experience for them, by far, was beholding the awe-inspiring expanse of stars at night, an encounter as can only be had far from city lights.

Beyond talking about the sheer magnificence of seeing the heavens aglow with countless specks of light, the students held late-night conversations about the rarity of our Earth—wondering at length how it even managed to come into existence. Like many of us who have experienced such wonder at some point in our lives, they began to grasp how relatively small and precious our home planet truly is.

Our perception and awareness of life and our living blue-green sphere can change profoundly when we gaze upon the stars and allow our imaginations to catch up to what it is that we are actually seeing and experiencing.

I cannot help but wonder what has happened to our consciousness as a species that, today, in our modern world, we are so devoid of this stellar dynamic. Perhaps the lack of star experiences has contributed—in ways more far-reaching than we credit—to contemporary people's sense of disconnection from the Earth community and lack of appreciation of our place in the greater universe. Without the measure of the stars, we miss the immensity and gift of our existence, and instead are confined to a very small and dwindling understanding of life and our meaning within it.

Until fairly recently, we humans have commonly looked to the stars for guidance. Seagoing and nomadic peoples worldwide have navigated the open waters and vast continents by their knowledge of the stars. Mapping the sky has also taught us about the passage of Great Time, which has been a science and a tradition in every old culture, many of which persist and even thrive today.

Stars have long been a symbol of hope and destiny for humanity. We look to them still for inner guidance as we navigate the course of our lives, often heeding the suggestion of old to "wish upon a star."

Stars are the "nursery" to the elements of life. Hot blue-white stars like Rigel (the right foot of Orion) create many elements, among them silicon and calcium—the same calcium that is in our bones. The most massive blue-white stars explode as supernovas, which create the heavy metals: gold, silver, copper, nickel, mercury, lead, and the like. The iron in our blood was forged from these types of stars. Red giants like Betelgeuse, one of the largest known stars, create oxygen, nitrogen, and carbon—the essential building blocks of life.

In the lyrics to Joni Mitchell's famous song "Woodstock," she writes, "We are stardust, we are golden, and we've got to get ourselves back to the garden." As it turns out, we are indeed stardust, and if we stop to reflect upon this extraordinary fact, perhaps we can allow it to shift our perception toward understanding our common origins and ancestry with all of life, every living thing here that had its origins in the stars.

In a 2005 interview, Mitchell commented upon her "Woodstock" lyrics:

> At that time, I felt so desperately that we were placed here to be the custodians of the planet Eden. So for the first 10 or 20 performances of that song, I used to get a lump in my throat.... We need to get a grip on our original destiny and learn to love the wild and save what's left of it and not go paving over farmlands that we may need someday. This is the farmer in me speaking. I'm the first generation of my genealogy off the farm, so it's in my blood to think in terms of good soil and weather.[30]

And so I have come to sit with the fire.

The starlight above reminds me that there are many lights, some from flame, some from nuclear fission, some from reflected sunlight, and some from biochemical fire. There is sunlight. Moonlight. Gem light. Torch light. Rainbow light. Twilight. Lamplight. Incandescent light. Florescent light. Candlelight. The sudden light of a lightning bolt. The gentle light of dawn. The twinkling lights of fireflies. The light in your eyes. Our inner light.

Poets and philosophers, artists and leaders, have drawn upon symbolic lights for inspiration and hope throughout the darkest of times. Metaphoric beacons are fashioned to show us the way through hardship, shafts of sunlight appear after stormy times to signal that all will be well once again, and torches of knowledge are safeguarded to pass from one generation to the next.

There is also the light that shines when we least expect it and need it the most. Poet/songwriter Leonard Cohen sings of this unforeseen light:

> Ring the bells that still can ring
>
> Forget your perfect offering
>
> There is a crack in everything
>
> That's how the light gets in.
>
> That's how the light gets in.[31]

Many of us are hoping and intending that the extensive crack—a massive fracture in our social and ecological welfare—will be a time when the light of inspiration, imagination, and creativity will get in, along with an abrupt, if necessary, adjustment within society as a whole.

The light of creativity is a power we need to foster now more than ever. The human ability to imagine and create is a force that has shone brightly even in our darkest eras. We have survived tsunamis, earthquakes, and cataclysms of all sorts, rebuilding destroyed communities better than they were before. We have risked our lives marching for peace and thus ended wars. Suffering the hardships of refugee camps, we have yet written great litera-ture and composed magnificent music. We have created art in war zones and lifted ourselves out of the most desperate circumstances with our power to imagine. Even after decades or centuries of oppression and deprivation, this essential spirit within humanity continues to create a vision of something greater, something that sustains us even now. Creativity is perhaps the most distinctive attribute of the human spirit. Our creativity survives under the most severe conditions and offers us tremendous hope. Often we think the direction of our society rests in the hands of banks, corporations, military institutions, and governments, but the concerted power of people everywhere and our capacity to imagine and create is an unstoppable force once we decide to use it. Governments follow when humankind takes monumental steps toward the good—not that this occurs without tremendous struggle and courageous actions by many.

The creative human spirit is lighting up the world now in unprecedented ways. In his book *Blessed Unrest: How the Largest Social Movement in History is Restoring Grace, Justice, and Beauty to the World*, Paul Hawken describes organizations worldwide dedicated to restoring the environment and empowering social justice, and their growing influence in communities around the world. Hawken's work reveals the prodigious diversity of the movement and its innovative ideas, which, taken altogether, demonstrates humanity's collective brilliance and creativity when faced with extreme adversity.[32]

New thinking and creativity are also reflected in the very nature of light itself, which exists as a wave-particle duality. When physicists first began to study the nature of light, very little was known about it from a Western scientific perspective. There were debates about whether light was a particle or a wave. Numerous experiments ensued, in which scientists like Issac Newton in the 1700s demonstrated that light was a particle, while others, such as Thomas Young a century later, proposed that it was a wave.

What was the conclusion? Physicists have explained to us that, actually, light is both particle and wave because it is a "quantum vector field." This means that light behaves differently under different conditions. For instance, when we shine light through small slits, it behaves like a wave. When we shine it on metal and observe the resulting spray of electrons, it behaves like particles.

This phenomenon is called the "wave-particle duality," and it depends on what we do with light and what we try to observe. The Heisenberg uncertainty principle further boggles the mind by stating that it is impossible to observe accurately both the path and the object—the wave and the particle—at the same time.

As I let these light-filled thoughts bathe my mind, it occurs to me that the dual nature of light actually describes quite well my sense of how we might move through this daunting stretch in our history. While I work to be aware of and involved in resolving the many challenges of our day, I also want and need to appreciate the beauty of my garden, the peach-colored clouds at sunset, poetry read aloud, concerts with friends—all the culture and arts with which I am surrounded. In these challenging and sometimes very dark times, it would behoove us to adopt the model of light, with its ability to demonstrate contradictory properties at the same time. In other words, when we learn that there are 200,000 new environmental refugees worldwide each day and allow ourselves to really take this fact in and imagine/feel the suffering of these people and the planet we also need to allow ourselves to celebrate the love, joy, and success in our lives. In this way, we can have the strength and courage to face what is happening to our Earth's people. We can draw upon an inner reserve of appreciation in the midst of hardship and let this gratitude nurture our work and light the way.

Here's the twist: it is entirely possible, even while we know that making our way through the current "bottleneck" is not going to be easy or comfortable by our old standards, that in the long run we are going to create the kinds of social structures and economies on a large scale that many of us have been longing for in our deepest dreams—local, bioregional, ecologically sustainable, child-and-elder-friendly, self-directed communities rich with diversity and creativity. No, not utopias, but regenerative, functional communities linked by smart grids and the Internet. Already we are seeing a plethora of creative, self-organizing groups and high-level initiatives on the move with this concept: Transition Towns, Cool Cities, Eco-builders, The Oberlin Project, C40 Cities, Carbon-Neutral Cities, Eco-villages, Eco-Cities, Bio-mimicry projects, permaculture communities—the list grows daily with working concepts and practical models in every part of the country and many parts of the world. As further inspiration for us, longstanding sustainable Indigenous communities have much to offer in the way of expertise, if we of the larger matrix can but accept it with the appropriate respect.

And so I have come to sit with the fire.

Another creative light is streaming through the fissure of this stress-induced crack in our current reality, one that is crucial to our human spirit and the decisions we make: the power of story.

Today there is a great hunger for stories of both old-time and newly emergent varieties. We humans live by story; it is an essential part of our experience. Since ancient times, people have sought to understand the great mysteries of life, and stories are a means to address these profound inquiries. Such tales present us with a worldview and values that can guide our understanding of life and how we perceive reality. Our parents, teachers, religious leaders, and other elders pass them on to us when we are children, and they provide a framework, a blueprint, for interacting with our human family and understanding our place in creation. Stories become the very essence of our life dreams, both personally and collectively.

Yet, what happens when our cultural story no longer encompasses the time we live in or no longer addresses the needs of the people or, in some cases, becomes a damaging story?

Thomas Berry writes, "The deepest crises experienced by any society are those moments of change when the story becomes inadequate for meeting the survival demands of a present situation."[33]

At one time, the hearth fire in the home or village was a gathering place for storytelling, both the sharing of our daily lives and the bigger stories of who we are as a people. Today, all too often the television "fire" has replaced this older storied hearthside. To be clear, television is not innately a bad thing. In and of itself, television is a remarkable human invention that can hold a place of great educational, cultural, and entertainment value in our society. The first issue of concern, of course, is about the hours and hours spent watching TV and that it can so easily become a substitute for actual experiences. Americans today watch an average of four to five hours of television a day.[34] We cannot learn about the full, sensuous, alive beauty and grandeur of the ocean by simply watching a television special about the sea. There is no substitute for sitting on the ocean cliffs and seeing, smelling, and hearing the waves, listening to the seagulls cry, feeling the wind and salt spray on our faces, watching the sun glistening on the water's surface. This direct experience simply is not replicable virtually. Our bodies, minds, and spirits cannot benefit from the synthetic experience of nature captured on an electronic screen. And, importantly, the content and purpose of commercial media messaging can be a huge problem in itself.

Our personal stories, as *not* seen on TV, are very important to our children, as Marian Wright Edelman, founder and director of the Children's Defense Fund, comments:

> … we should teach our children as much as we can about the heroes in their own families and try to be the people we want our children to become: the grandparents and great-grandparents who came before them and paved their way. Why is this so important? Family stories are often the most memorable inspiration of all. They bring history alive and reinforce the idea that anyone and everyone can use their lives to make a difference.[35]

Watching a story on TV is just not the same as hearing stories shared orally that come from particular people and places, alive in the moment of telling, and thus renewed and attuned to the audience and the times. There is a unique and irreplaceable living relationship, a sense of community, that such stories create between living, breathing people.

In 1984, Jerry Mander, director of the International Forum on Globalization, was invited to visit First Nations people in the MacKenzie River Valley in Canada. His experience is one from which we can all learn and take to heart in our own lives. Here is how he tells the story to Scott London in a *HopeDance* magazine interview:

> I was invited by an organization called the Native Women's Association of the Northwest Territories, an organization of Diné and Inuit women. The MacKenzie River Valley is where the Russian nuclear satellite came down some years ago. At the time, everybody was worried that it would fall on London or New York, but instead it fell on a so-called icy wasteland up in Canada. That's the place where I was invited to go. It was 40 degrees below zero the day I arrived. The MacKenzie River Valley has 22 communities of native people. They are spread over an enormous area. They still have a very successful traditional economy based on hunting and fishing and live in a communal manner in log houses.
>
> I was invited up there because television had begun to arrive in the area. The Women's Association was noticing startling changes in the communities where television had arrived. The men didn't go out on the ice to fish as often. The animals weren't being taken care of as well. The kids didn't want to go out and play traditional games. The kids were starting to want things—like cars (even though there are no roads there). The neighbors weren't hanging out together, working on the nets together, cooking together, eating together and so on. The community life was break-ing down.
>
> The most important thing, they told me, was the loss of story-telling. In the evenings, it used to be that the very old would gather with the very young in a corner of the

house—several families together—and the old people would tell traditional stories and stories from their past. By hearing those stories, the young people could remember who they are, what's good about their people, and how to live in that very harsh environment. The stories were a window to their roots. Also, the process of young and old hanging out together in that way was very important. There was a lot of love flowing back and forth and the kids were proud to be connected to their grandparents.

Apparently, all of this has been wiped out by television.[36]

It is a deeply disheartening story, and it seems we cannot stop the cold wildfire of television. What we *can* do is support and protect Indigenous communities and their languages so that they can save their stories and their culture, despite the current conditions. Additionally, as people from an industrialized culture who have grown up at the flat hearth of the television- fire, we can work to find our way, once again, to the community fire (both the real one and the metaphoric one) and say, "This community fire is good and of great value." At the fire, meeting together in our local community, we can learn the stories of our own bioregion and families. We can relearn and renew our tattered histories, including those from distant shores. We can find and reconnect with our orphaned big stories, in which our ancestors revered the Earth— the ones that tell of our essential relationship to the natural world, to grasses and trees, rivers and seas, meadows and mountains, and the greater universe. This is our great task, one that must be done in a modern way. Doing this might then help transform the stories commonly told on television, film, and the Internet. I think this is already happening to some degree through independent films, viral videos, short, widely-distributed documentaries, citizen-generated event and news images, text messages, communication between hand-held devices, and the Internet today.

Thus, it is not that modern media is detrimental; in fact, to the contrary, the Internet has enabled us to connect more powerfully and create community and mass innovation at great distances and with many more people. Books such as *Here Comes Everybody, Crowdsourcing, Smart Mobs: The Next Social Revolution*, and *We-Think* all demonstrate the unprecedented innovative thinking and effective results that have come about because of Web-based global communication and collaboration. The catch is how to use the technology discerningly: according to a 2010 Kaiser Family Foundation Study, pre-teens and teens in the U.S. are now spending an average of 7.5 hours per day watching videos, playing games, and listening to music on mobile devices.[37] As with television, we need to pay attention to the effects of substituting virtual experiences for real life because entertainment media consumption cannot fulfill the essential human need for intimacy, personal care, experiences, and humanity of the shared, living community fire.

Being mindful of content is another great challenge as we reconstitute or remember our stories, for a great deal of our commercial media, in addition to always trying to make us feel inadequate so that we will purchase something new, often tells us a negative story about our Earth.

In the aftermath of the Hurricane Katrina disaster in New Orleans and surrounding areas, I came across a startling national magazine advertisement from an insurance agency. Large, bold text read: "How do you deal with an enemy that has no government, no money trail and no qualms about killing women and children?" The answer: "The enemy is Mother Nature. And on August 29, 2005, in the form of Hurricane Katrina, she killed 1,836 people... ." The ad goes on to tell us that "It's time we started fighting back."[38]

Is it any wonder, then, that we are estranged from our beautiful home planet, our precious and only place in the universe, considering this kind of deleterious and Earth-fearing narrative?

Nigerian poet and author Ben Okri offers these wise words: "Beware of the stories you read and tell: subtly, at night, beneath the waters of consciousness, they are altering your world."[39]

Rather than demonizing the planet or viewing our living world as a commodity, we can uplift Earth-honoring stories again, stories that need to be renewed and retrieved after having been blurred by too many artificial lights of the industrial world. This profusion of harsh lights glare in our eyes, blinding us to the things that feed us, that sustain us, and that would fill us with the desire to contribute instead of consume, cooperate instead of compete.

We can invite to our hearth fires the storytellers, artists, and poets who are ushering in a new cultural narrative. Rachel Carson, Thomas Berry, Martín Prechtel, Maya Angelou, Jaime D'Angelo, Terry Tempest Williams, Brian Swimme, Alice Walker, Gary Snyder, Riane Eisler, Greg Mortenson, Mary Oliver, Jiang Rong, Barry Lopez, Joanna Macy, David Orr, Leonard Cohen, Janine Benyus, Michael Pollan, Clarissa Pinkola Estes, Wendell Berry, Malidoma Somé, Barbara Kingsolver, James Cameron, Annie Dillard—these are but a few of the better-known voices of the many who come to mind. Every home and hearth of every size and place will find its own, and with them, the stories that make the lives of each participant meaningful within that community, place, and world.

Some of the essential elements these good storytellers convey to us are important lessons about our own nature and real-life challenges. As in the older teaching stories whose remnants remain in some of our fairytales, the storytellers know that the hearth fire in the woodland cabin not only symbolizes and emanates light but also casts shadows. The questing forest-wanderer, too, must wrestle internally with her or his light and dark human facets. Central characters or kind creatures in the stories sometimes die and the wanderer can make grave errors that cannot be remedied. Not all the mysteries and conflicts are always resolved; not all obstacles are overcome, or at least not easily. All this is to say that our falsely purified stories are no longer working for us because they do not teach us of our nature, which is both light and shadow—and much more. When light touches the physical realm a shadow is cast; this is its nature. What makes firelight and sunlight alike so vital is that they need darkness to bring forth their full illumination. When vigil candles cast their shadows, our faces are illuminated but the Earth receives the silhouette of our care and grief. Shadows, the storytellers say, are there for our inward reflection. In the darkness, we can turn our vision inward; there, with introspection, we can learn about ourselves and transform. These are the kinds of mysteries revealed in the tales, which fill our souls with meaning, inspiration, and enchantment.

The old tales, as well as the new emerging stories, prompt us to get to know our local bioregions and neighborhoods: the trees, birds, and grasses, as well as the people on our streets. They encourage us to come to know our longtime ancestry and integrate these histories into our present time and place. These stories confirm that we are related in some way to each other and to all of life. They stimulate conversations about race and religion, place and purpose, dreams and design. The stories guide us to look to the stars, as Thomas Berry and mathematical cosmologist Brian Swimme convey in *The Universe Story*, reminding us of our origins within the 14.5-billion-year history of the cosmos. All these stories and more are unfolding as we re-imagine our world.

I gently stir the quieting fire now, and the rising smoke swirls in cadence with my thoughts. The fire asks to be fed—not with more wood, for it is well stoked, but with an old story. I offer this tale to the bright flames, a Nart saga from the ancient people of the Caucasus region, for it carries in it wisdom, boldness, and courage—all of use to us today. Here is the tale as retold by anthropologist John Colarusso:

If Our Lives Be Short, Let Our Fame Be Great

The Narts were courageous, energetic, bold and good-hearted. Thus they lived until God sent down a small swallow.

'Do you want to be few and live a short life but have great fame and have your courage be an example for others forevermore?' asked the swallow. 'Or perhaps you would prefer that there will be many of you, that your numbers will be great, that you will have whatever you wish to eat and drink, and that you will all live long lives but without ever knowing battle or glory?'

Then without calling a council, but with a reply as quick as thought itself, the Narts said, 'We do not want to be like cattle. We do not want to reproduce in great numbers. We want to live with human dignity.

If our lives are to be short,

Then let our fame be great!

Let us not depart from truth!

Let fairness be our path!

Let us not know grief!

Let us live in freedom!'

In this way they chose to be small in numbers but to perform deeds of courage and boldness. This was the answer they gave to that small swallow to take back to God. And so their fame has remained undying among people.[40]

In our case today, I would simply add that our battles be not of physical combat but of courageously fighting against our ignorance, apathy, and lack of imagination wherever we encounter it.

Just as a fallen rider cannot make it far on foot, I do not think we can make it very far without a good story. Part of building cultural resilience will be in retrieving and refashioning our stories—stories that remind us of our courage and boldness of purpose in meeting the future without fear and with enthusiastic solutions to today's biggest problems.

And so I have come to sit with the fire.

In 2009, when Al Gore received the Global Humanitarian Award in the heart of Silicon Valley, he reminded the audience, mostly people of wealth and success, that "one of the secrets of the human condition is that suffering binds people together."[41] His talk, unsurprisingly, focused on the climate crisis.

He told the story of President Mohamed Nasheed of the Maldives and his ministers, who held a cabinet meeting in scuba gear underwater. At first glance, the humor and peculiarity of the act strike our funny bone, but in actuality, it is anything but a joke. The aquatic meeting was held in a desperate attempt to grab the attention of the world and dramatize, through universal media, their awful plight and fight for survival. In 2008, as sea levels rose due to global warming, the Maldives added a new line item to their budget: "Fund to purchase a new country."

Gore also spoke about the rapid ice- and snow-melt of the Himalayas. The numbers of people in danger of losing their water once this source is drastically diminished is startling: because the seven great rivers of Asia originate in the Himalayas and the Tibetan Plateau, we are talking about a staggering forty percent of our human family in danger—women, children, men. Gore remarked: "Each one meter of sea level rise puts 100 million climate refugees on the move. Where do they go?"[42]

The word emergency came to me. "Emergency" and "emergence" share the same origin in the Latin *emergere*, meaning "bring to light." It is often said that we won't change our unhealthy or unsustainable ways until disaster hits. When a tragedy occurs, we know we are in an emergency and then act accordingly. I'd like to think that enough disaster has struck by now for us to collectively change course (we are brewing a big emergency by any standards)—or, on a more hopeful note, that we have the capacity as a species to use our remarkable ability to imagine, care, and respond appropriately and immediately, simply because it is the right thing to do—before we cause any more destruction to ourselves and our only, sustaining, Mother Planet. In this critical time, we need to ask ourselves what the most vital ways are to activate the necessary emergence of positive change in our lives and to bring our collective emergency to light.

This is both an individual and a collective query.

How we decide to move through the uncertain passage ahead can only be answered by each of us individually. As it stands, every facet of our current ecological, economical, and societal problems reflect the same imbalance and misunderstanding in the human project. We must transform a dominator and destructive model of society to one of partnership and life enhancement. Because of this, every action is equally important, whether it builds resilient and sustainable communities; protects and restores forests, water, and soils; defends the rights of Indigenous people, all children, and all species; establishes solar, wind, or geothermal technologies—or contributes in some other meaningful, positive way we have not yet imagined.

Put simply, because every arena of work is essential to the whole outcome, the things to do are the things that calls to us most, that lights our inner fire—those are the areas where we can contribute the most and where our passion will not be so likely to wane in the long years ahead.

The key is getting involved, and this is our way forward. As David Orr comments, "We've been playing fast and loose with life for a while now, and it's time to discuss the changes we must make in order to conduct the public business fairly and decently over the long haul."[43] He also reminds us that "... the job of building a decent world will come down to how well we understand ourselves... ."[44]

In respect to reducing our carbon emissions, each household, community, city, state, country, and continent will have different challenges and requirements depending on its unique bioregional, social, and economic circumstances. Local conditions will naturally lead to decentralized and varied solutions. These diverse solutions are integral to our new approach and can foster the creativity and collaboration required to move together toward not only reducing our carbon emissions overall, but also creating the world we want for our children and grandchildren. Likewise, we must not forget that in low-lying communities such as that of the Lapita Navigators or drought stricken regions across Africa, climate change is already having a serious impact, and mitigation and adaptation solutions are urgently needed—not in the future, but right now.

We can each ask ourselves: what is the light I offer, the flame that is mine alone to give?

There may be times we feel that our one small, flickering flame, our one little light, is not adequate, not significant enough, to matter. We may well ask: will my actions be enough? This is especially true as we recognize the magnitude of our current and future world challenges.

We may wonder if, in measure to the bright torches carried by known leaders, our light is too small or dim. Or perhaps we are concerned that, if we really let our light shine, our most precious and vulnerable hopes and dreams will become prey to human folly, contempt, and cynicism.

This kind of thinking, this fear that bids us to hide and not shine, not act upon our better instincts, is what has caused us so much sorrow and only leads us further down a dangerous road.

Now, more than ever, every light—of *every* person—is needed and can kindle and brighten the fire of hope and enthusiasm, which can bring about change. This moment in history is about taking our creative expression to another level in our offerings to the world. It is about invigorating and feeding our inner flame and finding a way to shine brighter than ever, no matter the obstacles and circumstances. It is also important to remember that we are not alone in holding up our light; in fact, we cannot see our way ahead without the light of many others.

Several ancient traditions come to mind as I watch the dazzling fire before me—traditions generated from the dark time of the year:

On the eve of the winter solstice, the longest night of the year, people in many European cultures of old silently gathered in a field under the stars to honor the darkness. After some moments of shared quiet, it was time for the breaking of the darkness, which represented the coming of longer days, the return of the sun. This was done by the beckoning of the light, as gradually, one by one, each person lit a candle, passing the flame one to the next. It became clear to all that, with each new candle lit, the field of darkness became lighter and brighter as the Festival of Light welcomed the Sun, as well as each person's light, into the new season. Variations of this Festival of Light are still practiced to this day in lands around the world.

One of the ways ancient peoples connected their individual communities, just as they reconnected their individual homes annually into the larger community, was through the kindling of shared fires. In autumn, as the Earth moves into the darker half of the year, the ancient Celts, among others, held a ceremony to honor the Final Harvest of the Year. It was time to take stock of grain supplies and the animal herds, as well as to prepare food to survive the winter. Central to these festivities, called Samhain in Celtic Europe, was the lighting of large bonfires, a practice still observed in some rural areas of Europe. One aspect of these bonfires held particular significance for the well-being of the community. Once the central bonfire was lit and glowing bright in the night, the villagers extinguished all the fires in their home hearths. Community members then re-lit their families' hearth fires from the shared central flame and, in this way, all were unified anew as a community.

In ancient Greek colonies, a firebrand was brought from the mother city's fire to link the colony with the related metropolis; so, for instance, an outpost could receive a carefully tended flame-lit months before from the winter bonfire back home—carried over great distances, much like the Olympic torch, to connect related communities. One can tell from these efforts how much care, reverence, and ritual importance such fire-tending acts held, and for how long. Traditions have deeper significance than we commonly remember. What more beautiful way can there be to enter into a complete and satisfying sensory conversation with the community-building efforts of our ancestors and with the future yet to come than with an experience with the flame of history, humanity, and eternity?

Fire once was the central feature of every home. The words "hearth" and "heart" share a similar root because the hearth was the heart—and, I will add, the health—of each home: the fire that glowed in the fireplace or stove or hearth was the same one that warmed the lodge, cooked the food, heated the bathing water, and brought the light. In turn, the light and warmth of each home was a reflection of the sun at the center of our home solar system as well as the common flame at the center of the community. I think it still is; we just need to retrieve and rekindle the fire.

We can find ways to reawaken the intimacy of the hearth fire within our homes and communities once again. It is our choice. We can think of this collective flame symbolically as the renewed fire of community, collaboration, and cooperation. We can re-member that we all share the same home planet in a shared solar system. Many elders from spiritual and religious traditions around the world have said that this is truly the great testing time for humanity; thus, we will need to share our hearths and hearts with each other for the health of the Earth and all species.

In this great time of transformation, we can relight the com-munity fire that speaks of our oldest origins, our deepest dreams and values, our love for our children and our animal and plant relatives, our passion for life and beauty, our creative ability to imagine our world anew and act upon it. Perhaps, in this coming together, we can make our way through the aberrant darkness, brought about by our unacknowledged and unattended inner shadows, that has resulted in the chemical wildfire of climate chaos, and instead—together by the hearth fires of humanity—regenerate our world back to health before it is too late.

And so together, let us come and sit with the fire.

Endnotes

CHAPTER 1

1. Carson, Rachel. *Silent Spring* (Boston, Massachusetts: Houghton Mifflin, 1962), p. 277.
2. Hawken, Paul. *Blessed Unrest: How the Largest Social Movement in History is Restoring Grace, Justice, and Beauty to the World* (New York: Penguin Books, 2007), p. 4.
3. Berry, Thomas. *The Great Work: Our Way into the Future* (New York: Bell Tower, 1999).
4. After engaging in both these pathways for many years and articulating their components, I was excited, some years later, to come upon Joanna Macy's description of the different dimensions of what she calls the Great Turning. She distinguishes three areas in her inspiring book, *Coming Back to Life: Practices to Reconnect Our Lives, Our World* (New Society Publishers 1998): 1) actions to slow the damage to Earth and its beings; 2) an analysis of structural causes and creation of structural alternatives; 3) a fundamental shift in worldview and values.
5. Carson, Rachel. *Lost Woods: The Discovered Writing of Rachel Carson* (Boston, Massachusetts: Beacon Press, 1999), p. 89.
6. Wilson, Edward O. *Biophilia* (Cambridge, Massachusetts: Harvard University Press, 1984).
7. Louv, Richard. *Last Child in the Woods: Saving Our Children from Nature-Deficit Disorder* (New York: Algonquin Books, 2005), p. 3.
8. Waters, Frank. *The Man Who Killed the Deer* (Chicago, Illinois: The Swallow Press Inc., 1942), pp. 8–13, 17–29.
9. Thoreau, Henry David. *A Week on the Concord and Merrimack Rivers* (New York: Dover Publications, 2001), p. 179.
10. www.audubonmagazine.org/features0909/greenDesign-Intro.html
11. Eisler, Riane. *The Chalice and the Blade: Our History, Our Future* (San Francisco, California: HarperCollins, 1987).
12. "World Population Monitoring, 2001. Population, Environment and Development." (United Nations Publications. Department of Economic Social Affairs Population Division. New York: United Nations, 2001); "Women's Education and Fertility Behaviour: Recent Evidence from the Demographic and Health Surveys." (United Nations Publications. Population Division, Department for Economic and Social Information and Policy Analysis. New York: United Nations, 1995).

13. Krech III, Shepard and McNeill, J.R. *Encyclopedia of World Environmental History* (New York: Routledge, 2004), p. 877.
14. Carson, Clayborne and King, Jr., Martin Luther. *The Papers of Martin Luther King, Jr.* (Berkeley and Los Angeles, California: University of California Press, 2007), p. 484.
15. Suder, Gabriele G.S. *Corporate Strategies Under International Terrorism and Adversity* (Cheltenham, United Kingdom: Edward Elgar Publishing Limited, 2006), p.180.
16. Berry, Thomas. *The Dream of the Earth* (San Francisco, California: Sierra Club Books, 1988), p. 123.
17. Carson, Rachel. *Silent Spring* (Boston, Massachusetts: Houghton Mifflin, 1962).

CHAPTER 2

1. Rilke, Rainer Maria. *Letters on Life: New Prose Translations* (New York: Modern Library, 2006), p. 7.
2. Berry, Thomas. *The Great Work: Our Way into the Future* (New York: Bell Tower, 1999), p. 166.
3. Davis, Wade. Interview with Anthropologist Wade Davis: National Public Radio, May 2003.
4. Anderson, M. Kat. *Tending the Wild: Native American Knowledge and the Management of California's Natural Resources* (Berkeley and Los Angeles, California: University of California Press, 2005), p. 156.
5. Ibid., p. 58.
6. Winn, Robert. "The Mendocino Indian Reservation" (*Mendocino Historical Review*. Mendocino Historical Research, Inc., 1986).
7. Levine, Donald and Phillip. "The Real Biodiversity Crisis" (*American Scientist Magazine*. January-February, 2002).
8. Andersen, Hans Christian and Owens, Lily. *The Complete Hans Christian Andersen Fairy Tales* (New York: Avenel Books, 1981), p. 724.
9. Ibid., p. 725.
10. Melville, Herman. *Moby-Dick, or The Whale* (Berkeley and Los Angeles, California: University of California Press and Arion Press, 1979), p. 57.

CHAPTER 3

1. Fuller, R. Buckminster. *Critical Path* (New York: St. Martin's Press, 1981), p. 142.
2. Ibid., p. 512.

3. Ibid., p. 324.
4. Ibid., pp. 262–263
5. www.tpl.org/tier3_cdl.cfm?content_item_id=1242&folder_id=905. "Benefits of Urban Open Space," 2010, The Trust for Public Land.
6. Neihardt, John G. *Black Elk Speaks: Being the Life Story of a Holy Man of the Oglala Sioux* (Lincoln, Nebraska: University of Nebraska Press), pp. 194–196.
7. Jensen, Derrick. "Saving the Indigenous Soul: An Interview with Martín Prechtel" (*The Sun Monthly*, April 2001).
8. McDonough, William. "Buildings Like Trees, Cities Like Forests" (*The Catalog of the Future*: Pearson Press, 2002).
9. Berry, Thomas. *The Great Work: Our Way into the Future* (New York: Bell Tower, Crown Publishing Group, 1999), p. 19.
10. Ibid.
11. Hawken, Paul. "A Declaration of Sustainability " (*Utne Reader*, September/October, 1993), p. 54–61. Zimmerman, Michael E.; Callicott, J. Baird; Clark, John; Warren, Karen J.; and Klaver, Irene J. *Environmental Philosophy: From Animal Rights to Radical Ecology* (Upper Saddle River, New Jersey: Prentice Hall; 4 edition, 2004), p. 427.
12. Snyder, Gary. *Turtle Island* (New York: New Directions Books, 1969), p. 101.
13. Elk, Black; DeMallie, Raymond J.; and Neihardt, John G. *The Sixth Grandfather: Black Elk's Teachings Given to John G. Neihardt* (Lincoln, Nebraska: University of Nebraska Press, 1984), pp. 291–292.

CHAPTER 4

1. "President's Commission on the Celebration of Women in American History." Minutes of the September 25, 1998, Commission Meeting. (Albuquerque Museum: Albuquerque, New Mexico. http://govinfo. library.unt.edu/whc/whc0925.htm).
2. "About two million women trafficked every year: UN" (*Thaindian News*. June, 2008).
3. Raymond, Janice G. and Hughes, Donna M. "Sex Trafficking of Women in the United States" (*Coalition Against Traffic of Women*. March, 2001). www.scribd.com/doc/28615682/Sex-Trafficking-of-Women-in-the-USA.
4. Eisler, Riane. *The Chalice and the Blade: Our History, Our Future* (San Francisco: HarperCollins,1987), p. xvii.
5. "World Population Monitoring, 2001. Population, Environment and Development" (United Nations Publications. Department of Economic

Social Affairs Population Division. New York: United Nations, 2001).

6. "Women's Education and Fertility Behaviour: Recent Evidence from the Demographic and Health Surveys" (United Nations Publications. Population Division, Department for Economic and Social Information and Policy Analysis. New York: United Nations, 1995).

7. Mortenson, Greg. "Fighting Terrorism With Schools" (*Parade Magazine*. November 22, 2009).

8. Kristof, Nicholas and WuDunn, Sheryl. *Half the Sky: Turning Oppression into Opportunity Worldwide* (New York: Alfred A. Knopf, 2009), p. xxi.

9. Tarr-Whelan, Linda. *Women Lead the Way* (San Francisco, California: Berrett-Koehler, 2009), pp. 51–52.

10. Chen, Lisa and Witter, Lisa. *The She Spot: Why Women Are the Market for Changing the World — And How to Reach Them* (San Francisco, California: Berrett-Koehler, 2008), pp. 14–18.

11. Ibid. p, xvi.

12. Eisler, Riane. *The Real Wealth of Nations* (San Francisco, California: Berrett-Koehler, 2007), pp. 31, 84.

13. Wagner, Sally Roesch. *Sisters in Spirit: Haudenosaunee (Iroquois) Influence on Early American Feminists* (Summertown, Tennessee: Native Voices Book Publishing Company, 2001), p. 10.

14. Weatherford, Doris. *American Women's History: An A to Z of People, Organizations, Issues and Events* (New York: Prentice Hall, 1994), p. 364.

15. Adams, Abigail; Adams, John; and Shuffelton, Frank. *The Letters of John and Abigail Adams* (New York: Penguin Group, 2003), p. 339.

16. Harris, Bill. *The First Ladies Fact Book* (New York: Black Dog and Leventhal, 2005), p. 25.

17. Stanton, Elizabeth Cady; Anthony, Susan B.; and Gage, Matilda Joslyn. *History of Woman Suffrage* (New York: Charles Mann, 1889), pp. 115–116.

18. Ibid., p. 116.

19. Black, Allida M. *Courage in a Dangerous World: The Political Writings of Eleanor Roosevelt* (New York: Columbia University Press, 1999), p. 190.

20. http://greenbeltmovement.org/a.php?id=146

21. Sideris, Lisa H. and Moore, Kathleen Dean. *Rachel Carson: Legacy and Challenge* (Albany, New York: State University of New York Press, 2008), p. 21.

22. Krieger, Richard Alan. *Civilization's Quotations: Life's Ideal* (New York: Algora Publishing, 2002), p. 298.

23. Carson, Rachel. *Silent Spring* (Boston, Massachusetts: Houghton Mifflin, 1994), p. xviii.
24. Campbell, Joseph and Moyers, Bill. *The Power of Myth* (New York: Anchor Books, 1991), p. 231.
25. Maher, John M. and Briggs, Dennie. *An Open Life: Joseph Campbell in Conversation with Michael Toms* (New York: New Dimensions Foundation, 1989), p. 22.
26. Eisler, Riane. *The Chalice and the Blade: Our History, Our Future* (San Francisco, California: HarperCollins, 1987). Gimbutas, Marija. *The Goddesses and Gods of Old Europe: Myths and Cult Images* (Berkeley and Los Angeles, California: University of California Press, 1982).
27. Berry, Thomas. *The Great Work: Our Way into the Future* (New York: Bell Tower, 1999). pp. 69-70.
28. Mackey, Albert G. *A Lexicon of Freemasonry* (London and Glasgow: Richard Griffin and Company, 1860), p. 156.
29. www.archives.premierministre.gouv.fr/villepin/en/acteurs/symbols_of_ the_republic_185/marianne_and_the_motto_50225.html
30. King Jr., Martin Luther. *I Have a Dream: Writings and Speeches That Changed the World* (New York: HarperOne, 1992), p. 91.
31. Wright, Kai. *The African-American Experience* (Black Dog and Leventhal, 2001), p. 609.
32. Boime, Albert. *Hollow Icons: The Politics of Sculpture in the Nineteenth-Century* (Kent, Ohio: Kent State University Press, 1987), p. 137.
33. www.bioneers.org/

CHAPTER 5

1. Weatherford, Jack. *Indian Givers: How the Indians of the Americas Transformed the World* (New York: Fawcett Columbine, Ballantine Books, 1988) pp. 64–73.
2. Popovsky, Mark. *The Vavilov Affair* (Hamden, Connecticut: Archon Books, 1984). Vavilov, N. I. *The Origin, Variation, Immunity, and Breeding of Cultivated Plants* (Moscow/Leningrad: 1935. Translated from the Russian by K. Starr Chester, Ph.D., Battelle Memorial Institute: Columbus, Ohio, 1949–1950).
3. Levin, Gregory. *Pomegranate Roads* (Forestville, California: Floreant Press, 2006), p. 20.
4. Reid, Anna. *The Shaman's Coat: A Native History of Siberia* (London: Weidenfeld & Nicolson, 2002), p. 2.
5. Ibid., p. 7, 37.
6. Buñuel, Luis. *My Last Sigh* (London: Jonathan Cape, 1984), p. 174.

CHAPTER 6

1. Kennedy, Mary and Xue, Tao. *I Am a Thought of You* (New York: Gotham Book Mart, 1968).

CHAPTER 7

1. "Safe Water System: A Low-Cost Technology for Safe Drinking Water" (U.S. Center for Disease Control and Prevention. Fact Sheet, World Water Forum 4 Update, March 2006). www.cdc.gov/safewater/publications_pages/fact_sheets/WW4.pdf
2. Hegel, Georg Wilhelm Friedrich. *Encyclopedia of the Philosophical Sciences* (Oxford, England: Clarendon Press, 1970. Originally published in 1817).
3. Ball, Philip. *Life's Matrix: A Biography of Water* (Berkeley and Los Angeles, California: University of California Press, 2001), p. 327.
4. Zürcher, Ernst. "Lunar Rhythms in Forestry Traditions—Lunar-correlated Phenomena in Tree Biology and Wood Properties," article published in *Earth, Moon and Planets* (Netherlands: Kluwer Academic Publishers, 2001), pp. 463–478.
5. National Geographic Society. *The National Geographic*, Volume 202, 2002, p. 108.
6. Postel, Sandra. *Last Oasis: Facing Water Scarcity* (New York: W.W. Norton and Company, 1992, 1997) p. xix.
7. Schwenk, Theodor. *Sensitive Chaos, The Creation of Flowing Forms In Water and Air* (United Kingdom: Rudolf Steiner Press, First English Edition, 1965), p. 10.
8. "World Water Day 2010 Highlights Solutions and Calls for Action to Improve Water Quality," United Nations Environment Programme. Yuba Net (March 2010). http://yubanet.com/world/World-Water-Day-2010-Highlights-Solutions-and-Calls-for-Action-to-Improve-Water-Quality-Worldwide.php
9. www.worldwaterday.org/page/2997
10. Alaerts, G.J. and Dickinson, N.L., editors. *Water for a Changing World* (London: Taylor and Francis Group, 2009), p. 81.
11. Raskin, Paul et al., "Water Futures: Assessment of Long-Range Patterns and Problems," Comprehensive Assessment of the Freshwater Resources of the World (Stockholm Environment Institute, Stockholm, 1997), p. 23.
12. Swanson, Peter. *Water: The Drop of Life* (Minnesota: NorthWord Press, 2001), p. 7.

13. Fishman, Robert. *The American Planning Tradition: Culture and Policy* (Washington, DC: Woodrow Wilson Center Press, 2000), p. 152.
14. Priscoli, Jerome Delli. *Water and Civilization: Conflict, Cooperation and the Roots of a New Eco Realism, keynote address for the 8th Stockholm World Water Symposium,* 1998. www.genevahumanitarianforum.org/docs/Priscoli.pdf
15. Ibid.
16. Tolkien, J.R.R. *The Lord of the Rings* (Boston, Massachusetts: Houghton Mifflin, 2004), p. 362. Originally published 1954–55.
17. Windling, Terri. "Sacred Springs and Other Water Lore," *Endicott Studio* (2005).
18. Lawrence, D.H. *The Complete Poems of D.H. Lawrence* (Hertfordshire, United Kingdom: Wordsworth Editions, 1994), p. 428.

CHAPTER 8

1. Kakuzo, Okakura. *The Book of Tea* (BC, Canada: Serenity, 2008) pp. 40, 49.
2. Couturier, Andy. "Ikebana: Asymmetry and the Mind." *Ikebana International Magazine* (Spring 2000).
3. Muir, John. *My First Summer in the Sierra* (New York: Houghton Mifflin Company; first edition, 1911), p. 211.
4. Harvey, Karen and Harjo, Lisa. *Indian Country: A History of Native People in America* (Golden, Colorado: Fulcrum Publishing, 1998), p. 41.

CHAPTER 9

1. Edwards, Tryon. *A Dictionary of Thoughts* (Detroit Michigan: F.B. Dikerson, 1908), p. 403.
2. Whitman, Walt. *Complete Prose Works* (Boston, Massachusetts: Small, Maynard, and Company, 1901), p. 222. *Democratic Vistas* originally published in 1871.
3. Mann, Charles C. *1491: New Revelations of the Americas Before Columbus* (New York: Alfred A. Knopf, 2005), p. 334.
4. Franklin, Benjamin and Smyth, Albert Henry, editor. *The Writings of Benjamin Franklin Volume Three* (New York: Macmillian Company, 1905), p. 42.
5. Whitman, Walt. *Complete Prose Works*, p. 222.
6. Justice, Daniel Heath. *Our Fire Survives the Storm: A Cherokee Literary History* (Minneapolis, Minnesota: University of Minnesota Press, 2006), p. 40.

7. Graves, Robert. *The White Goddess: A Historical Grammar of Poetic Myth* (New York: Farrar, Straus, Giroux, 1966), p. 371.

8. Edward, Gibbons. *Epitaph for the People of Ancient Athens* (attributed). Gerhart, Eugene C., editor. *Quote It Completely: World Reference Guide to More Than 5,500 Memorable Quotations from Law and Literature* (New York: William S. Hein, 1998), p. 69.

9. Annan, Kofi. "Secretary-General Extols Role of Artists in Global Struggle for Peace, Development and Human Rights" (United Nations Information Service, November 2002). www.unis.unvienna.org/unis/pressrels/2002/sgsm8516.html

10. Dzielska, Maria. *Hypatia of Alexandria* (Cambridge, Massachusetts: Harvard University Press, 1995).

CHAPTER 10

1. Bachelard, Gaston. *The Psychoanalysis of Fire* (Boston, Massachusetts: The Beacon Press, 1964), p. 7. Originally published in 1938.

2. Archer, David. *Global Warming: Understanding the Forecast* (Malden, Massachusetts: Blackwell Publishing, 2007). Brown, Lester. *Plan B 4.0: Mobilizing to Save Civilization* (New York: W.W. Norton and Company, 2009).

3. "Absolute Must Read IPCC Report: Debate over, further delay fatal, action not costly," Center for American Progress. (Climate Progress, November 2007). http://climateprogress.org/2007/11/17/must-read-ipcc-synthesis-report-debate-over-delay-fatal-action-not-costly/

4. [sic] "Anjelina Jolie and Jane Goodall are in the Building!" Center for American Progress. (Climate Progress, September 2007). http://climateprogress.org/2007/09/26/anjelina-jolie-and-jane-goodall-are-in-the-building/

5. Hansen, James. *Storms of My Grandchildren: The Truth About the Coming Climate Catastrophe and Our Last Chance to Save Humanity* (New York: Bloomsbury, 2009), pp. xi, 10–13.

6. Robinson, Nia. "Proud, Concerned and Hopeful"(http://ejcc.org/issues/proud_concerned_and_hopeful/).

7. Orr, David. *Down to the Wire: Confronting Climate Collapse* (New York: Oxford University Press, 2009), p. x.

8. Wilson, Edward. *The Future of Life* (New York: Vintage, 2003), p. 23.

9. Orr, David. *Down to the Wire: Confronting Climate Collapse*, p. 21.

10. Kormann, Carolyn. "Retreat of Andean Glaciers Foretells Global Water Woes" (*Yale Environment* 360, April 2009). http://e360.yale.edu/content/feature.msp?id=2139

11. Prescott, W.R. "Breaking the Spell: An Interview with Joanna Macy" (*Global Climate Change*, IC #22, Summer 1989).

12. Gore, Al. *Our Choice: A Plan to Solve the Climate Crisis* (Pennsylvania: Rodale Books, 2009), p. 394.

13. Brown, Lester. *Plan B 3.0: Mobilizing to Save Civilization*, p. 239.

14. Ibid.

15. Lyons, Chief Oren and Ewen, Alexander. *Voice of Indigenous Peoples: Native People Address the United Nations* (Santa Fe, New Mexico: Clear Light Books, 1993).

16. Gould, Stephen Jay. *Eight Little Piggies: Reflections in Natural History* (New York: W.W. Norton, 1993), p. 40.

17. Leonard, Annie. *The Story of Stuff* (referenced and annotated script by Annie Leonard, released online 2007. http://www.storyofstuff.com/pdfs/annie_leonard_footnoted_script.pdf).

18. Ibid.

19. Klinke, Andreas and Renn, Ortwin. "Prometheus Unbound: Challenges of Risk Evaluation, Risk Classification, and Risk Management" (No. 153 / November 1999 Working Paper ISBN 3-932013-95-6. http://elib.uni-stuttgart.de/opus/frontdoor.php?source_opus=1712).

20. Ibid.

21. Fenkl, Heinz Insu. "Fire and The Fire Bringer" (Online Essay, 2005. www.endicott-studio.com/rdrm/rrfirebringers.html).

22. Reid, Senator Harry. "National Clean Energy Summit 2.0" (Transcript, August 10, 2009. Copyright © 2009 Federal News Service, Inc., Washington, DC).

23. Ibid.

24. Hansen, James. "Copenhagen has given us the chance to face climate change with honesty" (*The Observer*, December 2009).

25. Ibid.

26. Kirsch, Steve. "New Poll Shows Americans Prefer Fee-and-Dividend," (www.huffingtonpost.com/steve-kirsch/new-poll-shows-americans_b_377142.html).

27. Gore, Al. *Our Choice*, p. 21.

28. Ostrom, Elinor. "Climate Rules Set from the Top Are Not Enough" (www.spiegel.de/international/world/0,1518,667495,00.html).

29. Daly, Herman E. *Ecological Economics and Sustainable Development: Selected Essays of Herman Daly* (Northhampton, Massachusets: Edward Elgar Publishing, 2007), p. 251.

30. Paglia, Camille. "Joni Mitchell: we are stardust, we are golden" (*Interview Magazine*, Brant Publications, Inc., August 2005).

31. Cohen, Leonard. *Stranger Music: Selected Poems and Songs* (New York: Vintage, 1994), p. 374.

32. Hawken, Paul. *Blessed Unrest: How the Largest Social Movement in History Is Restoring Grace, Justice, and Beauty to the World* (New York: Penguin, 2008).

33. Berry, Thomas. *The Dream of the Earth* (San Francisco, California: Sierra Club Books, 1988), p. xi.

34. Winter, Richard. *Still Bored in a Culture of Entertainment* (Downers Grove, Illinois: Intervarsity Press, 2002), p. 34.

35. Edelman, Marian Wright. "Making Sure Our Children Know Their History" (*Child Watch® Column*, February 8, 2008).

36. London, Scott. "The Perils of Technology: An Interview with Jerry Mander" (*HopeDance Magazine*, January 2000).

37. Foehr, Ulla; Rideout, Victoria; and Roberts, Donald. *GENERATION M2 Media in the Lives of 8- to 18-Year-Olds: A Kaiser Family Foundation Study* (Kaiser Family Foundation, Menlo Park, California, January 2010).

38. "How do you deal with an enemy that has no government...?" (advertisement, ProtectingAmerica.org., *Time* magazine, September 25, 2006).

39. The 2008 Shift Report: Changing the Story of the Future (Petaluma, California: Institute of Noetic Sciences, March–May 2008).

40. Colarusso, John. *Nart Sagas from the Caucasus* (Princeton, New Jersey: Princeton University Press, 2002), p. 11.

41. Temple, James. "Gore to techies: Shake off the lethargy" (online, SFgate, November 20, 2009).

42. Ibid.

43. Orr, David. *Down to the Wire: Confronting Climate Collapse*, p. 189.

44. Ibid., p. 162.

Resources

CHAPTER ONE

Benyus, Janine. *Biomimicry: Innovation Inspired by Nature*. (New York: Morrow, 1997).

Carson, Rachel. *The Sea Around Us* (New York: Oxford University Press, 1951).

Schaefer, Carol. *Grandmothers Counsel the World* (Boston, Massachusetts: Trumpeter, 2006).

Snyder, Gary. *The Practice of the Wild* (San Francisco, California: North Point Press, 1990).

CHAPTER TWO

Davis, Wade. *Light at the Edge of the World* (Washington, DC: National Geographic Society, 2002).

Eifert, Larry (*The Distinctive Qualities of Redwoods* (Redcrest, California: FVN, 1991).

Hogan, Linda and Peterson, Brenda. *Sightings: The Gray Whales' Mysterious Journey* (Washington, DC: National Geographic Society, 2002).

Margolin, Malcolm. *The Ohlone Way: Indian Life in the San Francisco-Monterey Bay Area* (Berkeley, California: Heyday Books, 1978).

Purdy, Carl. *Pomo Indian Baskets and Their Makers* (Montana: Kessinger Publishing, 2007. Originally published by Out West Company Press, 1902).

Trees Foundation. "InterTribal Sinkyone Wilderness Council" (*Forest & River News*, December 10, 2007).

Tucker, Wilma. Mendocino—From the Beginning: Twenty Billion Years of History of a Small Town" (*Mendocino Historical Review*, Mendocino Historical Research, Inc., 1992).

Varner, Gary R. *Menhirs, Dolmen, and Circles of Stone: The Folklore and Magic of Sacred Stone* (New York: Algora Publishing, 2004).

Walker, Barbara G. *The Woman's Encyclopedia of Myths and Secrets* (New York: Harper and Row Publishers, 1983).

CHAPTER THREE

Bozovic-Stamenovic, Ruzica and Lu, Yi. "The Spatial Concept of Chinese Architecture." *The Cultural Shaping of Architectural and Urban Spaces* (Singapore: Built Spaces Vol. 9, No. 1, November, 2004).

Klemp, Herwig and Lenarduzzi, Marco. *Der Hohe Meissner: Unterwegs im Reich von Frau Holle* (Mainz, Deutchland: Fachverlag Dr. Fraund GmbH, 2006).

Kollman, Karl. *Frau Holle und das Meissnerland: Einem Mythos auf der Spur* (Eschwege, Deutchland: Herausgegeben von der Historischen Gesellschaft des Werralande und dem Werratalverein, 2005).

Krupp, E.C. *Echoes of the Ancient Skies: The Astronomy of Lost Civilizations* (New York: Harper and Row,1983).

Paetow, Karl. *Frau Holle: Volksmarchen und Sagen* (Husum, Deutchland: Husum Druck-und Verlagsgesellschaft mbH u. Co. KG, 1986).

Rogers, Elizabeth Barlow. *Landscape Design: A Cultural and Architectural History* (New York: Harry N. Abrams, 2001).

Singh, Madanjeet. *The Sun: Symbol of Power and Life* (New York: Harry N. Abrams, 1993).

Wheatley, Paul. *The Pivot of the Four Quarters: A Preliminary Enquiry Into the Origins and Character of the Ancient Chinese City* (Chicago, Illinois: Aldine Publishing Co., 1971).

CHAPTER FOUR

Akers, Charles W. *Abigail Adams: A Revolutionary American Woman* (Upper Saddle River, New Jersey: [Library of American Biography Series] Prentice Hall, 2007).

American Studies at the University of Virginia. *The Agendas Behind the Monuments.* http://xroads.virginia.edu/~CAP/LIBERTY/politics.html

Berkin, Carol. *Revolutionary Mothers: Women in the Struggle for America's Independence* (New York: Alfred A. Knopf, 2005).

Bodnar, John; Burt, Laura; Stinson, Jennifer; and Truesdell, Barbara. "The Changing Face of the Statue of Liberty," A Historical Resource Study for the National Park Service, Center for the Study of History and Memory: Indiana University, December, 2005.

Burns, Ken. "The Statue of Liberty" (PBS American Stories. Original Broadcast Date, October 28, 1985).

Costanza, Robert. "The Value of the World's Ecosystem Services and Natural Capital" (*Nature Magazine.* Volume 387, May 15 1997).

Gage, Frances D. "Reminiscences by Frances D. Gage of Sojourner Truth"

Akron Convention, Akron, Ohio, May 28-29, 1851. http://womenshistory. about.com/gi/dynamic/offsite.htm?site=http://www.sscnet.ucla.edu/ history/dubois/classes/995/98F/doc7.html

Han, Minzhu, and Sheng, Hua. *Cries For Democracy: Writings and Speeches from the 1989 Chinese Democracy Movement* (Oxford, England: Princeton University Press, 1990).

Kramer, Lloyd. *Paine and Jefferson on Liberty: By Thomas Paine and Thomas Jefferson* (New York: The Continuum Publishing Company, 1988).

Nash, Roderick. *The Rights of Nature: A History of Environmental Ethics* (Wisconsin: University of Wisconsin Press, 1989).

National Women's History Project Resource Center: www.nwhp.org/resourcecenter/index.php

Conversation with National Women's History Museum President Joan Wages, March 2007.

Trachtenberg, Marvin. *The Statue of Liberty* (New York: Penguin Books, 1977).

Warner, Marina. *Monuments and Maidens: The Allegory of the Female Form.* London, Great Britain: Random House Vintage Books,1985.

Weatherford, Doris. *A History of the American Suffragist Movement* (New York: MTM Publishing, 2006).

CHAPTER FIVE

Palmer, Martin and Ramsay, Jay. *Kuan Yin: Myths and Prophecies of the Chinese Goddess of Compassion* (San Francisco, California: Thorsons, 1995).

CHAPTER SIX

Saier Jr., M. H. and Trevors, J. T. "First Nations/Indigenous People's Wisdom" (Published online: *Springer Science + Business Media B.V. 2008,* April 2008).

CHAPTER SEVEN

Barlow, Maude and Clarke, Tony. *Blue Gold: The Fight to Stop the Corporate Theft of the World's Water* (New York: The New Press, 2002).

Barlow, Maude. *Blue Covenant: The Global Water Crisis and the Coming Battle for the Right to Water* (New York: The New Press, 2007).

Croutier, Alev Lytle. *Taking the Waters* (New York: Abbeville Press, 1992).

Postel, Sandra. *Pillar of Sand: Can the Irrigation Miracle Last?* (New York: W.W. Norton & Company, 1999).

Roddick, Anita. *Troubled Water* (United Kingdom: Anita Roddick Books, 2004).

Schwenk, Theodor and Schwenk, Wolfram. *Water: The Element of Life* (USA: Anthroposophic Press, Inc., 1989).

Warshall, Peter. "The Morality of Molecular Water," *Whole Earth Review* (Spring 1995).

CHAPTER EIGHT

Hesse, Hermann. *Siddhartha: An Indian Tale* (Rockville, Maryland: Wildside Press, 2009. Originally published 1922).

Melville, Herman. *Moby-Dick or The Whale* (New York: New American Library, Signet Classic, 1955).

CHAPTER NINE

Allen, Paula Gunn. *The Sacred Hoop: Recovering the Feminine in American Indian Traditions* (Boston, Massachusetts: Beacon Press, 1986).

Dashu, Max. *Women's Power*. DVD http://www.suppressedhistories.net/womenspowerdvd.html

Gibbon, Edward. *The Decline and Fall of the Roman Empire* (United Kingdom: Wordsworth Editions Ltd, 1999). Originally published between 1776 and 1788.

Jones, David E. *Women Warriors: A History* (Dulles, Virginia: Potomac Books Inc., 2002).

Kalter, Susan. *Benjamin Franklin, Pennsylvania, and the First Nations: The Treaties of 1736-62* (Champaign, Illinois: University of Illinois Press, 2006).

Korten, David. *The Great Turning: From Empire to Earth Community* (San Francisco, California: Berrett-Koehler Publishers, 2006).

Patai, Raphael. *The Hebrew Goddess* (Detroit, Michigan: Wayne State University Press, 1990).

Stone, Merlin. *Ancient Mirrors of Womanhood* (Boston, Massachusetts: Beacon Press,1984).

Walker, Barbara. *The Woman's Encyclopedia of Myth and Secrets* (New York: Harper and Row Publishers, 1983).

Weatherford, Jack. *Indian Givers: How the Indians of the Americas Transformed the World* (New York: Fawcett Columbine, 1988).

CHAPTER TEN

Bachelard, Gaston. *The Flame of a Candle* (Dallas, Texas: The Dallas Institute Publications, 1988).

Berry, Thomas. *Evening Thoughts* (San Francisco, California: Sierra Club Books, 2006).

Berry, Thomas and Swimme, Brian. *The Universe Story* (New York: HarperOne, 1994).

Environment News Service, "Occidental Petroleum Abandons Oil Development on U'wa Land" (Synthesis/Regeneration 30, Winter, 2003).

Frazer, James George. *The Golden Bough: A Study in Magic and Religion* (New York: Macmillan Company; Abridged Edition, 1951).

Frazer, James George. *Myths of the Origin of Fire* (London, England: Macmillan Company, 1930).

Friedman, Thomas. *Hot, Flat, and Crowded: Why We Need a Green Revolution—and How It Can Renew America* (New York: Farrar, Straus and Giroux, 2008).

Hansen, James. *Storms of My Grandchildren: The Truth About the Coming Climate Catastrophe and Our Last Chance to Save Humanity* (New York: Bloomsbury, 2009).

Korten, David. *The Great Turning: From Empire to Earth Community* (San Francisco, California: Berrett-Koehler, 2006).

Mander, Jerry. *In the Absence of the Sacred* (San Francisco, California: Sierra Club Books, 1992).

Singh, Madanjeet. *The Sun: Symbol of Power and Life* (New York: Harry N. Abrams Publisher, 1993).

Index

About the Author

Osprey Orielle Lake is a life-long advocate of social and environmental justice issues. She is the Director of the Women's Earth and Climate Caucus and on the governing Board of Praxis Peace Institute. Osprey has traveled to five continents studying ancient and modern cultures while making presentations at international conferences and universities. She is the Founder/Artist of the International Cheemah Monument Project and is creating eighteen-foot-tall bronze sculpture monuments for locations around the world, which are places to ponder a better future for the earth and humanity. Three have been placed in Germany, Spain and the United States. With a unique perspective as a renowned international sculptor and public speaker for environmental issues, Lake has been featured on both national and European television.

Lake's writing is informed by the American nature-writing tradition that arises from Henry David Thoreau, Walt Whitman, John Muir, and Rachel Carson, as well as from cultural and natural historians Riane Eisler, Thomas Berry and Terry Tempest Williams.

Lake lives in Northern California.